Bent

Australia's Crooked Cops

James Morton & Susanna Lobez

16

EasyRead Large

RHYW

Copyright Page from the Original Book

MELBOURNE UNIVERSITY PRESS
An imprint of Melbourne University Publishing Limited
11–15 Argyle Place South, Carlton, Victoria 3053, Australia
mup-info@unimelb.edu.au
www.mup.com.au

First published 2014

Cover design by Nada Backovic
Typeset by J&M Typesetting
Printed in Australia by McPherson's Printing Group

National Library of Australia Cataloguing-in-Publication entry

Morton, James, 1938– author.

Bent: police corruption in Australia/James Morton and Susanna Lobez.

9780522862256 (paperback)
9780522866506 (ebook)

Police corruption—Australia.
Police misconduct—Australia.
Judicial corruption—Australia
Organized crime—Australia.
Crime—Australia.
Lobez, Susanna, author.

364.1323

TABLE OF CONTENTS

But that was in another country, and besides, the wench is dead.

Christopher Marlowe, *The Jew of Malta,* Act IV, i.

ACKNOWLEDGEMENTS

This is another of our books which could not have been completed without the endless hours of research, advice and encouragement of Dock Bateson. To misquote, 'This poor thing is not ours alone but hers as well'.

Our thanks are due to many people. They include in strictly alphabetical order: Gary Adsworth, Sunil Badami, JP Bean, Bob Bottom, Keith Bottomley, the late Clive Coleman, Sean Cowan, Nicholas Cowdery QC, Professor David Dixon, Michael Drury, Walter Easey, Dr Richard Evans, Tim Girling-Butcher, Sally Heath, Simon Illingworth, Barbara Levy, Damian Marrett, Bernie Matthews, Brian Murphy, Christine Nixon, Sybil Nolan, Leonard 'Nipper' Read, John Rigbey, Russell Robinson, the late CH Rolph, Geoff Schuberg, Adam Shand, Clive Small and Joe Swickard, as well as many others who have asked not to be named.

Our thanks are also due to the staff at the National Library of Australia, the state libraries and archives of New South Wales, Queensland, South Australia, Victoria and Western Australia, as well as the National Archives in London, the British Library and the Newspaper Library formerly at Colindale.

1

FROM 'BENT FOR THE JOB' TO DOWNRIGHT CRIMINAL: THE FIVE STAGES OF CORRUPTION

Over the years and around the world there have been many examples of brilliant cross-examinations. They include the destructive opening question of prosecutor Norman Birkett, 'What is the co-efficient of the expansion of brass?', put to a self-proclaimed engineering expert in the 1928 Rouse murder trial in England. He was unable to answer and the defence case was destroyed. But there can be few which have matched the brilliance of that of Virginia Bell, assistant counsel to the 1995 Royal Commission into the New South Wales Police Service chaired by Justice James Wood.

On 11 December 1995 Wayne Eade, the former head of the Gosford drug squad, was in the witness box and doing nicely. Yes, he thought he was an officer 'of impeccable integrity'. No, he certainly did not have an interest in child-porn videos. Nor had he tried to buy ecstasy for colleagues; of course he knew that it was an illegal drug. He had certainly never visited a witness codenamed GDU7, a former prostitute and drug dealer, while on duty.

It was a classic piece of cross-examination and one that should go down in any textbook. Eade was then invited to look at a film taken when he was on duty at 10.40p.m. on 27 August that year. Up on the room's television screens appeared a film of GDU7 (who had been given anonymity) pouring a line of cocaine on the officer's penis and proceeding to lick it off. She then started to talk about a shipment of cocaine before they moved to a couch, where he began masturbating and talking about buying ecstasy and a porn video of children. The screen went blank as GDU7 was about to provide more oral sex.

Wood asked Eade if he wished to see more of the film, adding:

> I'm not saying that by way of a threat. I'm not suggesting I want to show it publicly, but you and your solicitor are free to view the entirety of the tape, including the sexual relations depicted, if you wish to do so.

Eade did not. Before the end of the day the man about whom there had been suspicions for the previous ten years and who had survived a number of internal investigations had been dismissed by beleaguered police commissioner Tony Lauer. That half-hour broke the resistance of corrupt officers. Who could tell who was on film and in what position? It was no longer a question of solidarity. In the words of the old gospel hymn, it was a case of 'Lord, let me in the lifeboat'.

Eade was later sentenced to twenty-two months' imprisonment for inciting and procuring the supply of prohibited drugs and knowingly giving false evidence to the commission. In 2006 he was ordered to pay in excess of $286,000 to the state, which had settled an action by Michael O'Sullivan, who claimed that Eade had threatened to load him up (plant) with heroin.

There is an old story of a school class allowed an hour to write an essay on the police. One child finished within the first few minutes. When he handed in the composition it consisted of one sentence, 'All coppers are bastards'. Although whole swathes of the community would, quite wrongly, agree with the sentiments, it was decided that this viewpoint should be changed in one so young. It was arranged that the boy should visit the local police station for a day, after which he would write another essay. The visit passed off well enough. He was shown how fingerprints were taken, went down to the cells, was allowed to pat the police horses, was given a police tea mug to take home and so on, but the revised essay took hardly longer to write. It read, 'All coppers are cunning bastards'.

As the years pass, for good and bad reasons, large sections of the public have become disaffected with the police, if indeed they were ever affected. Many would now subscribe to the boy's generalisation or, to use a sociological term, stereotypicalisation, which means just about the same thing but looks and sounds better. As a result, continuing the sociological trend, the police tend to close ranks around themselves and develop a 'no one loves us, so why should we do anything about our image?' culture, which sociologists like to call labelling or anomie. This can arise over really petty matters and in turn shows how statistics can be made to lie.

For example, in London after the First World War arrests of women on charges of soliciting for the purposes of prostitution remained at a consistent level. In 1922 there were 2231 convictions, but that figure suddenly dropped the following year, to under 600. However, that did not mean that there had been a drop in soliciting. Rather, a decision at Quarter Sessions had ruled that there was insufficient evidence to show that the man solicited in a particular case had been annoyed—a requirement for the conviction—rather than flattered by the solicitation. The case was dismissed. As a result the police downed tools, staging a go-slow and refusing to arrest the women. A not dissimilar example happened in 1946 in Sydney, when statistics appeared to show that vice in the city was in major decline. All that had happened was that the working girls had shifted their beats from the inner city to the outer suburbs.

What is police corruption? Getting a daily floater in the local cafe—or is that simply a good example of keeping a finger on the pulse of the local community? After all, in the 1930s New South Wales commissioner Bill MacKay was said regularly to eat on the arm at Romano's, the fashionable Sydney restaurant where he later arrested one of the waiters, Antonio Agostini, for the murder of the man's wife, Linda. Is it a ticket for the Grand Final? A hotel stay in Honolulu? An expensive bottle of wine? Taking a few dollars from a dead derro? And where in the spectrum do you place officers who in 2012 were paid $100 each to open accounts in their own names so that gambler Steve Fletcher could place bets? What about so-called noble cause corruption: bricking a suspect when you KNOW the man is guilty but there isn't sufficient evidence to send him down? Is that really corruption? What would most people say about the practice in 1960s Queensland of taking interstate criminals released from Boggo Road Gaol to the New South Wales border and dumping them with firm instructions not to reappear in the state? Don 'Shady' Lane, a former member of the consorting squad and special branch as well as a Bjelke-Petersen cabinet minister in Queensland from 1983, thought that this was a good example of the oldest form of community policing.

Sociologists have used up the equivalent of forests in trying to formulate an answer. In 1979 Dr Keith Bottomley, in his *Criminology in Focus,* devoted the first thirty-eight pages to a discussion of the definition, and many more after him have been similarly puzzled.

However, corruption was neatly defined in the Wood Royal Commission as deliberate unlawful conduct (whether by act or omission) on the part of a member of the police service who is utilising his or her position, whether on or off duty, and the exercise of police powers, in bad faith. The commission went on to say that this included:

> [t]he receipt of bribes, green-lighting, franchising and protecting or running interference for organised crime; releasing confidential information and warning of pending police activity; 'gutting' or 'pulling' prosecutions; providing favours in respect of bail or sentencing; extortion; stealing and recycling drugs, money, property obtained during the course of otherwise legitimate police operations; various forms of direct participation in serious criminal activity the commission of which is facilitated by virtue of the office held; and the deliberate misuse of an office to procure an advantage or disadvantage in matters of promotion, discipline, transfer and the like, through patronage, friendship or personal prejudice.

There has long been a defence mechanism among police management that a corrupt officer is a rotten apple and there are no such things as rotten barrels or, even worse, rotten orchards. One study (quoting former New York police commissioner Patrick Murphy) surmises that most of the major inquiries into police corruption reject the 'bad-apple' theory:

> The rotten-apple theory won't work any longer. Corrupt police officers are not natural-born criminals, nor morally wicked men, constitutionally different from their honest colleagues. The task of corruption control is to examine the barrel, not just the apples, the organisation, not just the individual in it, because corrupt police are made, not born.

> The 'bad apple' theory of corruption has been all but fully discredited. Successive major commissions of inquiry have catalogued the ways in which corruption is frequently highly organised and systematic.

The rotten-apple theory of police corruption, that it is one of individual moral failure, was discredited at least back in the 1990s and probably a century before that. Any attempt by government or the police hierarchy to defend the rotten-apple theory can only be seen as a face-saving, papering-over-the-cracks exercise doomed to failure.

The question of free food raised its head from the plate, or at least the wrapper, yet again in January 2013 when McDonald's and Krispy Kreme, along with a number of other fast-food outlets, acknowledged that they gave free or heavily discounted food to police and emergency-services staff.

Former McDonald's employees, including managers, told online news publication *Crikey* that a key motivation was to entice police to visit more frequently, to provide high-visibility and free security at taxpayer expense. It is in no way different from the London casinos of the 1960s, which used to hire well-known hard men to keep out potential predators. One look at men such as 'Mad' Frank Fraser sitting on a stool was sufficient to deter all but the most committed robber or cardsharp.

Professor Leslie Holmes of the University of Melbourne's School of Social and Political Sciences, who is researching international attitudes to police corruption, says the fast-food perks pose a 'potential problem' and the practice isn't allowed in countries like Singapore due to the potential for corruption.

'They should not be allowed to accept anything, they're not paid that badly', Holmes told *Crikey.* 'It would be much clearer if there were rules saying, "we don't accept it".' It is not a problem confined to McDonald's. On the Gold Coast officers were receiving free drinks and skipping queues at nightclubs and discos until the practice was barred in 2012.

Holmes cites the work of pioneering US researcher Lawrence Sherman, who wrote in the 1970s on the 'slippery slope' of public officials accepting free gifts, however small. Holmes posed a hypothetical example in a small town: if a cop receives free food, then pulls over the store manager for speeding, will he issue a fine or wave the manager through due to their cosy relationship? Perhaps more significantly, what would be the attitude of a police officer who eats on the arm regularly and is then called to the outlet to deal with a dispute with a customer?

Holmes' research on public attitudes to police corruption in Germany and Bulgaria found that just under 60 per cent of respondents thought it was unacceptable for officers to receive minor perks. He hoped the survey could be replicated in Australia.

Olivia Monaghan, a PhD candidate studying with Holmes who is looking at police corruption in Australia, raises other concerns about officers providing free security for McDonald's: it may not be fair to competing businesses and could detract from the police officers official capacities. If McDonald's wants security officers it should hire them, she argues.

At its most simple, police corruption can be divided into two categories. First, there is 'bent for self' and, second, there is 'bent for the job'—so-called noble cause corruption. Unfortunately, 'bent for the job' is not as altruistic as it first seems. A high conviction rate leads to promotion, and better pay and status. There is also the possibility of a share in the now considerable reward money that is often on offer but not necessarily available to the rank and file. At the end of a career in the police force a higher rank will result in better retirement pay and the chance of a better job in security, far higher up the food chain than what is available to the routine jobsworthy. Officers can sometimes be bent for both self and job: adopt noble cause corruption and also behave in a corrupt way for their own financial advantage. Into this category would certainly fall Ray Kelly, the great New South Wales thief taker of the war and postwar years, and a generation later, the same force's talented but wholly corrupt [redacted].

After looking at patterns of police corruption in New York, Marseille, Hong Kong, Bangkok and Sydney, 1970s sociologist Alfred McCoy propounded a five-stage model for the scale and quality of police corruption. However, academic critics such as Dr Richard Evans have suggested that this may be too basic:

> I think his model is a bit simplistic—corruption is much more a matter of networks, and there is a continual process of jostling for position and influence. Extensive corrupt networks can and do co-exist with comparatively effective and honest policing—indeed really effective corruption thrives best behind a good 'shopfront' of policing.

American sociologist ER Stoddard has suggested that there may be as many as ten stages of corruption, but McCoy's five-point plan seems to provide an eminently workable and relatively uncomplicated structure and, at the risk of offending our betters, we consider this as good a basis as any upon which to begin.

McCoy suggests that the first stage is what he calls honest graft, such as accepting fees from accident tow-truck drivers in return for sending work in their direction. Getting an informal bonus for doing their job of keeping the streets clear: what harm is there in that? Probably not a great deal, except that it can be turned into a business, as Victorian police did in similar circumstances in the 1980s. This leads to step two, which is taking an actual bribe not to report a speeding or similar minor offence. Unfortunately, at a higher level this may lead to sharing the proceeds with an armed robber or splitting the drugs with a dealer, either to be resold for the officer's profit or to be given to their informers.

McCoy's third step is obtaining a regular fee from club and brothel owners, abortionists and illegal gamblers to allow them to continue unmolested or to warn them of impending raids. The fourth is a giant leap. Now officers at a senior level become criminal entrepreneurs, licensing certain criminals to commit serious offences. The fifth stage is the one reached in the Royal Hong Kong Police in the late 1960s, when corruption was rife throughout the country. Hospital patients had to pay so-called 'tea money' to be brought a bedpan or have their sheets changed. Ambulance staff required money to collect a patient. Bribes were required when applying for housing and schooling. Police officers had to pay for promotion to vice or drug squads, where protection was on offer for payment. So far as the police were concerned, drug dealers, brothel keepers and gamblingpalace owners paid a fixed share of their income to senior officers, which was then divided among themselves and junior officers.

In the ensuing Hong Kong investigation around forty Chinese officers left the colony. During the week granted him to explain his assets of HK$4.3 million, Deputy District Commissioner Peter Fitzroy Godber managed to get out of the territory, using his police airport pass to bypass immigration and passport checks. His escape, however, brought on a public outcry, with students at a mass rally in Victoria Park protesting against the government's failure to deal with corruption, and Godber was extradited from England in April 1974. Found guilty, he served a four-year sentence. He was thought to have accumulated some US$600,000 through bribes. The upshot was the establishment of the Hong Kong Independent Commission Against Corruption that year.

McCoy thought that over the years Australian police in general, and officers in the New South Wales, Victorian and Queensland forces in particular, had consistently operated at levels three and four. However, as the Fitzgerald inquiry in Queensland showed, they had also operated at level five in the 1970s and 1980s, and it may well be that there was a similar situation in New South Wales in the 1940s, 1950s and 1990s, and in Victoria in the late 1990s.

Any police force worldwide will try to explain that any corruption (which anyway is not admitted) is a thing of the past.

In this book we have mostly concentrated on fourth and fifth level corruption, where other officers must have known what was happening but turned a blind eye or became passive participants.

Sometimes is it clear that colleagues did not know what was happening. If it seems inconceivable that an officer could go off and rob a bank in his lunch hour, then attention should be paid to South African police captain Andre Charles Stander. The handsome son of retired police officer Major General Frans Stander, he had been Pretoria police college's dux of 1964 and, as captain at the CID branch of Kempton Park police station, he was destined for a career that might have led all the way to the top. But then he took to robbing banks after, he claimed, he was sickened when he shot up to twenty-two unarmed demonstrators in the Tembisa township uprising of 1976. Others say he had never been at Tembisa and that, forced into the police by his father, he had resented the discipline required when he joined the drugs squad.

The first robbery seems to have been after he gave out the morning assignments to his staff. He then drove to Jan Smuts airport to catch a plane to Durban, where he hired a car. He put on a wig and a false beard, then drove to a bank. South African banks in the late 1970s were open plan with little security. Stander approached a cashier, sat down and quietly pulled a gun on her, asking her to fill a bag with money. Terrified, she did. Stander took the money, left the bank before anyone realised what had happened, got in his car and drove back to Louis Botha airport, peeling off his disguise on the way. Then he flew back to Johannesburg in time for an afternoon's work. Buoyed by his success, very often he would carry out a robbery in his lunch break and return later in the day as the investigating officer.

When police officers go off the rails it is often in a spectacular fashion. None illustrates this better than South Australian fraudsquad detective Colin Creed, also the dux of his intake class. Perhaps his superiors should have paid closer attention because, a connoisseur of wine and 'always flash with cash' when in the squad, Creed would spend $60 – a substantial sum in the 1970s – on a bottle of Riesling.

In April 1974 a young woman was raped at knifepoint in her own home. When she went to Hindmarsh police station the next day she identified Creed, whom she saw in the station, as her attacker. He had been at her house some months previously when he investigated a minor burglary. He was found not guilty, but after that his first marriage broke up. A year later he married a policewoman. On 10 April 1980 security cameras picked out a man in a Torrensville bank robbery and, to the shock of officers, it appeared to be Creed. He was questioned, brazened things out and, when he was not identified in a parade, was allowed to go home. That night he vanished. Two rapes followed immediately, both at knifepoint, and he carried out a bank robbery at Glenelg the following month. While on the run he wrote a letter of resignation from the force. After that he went interstate and was said to have teamed up with New South Wales robber and escaper Russell 'Mad Dog' Cox.

His career on the run was marked by near misses. First there were suggestions he had been standing over women in Victorian massage parlours and that the underworld had put out a $15,000 contract on him. If the latter was correct, he survived. Then he was seen by police sitting in a car in Coburg for what appeared to be an inordinately long time. When questioned he again toughed it out, saying that he was waiting for an assignation with a married woman.

He certainly should have been caught in Queensland on 4 January 1982, when police were alerted by a hotel manager who had seen green dye on Creed's hands and suspected that he had touched banknotes marked by the authorities. Creed was also in possession of a large sum of money but, after three hours of police questioning, he was released.

He also survived the police raid following a shootout at Mad Dog Cox's safe house on the Mornington Peninsula in which painter and docker turned bank robber Ian Revell Carroll was killed. By the time police searched the house, finding an arsenal of weapons and Creed's fingerprints, he was long gone.

By the spring of 1983 the hunt for him stepped up, with women's magazines being asked to refer specifically to the rape, and medical magazines to the fact that Creed was suffering from a bowel disorder which, his family thought, might kill him unless he had long-term treatment. Restaurants were canvassed in case a waiter remembered a man buying expensive wine.

He was finally caught in an ABC bookshop in Hay Street, Perth, on 6 September that year, when he was recognised by Ian Goldsmith, a South Australian police officer on holiday, who said, 'It's been a long time, Colin, hasn't it?' Creed was charged with possession of implements of disguise—a wig and a balaclava—along with possession of a .32 Smith & Wesson at the north-eastern Perth suburb of Bayswater. Creed pleaded guilty to charges relating to two armed hold-ups on 10 April 1980 at Underdale.

The authorities were singularly reluctant to pay the reward money to the holidaying police officer who had caught him, arguing that it was only part of the officer's duty. Eventually, with the help of his union, an ex-gratia payment was negotiated. Perhaps this sort of attitude does not encourage honest officers.

In November 1984 Creed's South Australian sentence of twentyone years for the rapes and bank robberies, with a pre-parole term of twelve years, was increased on appeal by the Crown to a minimum of seventeen. A psychological report suggested that at the time he went off the rails he was 'in a state of depression and anxiety and that contributed to his offences'. In early June 1986 the Victorian Supreme Court sentenced Creed to forty-five years in jail on charges relating to six robberies, three of them armed, to be served concurrently.

Throughout his sentence Creed's behaviour was exemplary, but—like all former police officers—he was at risk of attack from other prisoners. In February 1988 his cell was firebombed, destroying his computer equipment. Two months later, with his security rating downgraded, he was transferred to Mobilong Prison. In 1995, now deemed a model prisoner and with no objections from the police, he was granted parole. When he spoke of his time on the run he said, 'You may as well be in prison. It's a pretty terrible lifestyle.' Multiple jail escapees such as Brenden Abbott might disagree.

Police who turn corrupt are, like fallen angels, often fascinating, and Australia has provided rather more than its fair share of them. This book is an informal, to an extent selective, and certainly condensed, account of corruption by police, politicians and lawyers from the arrival of the First Fleet to the present, with an added glimpse of the future. It is not a reflection on the hundreds of thousands of honest and decent officers who have struggled to maintain the integrity of their forces. Indeed it is an account of how they have been betrayed by their colleagues, superior officers and management.

The naming of an individual in this book should not in any way be taken to imply that he or she is guilty of an offence or improper behaviour; in many cases it is quite the reverse.

2

DOOMED TO BE BAD

It was never likely that the police in Australia would get off to a good start. Initially, the police force comprised the marines sent out with the First Fleet. Conditions in Sydney town were terrible: food was at a premium and theft was rife. Damper was all there was to mark the celebrations for the birthday of the Prince of Wales after it was discovered that some of the sheep scheduled for roasting had already been stolen and eaten. Within three weeks of the arrival of the First Fleet in 1788, Governor Arthur Phillip appointed James Smith, said to be the first recorded police officer in Australia, as constable. Smith did not last long. In 1789 he was forced to resign amid allegations that he had pilfered the government stores at Rose Hill. Shortly afterwards, Private Hunt of the marines was caught looting. It was something he and six colleagues—all of whom, as marines, were supposed to be enforcing the law, not breaking it—had been doing for a period of eight months. He saved himself from the gallows by turning King's evidence, but five of his fellow looters were hanged.

The New South Wales Corps, known as the Rum Corps, was formed in England in 1789 for the purpose of travelling to Australia to relieve the marines of their police duties. Commanded by officers on half pay, and composed of a ragtag collection of soldiers released from military prisons and rapscallions who were happy to look for new hunting grounds, the corps arrived at Sydney Cove in 1790 with the Second Fleet. Their commander, Major Francis Grose, arrived two years later. A fourth company was raised from marines who wished to remain in New South Wales.

The night watch and the rowboat guard were appointed in 1789 from 'the ranks of the best behaved of the convicts'. In 1790 the night watch was replaced by the Sydney Foot Police, which continued as one of the organised forces until the amalgamation of New South Wales colonial police forces in 1862. Strangely, it was often not the 'best' of convicts who turned gamekeeper but the worst. For example, Thomas Chalkley had only been in the police a month before he was 'disarmed' by bushrangers. The suspicion, however, was that he had cooperated with them, for they were his associates.

It wasn't until 1 June 1811 that Governor Lachlan Macquarie established the first rudimentary police force in Sydney. Fifty constables appointed under a superintendent were empowered to punish all prisoners, freemen rogues and vagabonds. There were five district watch houses and the men were equipped with cutlasses and wooden rattles. In October of that year Macquarie felt able to write to the Earl of Liverpool back in England to tell him that '...thefts, burglaries and depredations' were largely a thing of the past:

> Happily these are now almost totally suppressed, and when such an occasional plunder does take place such is the vigilance of the police that justice speedily overtakes the delinquent.

Certainly, in the short term this new arrangement improved matters, but since the police were expected to combine the functions of judge, jury and executioner with power to whip miscreants, they were never popular and were frequently heavy-handed.

Hannibal Hawkins Macarthur, well-connected and successful nephew of the better-known soldier, entrepreneur and pastoralist Captain John Macarthur, wrote to his brother-in-law PP King in England in the 1820s that the police magistrate of Parramatta was said to be 'at the head in this unfortunate village, keeping up a most detestable system of Police, such as would never be imagined to exist in any English Town ... every stranger coming to the inns, however respectable, being questioned as to their name etc by the Convict Constables of this detestable fellow'.

A horse patrol, set up to deal with Aboriginal and settler disputes and to combat bushrangers, was established in 1825, but as the recruits were frequently drunk and disorderly, the patrol soon started recruiting its men from the British police, a move that succeeded in alienating it from the general population.

The irony was that the British recruits were no more honest than those recruited in New South Wales. Between 1825 and 1826, at a time when the average strength of the force was fifty, fifty officers were dismissed for misconduct and another twenty-five resigned.

In the 1840s three consecutive chiefs of police in Sydney were dismissed in fairly quick succession for a variety of indiscretions. The first was Henry Croasdaile Wilson, appointed in 1834 with a brief to devote his time to the supervision of recruitment and training. The plan foundered because of the increasing number of cases being brought before the bench, of which Wilson was also first magistrate. On the credit side of his tenure was his introduction of the beat system and his reorganisation of the force, which made the Sydney police something resembling London's Metropolitan Police: one of service, rather than a paramilitary force like the Irish Constabulary. On the debit side was his temper: governor Sir George Gipps was obliged to inquire into physical quarrels between Wilson and other officials. In 1838 Wilson survived allegations of a relationship with a female convict, but he did not survive complaints lodged the following year that he had used policemen to build his home and as liveried domestic servants. (His claims that the officers were necessary for his personal protection and that the liveries were a disguise were not accepted.) On 7 November 1839 Wilson was suspended from duty, and he was formally removed from office in July the next year. In 1841, after he had been defeated in an election for secretarytreasurer of the Australian Club by Major William Christie, he wrote a series of anonymous articles suggesting that Christie's wife was morally unsound. When Wilson's authorship was revealed, Christie horsewhipped him. In a later Supreme Court action Wilson was awarded £150 in damages for assault.

William Augustus Miles, who took over conduct of the police force in 1841, was reputedly the illegitimate son of William IV. He was no greater success than Wilson. Unfortunately, Miles was also a man of eccentric habits and, worse, a poor judge of character. When in October 1846 he employed George Hood as one of his 'runners' or *de facto* detectives, Sydney newspaper *Bell's Life* commented:

> about one of the most thorough knaves—one of the most convicted scoundrels in New South Wales. He has been in almost every iron gang in the Colony: and has been a leader in some of the greatest burglaries that were perpetrated in Sydney. When Joe Jennings and Watkins the publican were robbed, Hood (Miles's Police Runner) was the man who bailed them up. It would be absurd to suppose for a moment that Mr Miles could have been ignorant of the police history of this Hood. With the knowledge therefore that he must have had that the fellow was a knave of the deepest dye, why employ him? Why allow such a character to join the force? Why bring such

> a contaminated ruffian into connexion (sic) with a body of men, deserving and respectable? He (Hood not Miles) has been flogged for absconding—and it is actually proved now that he is at present a runaway from the Goulburn district. It is both an injustice to the public, and an insult to the force, to promote a criminal to such an appointment.

A select committee on police was formed in 1847 under the chairmanship of Charles Cowper. Miles appeared as a witness on 16 June 1847, answering a range of questions on his role and the manner in which his duties were carried out, the duties of his subordinates, alternative models for the organisation of the police force, the conflict with the Corporation of the City of Sydney and some specific questions relating to crime and order in Sydney. He testified that there were too few police officers and that too much of their time was occupied by 'casual duties'. He generally defended his men against charges of neglect of duty and corruption, although he admitted that there was difficulty in hiring and retaining an appropriate quality of man because of uncompetitive salaries and better opportunities in other callings.

The next year Miles' accounts were found to be out of order. He was dobbed in by what must be the first whistleblower, police sergeant James Robinson, who reported to the governor that Miles was appropriating police funds for his own use. Robinson was not believed and was sacked from the force.

In May 1848 a select committee was set up to inquire into the state of policing. The unfortunate Robinson's allegations had resurfaced when other constables also complained. Miles was now accused of inappropriate use of the police fund—made up of the fines of constables and the payment of half of the first week's pay of each constable, which was supposed to go toward their uniforms. Miles had used the fund to pay informers, for his own carriage hire and for other personal expenses. He had also taken money from the treasury that was intended to pay constables an extra stipend for night service in the bush. To compound this, he had wrongly dismissed an acting chief constable and he had been drunk on duty. In the Legislative Council, Robert Lowe accused Miles of being 'guilty of gross peculation and abominable tyranny'. Miles had become an embarrassment, and in a time-honoured move was shifted sideways and allowed to remain a police magistrate. *Bell's Life* thought him 'about as queer and as funny an old gentleman as this portion of the world contains'. He died three years later. On his tombstone in Newtown cemetery appears the epitaph:

> Here lies the remains of William Augustus Miles, Police Magistrate and Late NSW Commissioner of Police, whose parentage was derived from Royalty. He was born in Hampshire, England, and died

> April 24th 1851 in the 53rd year of his life, neglected and in poverty.

The third police chief, Captain Joseph Innes, had actually served for a short time in 1841 before Miles. But in 1848 he replaced Miles and, in turn, retired in 1849 because of 'irregular practices' when he had been a visiting magistrate at Darlinghurst Gaol, which was run as a private enterprise by Governor Henry Keck, his wife and his mistress.

Keck, Irishman, forger and all-purpose rogue, whose wife, Teresa, had reportedly sadly died in Ireland, arrived in Sydney in 1832 along with his six children. Also in tow was his mistress, Sarah Whitehouse, who was posing both as his wife and as a governess. Keck had obtained the post after presenting forged papers showing he was a British Army officer who had been governor of Dublin Castle prison. In reality he had only been a low-paid clerk. Once in office he conducted the prison as a model of private enterprise, helped by chief warder Elias Hibbs and Innes, who, for a small share of the takings, turned a blind eye to the goings on.

And takings there were. First Keck had the prisoners organise vegetable gardens, then a dairy farm, followed by poultry—he kept two emus—and a pigsty. The animals were fed with grain intended for the prisoners, but Keck did show some sort of communal spirit: the inmates were also allowed a small percentage of his profits. There was a hat-making cottage industry, with prisoners working at night and on Sundays to produce 200 cabbage-tree hats a week. For a fee, inmates were allowed out at night to go fishing at Woolloomooloo, and Keck sold their catch. The more talented male prisoners were hired out as musicians, and those inmates who had money to spare could spend it on the female prisoners, whom he organised into brothels. This was so successful that he recruited Sydney prostitutes to help out and even established other bordello premises in the courthouse. In this he was helped by both Sarah Whitehouse and the real Mrs Keck, who, far from being dead and buried in Ireland, had arrived in Sydney in 1835 and been appointed matron at the gaol. The trio must have got on well because between the two women he fathered another six children.

Of course it all ended in tears. At first tales from released prisoners were not believed—Keck was regarded as generous and good company. But an inmate was seen out and about in Sydney and the next day Keck's coachman, James Cox, was recognised as a serving prisoner. The final straw came when members of one of his orchestras were so drunk that they refused to return to the gaol. An inquiry, begun in June 1849, lasted nineteen days and evidence was given by thirty-five witnesses before a select committee of the Legislative Council, which found the gaol to be 'a nest of profligacy and corruption'. On 22 August chairman Charles Cowper wrote in his report:

> Evidence given by Mr Keck and Captain Innes so far from being calculated to make your committee acquainted with the real state of the gaol was framed expressly with the intention of keeping them in ignorance and defeating the object of their appointment.

The Sydney Morning Herald took a righteous stance:

> That burglaries should be fearfully on the increase, that life and property should be daily and hourly becoming less secure in this city and in the suburbs, can hardly surprise when the model gaol of the colony is converted from a prison into an hotel; from a house of mourning into a house of feasting; in short, from a place of restraint, discomfort, and hard-fare, to a place of luxury and no discipline.

Keck, his wife, Innes and the turnkey Hibbs were dismissed. Later Keck became the clerk of St George's markets. By then he was a rich man. He died on Christmas Day 1863 in Surry Hills.

It is generally accepted that the standards of serving officers are directly related to the standards of senior officers. Given this sort of leadership in the police force of the new colony, it is not surprising corruption flourished and that, between 1844 and 1847—at a time when the force averaged 100 men—eighty-two officers were dismissed. The police, as they were in Britain at the time, were thoroughly unpopular, combining as they did brutality and cowardice. There were, of course, exceptions.

However, on the Queen's Birthday holiday in 1848 crowds attacked the St James watch house on Elizabeth Street and released the prisoners, smashed furniture and destroyed the library. Two years later, after the New Year's Eve 1850 riots, in which the police lost control of a largely young crowd of rioters for up to four hours, a commission reported there was still a substantial criminal element in the force that collaborated with the men they were supposed to be arresting. When the ringleaders were finally arrested all but two were released by the police, and it was then that the force was described as being at an all-time low, with scandals, drunkenness and bribery prevalent among the constables.

In the 1850s CGB Lockhart, the commissioner for Crown lands, wrote in his *Sketch of a Proposed System of Police for the Colony of New South Wales* that the constables were 'such confirmed drunkards they could not be trusted out of surveillance', and 'many of them were either infirm old men or petty tyrants with itching palms'.

When at the beginning of the 1860s the New South Wales police system was being remodelled by Sir Charles Cowper, Edmund Walcott Fosbery was offered and accepted the position of secretary to the department and acting inspector-general, arriving in Sydney in 1862. Born in England in 1824, he had been a company secretary before he migrated to Victoria and the Mount Alexander goldfields, later joining the Victorian police force as a gentleman-cadet.

That year riots on the goldfields at Lambing Flat (near Young) in New South Wales saw police and the military deployed to restore peace and led to a new push for more effective policing in the colony.

In 1862 the *Police Regulation Act* was passed by the colonial parliament, and on 1 March that year all existing police forces amalgamated to establish the New South Wales Police Force under former Army captain John McLerie as inspector-general.

The force had its headquarters in Phillip Street, Sydney, and the colony was divided into districts and sub-districts. There were 800 policemen at the ranks of superintendent, inspector, sub-inspector, sergeant, senior constable and constable. The force was divided into foot police, mounted police and water police, and now Fosbery established a detective force.

Fosbery was appointed inspector-general of the police force in 1874, after the death of Captain McLerie. On his retirement in 1904 things had changed for the better, and he commented:

> A peaceful traveller, or even an armed escort, was not safe from highwaymen forty-three years ago. The police and mounted patrols, who were under control of various magistrates, were not

> always a class of men equal to coping with the villainy and criminality of the day.

During that time, however, there had been two contrasting boards of inquiry. The first, in 1867, into crime in the Braidwood district, had been censorious of both the magistracy and the police. Bail was being given far too often and derisory sentences imposed. One magistrate had effectively opted out of dealing with bushranging cases to avoid reprisals against his property. As for the police, officers were far too friendly with the families of bushrangers and were not under the proper control of their superintendent. The leniency of magistrates was an early example of the judicial and public behaviour that led to the police thinking they were underappreciated and unsupported, and therefore disinclined to take positive action against criminals.

The second was the 1892 Royal Commission on Alleged Chinese Gambling and Immorality and Charges of Bribery Against Members of the Police Force. It followed allegations that there had been corruption in dealings with the Chinese population, then centred on North George Street in Sydney, and regarded by the complainants as the best beat for obtaining money. The allegations against the police included wanting chests of tea, 'diamonds for their fingers' and, worse, 'gifts of women'. As for the Chinese immorality, that was the seduction of European girls, promiscuous intercourse with European women and opium smoking.

The commission reported favourably on the Chinese community, which it considered singularly peaceable and generally law abiding. It also approved of the way the Chinese dealt with their women. As for the allegations of immorality: there was no real evidence of seduction, the girls who lived with Chinese men were happy; and prostitutes were treated better than the drudges of some white families. But—and this was a big but—all succumbed to opium smoking. As for the allegations that police were turning a blind eye to Chinese gambling and were taking bribes, the commissioners, also a little myopically, found:

> With reference to the charges of bribery generally, the commissioners would state one consideration that renders the truth of them all extremely improbable. No beat is under the exclusive of any individual constable. On the contrary, not only are officers relieved from duty at stated intervals by other officers, but they are frequently shifted from one part of the district to another, so that for bribery to be effectual it would have to be, to a large extent, general, and that amongst so numerous a body of men who surely include a percentage of honest individuals, is practically out of the question. Thus, after the most searching inquiry, after plying witnesses with questions often verging in their bias upon unfairness to the police, the commissioners emphatically discredit the charges of bribery.

It was among the first of many exculpatory inquiries over the next century.

Sydney wasn't alone in police problems. Down south in Van Diemen's Land, a February 1853 newspaper recorded an early example of how police corruption was allowed to flourish.

> No less than six cases of police misconduct came before the Bench last week, the offenders being all convicts, and most of them fresh from Port Arthur. No free man is safe against the attacks of these infamous scoundrels, unless his position in life is such as to render it dangerous to meddle with him; strange to say, however, notwithstanding the daily exposures of police incompetence and misconduct, they are supported through thick and thin by magistrates, and punishment is administered in no homeopathic doses on the testimony of scoundrels who never tell the truth unless by accident.

For many years, well into the late twentieth century, Victorian politicians and high-ranking officers in the police believed that, while corruption thrived in New South Wales, when it came to the Murray River it drowned. They were deluding themselves and others with them. From the foundation of the force there were troubles at all levels. It was unsurprising. In their first seventeen years the police were paid less than road labourers; there were no standards of entry and there was no code to govern police conduct.

Before then, in August 1838, Henry Batman, chief constable of the Melbourne City Police, under whose tutelage some of these police services had grown, was dismissed for bribery. Between 1838 and the appointment of Superintendent EPS Sturt in 1850, no fewer than six chief constables were engaged to lead the city's police. One of these, William Sugden, embraced the new English model of detectives and devoted 10 per cent of his force to a detective branch.

In 1851, after Victoria separated from New South Wales, a finesharing policy was introduced in an effort to recruit constables. Naturally, this had disastrous consequences. The police were keen to weed out sly-groggers, whose convictions produced fines, but serious assaults, which would not, went undetected.

Reliance on informers became the fundamental means for detectives to solve crime. Informer payments came from the wages of detectives without reimbursement. The select committee on police in 1852 was told that 'there has been, in the case of several detective officers, a most suspicious suddenness in getting rich'.

However, magistrates were often perceived as being anti-police in licence cases. Constable Patrick Bourke said days of investigation and surveillance would come undone when the magistrate would 'dispose of the case and turn around and look at you as if you were a dog'. This was unsurprising: many of the licensing magistrates had financial holdings in the hotels the police were trying to prosecute. And of course many police disobeyed the 1853 regulation that forbade them to moonlight on night shift for publicans—an open invitation for corruption among the poorly paid constabulary. Frequenting brothels and drunkenness were endemic amongst police, and in 1854 a prison was built in Richmond specifically to hold offending officers.

After 1854 Victorian police were given enormous discretion to maintain what was referred to as 'moral order'. This was largely maintained by sporadic raids targeting the poor and working classes, whom many in the upper echelons saw as synonymous with the criminal class. Gambling, prostitution and illicit liquor only became the subject of police concern if conducted by those 'worthy of watching'. During the 1850s public houses were ubiquitous in Melbourne, and visitors noted that licensing laws were 'more honoured in the breach than the observance'. The laws were notoriously unpopular and the police, who relied primarily on their network of informants to solve crimes, did not want to alienate the locals by using trickery or disguises to secure sly-grog arrests, so in 1855 a force of 'revenue police' to suppress the sly-grog trade began operation.

The arrangement under which the police took a share of fines imposed by magistrates also brought trouble on the goldfields, where police tricked miners into admitting they had no licence and then arrested them. A witness to a parliamentary inquiry said, 'A trooper is looked upon as a devil, no better!' Police superintendent Armstrong was given the name The

Flying Demon because of his standover tactics, which, apart from the usual flogging and bashing, included tying recalcitrant miners to trees and burning the tents of sly-grog sellers. During his short time in the force he was said to have illegally amassed £1500.

It was after the April 1852 robbery of the barque *Nelson,* when some 232 kilograms of gold was stolen, that arrangements were made to recruit police from Britain. Fifty officers from the paramilitary Irish Constabulary, who were experienced horsemen, were recruited at the proposed pay of ten shillings a day. They were required to post a £50 bond—more than double the cost of a single man's passage—to remain in the force for three years from their arrival. It was thought that there should be an inspector, to be paid not less than £300 per annum, and three sergeants to keep them in order. London's Metropolitan Police, where the policy was policing by consent, was approached to provide these officers.

It was then that the first of many commissions and committees was appointed to examine policing in Victoria, and on 8 January 1853 the Legislative Council passed an act for the regulation of a police force, merging the then seven separate bodies into one. The next day the force, under its chief commissioner, William Henry Mitchell, dealt with two furious drivers, two saddle stealers, two robberies, a vagrancy and a murder.

Unfortunately for the force, Mitchell lasted little more than a year before he resigned his post due to increasing ill health. *The Argus* newspaper, never a supporter of the early police, paid him due tribute:

> Nothing could be worse than its condition when he took the reins. Corruption, perjury, ruffianism of every description were rife throughout the force, till it had become a public nuisance, not a safe-guard. In a few short months, with the aid of a strong will, a sense of duty and a competent intelligence, all this has been so far reformed, that to calm observers like ourselves, it appears little short of miraculous.

After his retirement as chief, Mitchell seems to have travelled to England, 'to avoid the local profiteers', he said, with a virtual blank cheque to acquire provisions. Although he spent hundreds of thousands of pounds for a force of 2010, there was no doubting his integrity. As he explained, 'I could have put aside £100,000 for myself and no one would have known'. His shopping skills, however, were less adroit and the department eventually sold piles of inappropriate uniforms, greatcoats and rifle bayonets at a huge loss.

Unfortunately, the first long-lasting commissioner—the gambler, drinker and womaniser Captain Frederick Charles Standish—was, unsurprisingly, not a success. In his native England there was said to be no more popular man on a racecourse, and in 1852 he sold his mortgaged properties to pay his gaming debts and set sail for the colonies. He became assistant commissioner of the goldfields and in September 1858 was appointed chief commissioner of police in Victoria, at a salary of £1200. He had already been rejected for the appointment in 1853, when he applied under an assumed name.

Standish was not a good choice. He certainly undertook some reforms, including the use of the telegraph and the railway for communication and transport, but his control was lax and he did not believe in any formal training for officers. There was also preferment for Irish Catholics (82 per cent of the force). Suppression of slygrogging was in Standish's view 'inoperable' and he continued the unofficial licensing system, under which favoured and well-controlled establishments went untouched by the police. Efforts to police gambling in Melbourne were as sporadic and discretionary as efforts to suppress other vices. Gaming was the domain of detectives, not beat police, and the focus was once more on 'low-class' establishments. By 1860 competition was rife among publicans, who set up skittle alleys and billiard rooms in their hotels, which also functioned as gambling venues. Tricksters setting up gaming tables at racecourses knew they had to pay detectives a fee. Just as half a century later Commissioner Blamey had a penchant for sly-grogging, Standish's enthusiasm for the tables and cockfights made it difficult for police to see gambling as a crime, and hence it was rarely prosecuted.

From 1860 to 1863 there were no fewer than three select committees looking into his administration; the third suggested he be replaced, but he survived. Standish also had a close personal interest in the leading brothels in the city and it was he who took the Duke of Edinburgh on a tour during his 1867 visit to Melbourne. Clearly, Standish had an artistic eye. One of his preferences in the brothels was for naked white women to be placed on black chairs. He did not, however, survive the Ned Kelly outbreak. Legend has it that the hunt for Kelly was suspended while the weights for the Melbourne Cup were declared.

After Kelly's capture there were serious worries about the inefficiency of the country police and, more importantly, about corruption among those in Melbourne. According to the 1881 royal commission on the police, Standish's conduct of the force was 'not characterised either by good judgment, or by that zeal for the interests of the public service which should have distinguished an officer in his position'. There were clear examples of favouritism and one officer, John Sadleir, thought it might be even worse. Standish had a tendency to 'form intimacies with some officers of like mind, and to think less of others who were much more worthy of regard', but his 'almost pathetic' affection for Superintendent Frank Hare, notable in the period of the Kelly pursuit, was a symptom of the mental trouble under which he eventually broke down:

> His devotion to Frank Hare was of another kind—it was like the love of Jonathan for David. It was

> almost pathetic to see, during the months Captain Standish spent at Benalla in the Kelly time, how restless and uneasy he became were Hare out of his company. I have seen Standish on the top rail of a fence watching anxiously for Hare's return from a short ride of a mile or two. He said to me that he was in constant fear lest some accident should happen to him.

After his resignation as commissioner in 1880 Standish continued his rackety ways. In November 1882 he was nearly thrown through the window of the Melbourne Club by honorary member Colonel Craigie Halkett, whom he had called by a 'provocative name'. He declined to prosecute, but the colonel duly resigned his membership. Standish died in the club on 19 March 1883 of cirrhosis of the liver. He is said to have converted to Catholicism on his deathbed. His appropriate legacy is the Standish Handicap, run at Flemington on New Year's Day.

Another Standish favourite was Superintendent Frederick J Winch, who had joined the force as a cadet in 1852. When Standish summoned Winch from Ballarat, he arranged for a house in Punt Road to be made ready for him, using police as labour and government supplies and materials. Winch was a gambling fanatic and had to be ordered by Standish to stop gambling at the depot; this did not stop him indulging his love elsewhere. At Beechworth he and Police Magistrate Barnard gambled with the elderly

Judge Cope. They allowed him to win a few times, then upped the stakes and eventually took the judge for £300. The judge told his wife, and she publicly denounced Winch and Barnard as swindlers and also had some terse words to say about Mrs Barnard, a former barmaid.

In July 1882 the vastly experienced Winch gave evidence to the Longmore Royal Commission on a variety of subjects, including the detective branch and the question of promotion from the ranks. Unfortunately, during his career Winch had conducted a system of organised corruption, allowing sly-grog shops, prostitution and gambling to flourish over a 20-year period. He had also blocked honest Melbourne police trying to stamp out these pursuits. Brought before a board as early as 1861, he was acquitted of charges except for borrowing money from a subordinate to balance the station's books. Now allegations against him included being found near brothels in a drunken state, appropriating bottles of brandy and whisky from hotels, borrowing money, being found (sober) in Madame Brussels' fashionable brothel in Lonsdale Street, permitting prostitution in hotels and improperly transferring a Sergeant O'Sullivan, who had been trying to clear the streets of prostitutes. The commission also looked into the affairs of Sub-Inspector Larner, whose chief fault seems to have been standing over publicans and 'borrowing' money that he never repaid.

Overall the detective branch was seen by the Longmore Royal Commission as 'so iniquitous that it may be regarded as little less than a standing menace to the community' and a 'nursery of crime'. It was institutionally corrupt and there were also complaints about the uncontrolled use of informers. The commission recommended that the branch be disbanded. Nevertheless, the force was still the place to be, and in 1888, 500 young men applied for the fifty positions available.

As for Winch and Larner, the chief secretary thought it undesirable that they should be allowed to resume public duty. But—setting an unfortunate precedent that has continued for 150 years—instead of facing at least disciplinary proceedings, they were allowed to retire. Winch retired in November 1882, when he was fifty-five, keeping his superannuation of £326 a year.

The dishonesty in the Victorian police of the time may be compared with that of the detective branch of London's Metropolitan Police of the same period. In 1877 one third of the branch, admittedly only seven officers, appeared at the Old Bailey charged with betting frauds. The men received sentences of up to two years apiece.

As always, what happens at the top influences the state of a force. Victorian chief commissioner Thomas O'Callaghan also led a chequered professional life. He joined the police in November 1867, aged twenty-two, and after becoming a detective was reduced to the ranks in 1871 for supplying liquor to a prisoner. Eleven years later he was accused of disrespectful behaviour to the Longmore Royal Commission, which declared him 'not trustworthy'. Despite this he was promoted to inspector in 1892. He became chief commissioner in 1902.

O'Callaghan was not supportive of the men under his command. During the 1890s he actively campaigned for police to retire at the age of sixty, thereby accelerating his own promotion. However, when he became chief commissioner he encouraged the government to raise the retirement age to sixty-five years. This both kept him in office and hampered promotion for his junior officers. The government's decision was given effect by an order-in-council in 1902, after which, feeling betrayed by O'Callaghan's about-face, officers met on 19 March 1903 to protest. With the newspapers of the time and politically unaligned politicians backing them, the order-in-council was cancelled.

A new requirement that confined police to barracks to provide an emergency response capability also met with hostility. Police openly disobeyed O'Callaghan's decision and a group went directly to the chief secretary to have the order annulled. With a rash of additional complaints from the community, Premier Thomas Bent appointed James Cameron as chairman of a royal commission to inquire into the force and its management.

The 1905 Cameron Royal Commission found 'many blemishes' in O'Callaghan's administration. He had caused dissent in the ranks when he refused to retire and, worse, he was alleged to have an improper interest in licensed premises in Carlton, something that, if proved, should have brought about his instant dismissal. Instead the committee merely referred the matter for a legal opinion. However, despite all this, he remained in office until he finally retired on 31 March 1913. He is the prototype of the corrupt commissioner Thomas Callinan in Frank Hardy's novel *Power without Glory.*

Even John Mitchell Christie, whose use of disguise and thenunorthodox methods led him to be called the Sherlock Holmes of the Melbourne police, was not above suspicion. The well-known thieftaker, sportsman and later customs officer was thought to have lived with the wife of Levi Walker while the skeleton-key maker and bank robber was in Pentridge in the 1860s. Worse, he had 'dressed her like a lady'. Christie, who resigned in dubious circumstances, was not a fan of the subsequent efforts of the force, writing in his diary:

> One does not expect the genius of a Sherlock Holmes for comparatively small wages but the pretensions of the Victorian force are such as to warrant the public in expecting a high average of successes.

However, it may simply have been a bit of sour grapes.

If the 1901 merger into a federation of the various colonies gave rise to expectations of better policing in the states and territories in the new century, these hopes were to be disappointed.

3

SPOOKS, STRIKES AND SCANDALS: VICTORIA 1920–1946

'A Police strike is a rare and beautiful thing', wrote Bertha Walker in *Solidarity Forever!,* her study of Australia's radical history. Whether a police strike is actually a beautiful thing is debatable, but it was not rare at all in the first quarter of the twentieth century, when there were strikes in London (1918, 1919), Liverpool in support of London (1918), Cincinnati (1918), Boston (1919), Long Beach (1920) and Quebec (1920). In 1924 in South Australia the entire force threatened to tender its resignation, in an attempt to obtain a wage increase.

By the early 1920s the reputation and morale of the dreadfully underpaid Melbourne police were in serious trouble. The chief commissioner was paid just over half that of his New South Wales counterpart, and at a time when a man's hat cost about half a pound, a suit just over £5, a dining-room suite £42 and the cheapest Vauxhall car £825, the basic wage for a Victorian policeman for a 47 1/4-hour week was a little over £5.

There were demands that officers should be given pensions. Victoria remained the only state not to provide these to police, the entitlement having been abandoned in 1902. Over the years the non-pensioners in the force had grown and by the 1920s totalled 74 per cent. The government, which had been warned that this balance was now a problem in the force—for one thing, pensioned officers responded to emergencies more swiftly than non-pensioned ones—disregarded the advice. Overtime payments were still outstanding from the policing of a long-running waterside strike. A semiofficial pension system for injured officers, which had been run by the Police Association, had been scrapped. Then, in the autumn and winter of 1923, militants led by Constable William Brooks were agitating for pay parity with New South Wales officers as well as to be given one Sunday in two off instead of only one in four.

Additionally, there were difficulties with the plainclothes licensing division, with allegations that some of its members were consorting with criminals, such as Leslie 'Squizzy' Taylor. There were also allegations that the police were leaning on the brothel madams, asking up to £50 a week protection, and more if they had lost at the trotting. At pavement level one girl was said to be paying a beat policeman half of every five shillings she earned.

There was a similar situation in Adelaide, where there were allegations of graft with police who enforced the Betting Act. It was suggested that no bookmaker could make a living without immunity from police interference. The going rate was alleged to be £4 a week to two constables, and when the bookmakers stopped paying arrests followed. Samuel Lampard gave evidence in support of bookmakers Eric and John Shannon. He said he had been paying for ten years. Plainclothes policemen were getting a staggering £40 a week 'under the lap' and were buying motorcars with the proceeds. *Truth* newspaper interviewed twenty-three bookmakers, and twenty-one said they were paying the police.

The Victorian officers had no confidence in their new commissioner, Alexander Nicholson. Appointed in 1922 over far more qualified men, he had never completed primary school and until just before his appointment had been stationed in Ballarat. Although a man of personal bravery, he had no conception of the problems confronting a city force, nor how to deal with them. To add to the officers' complaints, in November that year he reintroduced a system of secretly monitoring beat officers using special supervisors known as 'spooks', a system tried, tested, found flawed and discarded in the first few years of the twentieth century. Special supervisors were given a motorcar and, working in either plainclothes or uniform, would tour the city rooting out beat officers found indulging in unacceptable behaviour such as taking free meals or sleeping on their shift. The officers were reported and fined or more severely disciplined. There was no doubt there had been skiving. In the celebrated 1921 Gun Alley murder case, the beat officer admitted he had not patrolled the alley as he should have done on the night Alma Tirtschke was murdered. The long-running journal *Round Table* reported:

> [An] increase in burglaries in city premises upon beats regularly patrolled by constables had made many people doubtful of the integrity of some members of the force and the administration of the licensing law had not been above suspicion.

There was also more than just a hint of nepotism in Nicholson's appointments, which included his brother-in-law. Other appointments were of the 'set a thief' principle and, unfortunately, the men appointed as supervisors were not of the highest calibre or integrity. One man had himself been reported on two occasions as being drunk on duty, the second time just a year before his new appointment.

In February 1923 Nicholson transferred seventeen plainclothes licensing officers back into uniform. They included Constable Brooks, whom Nicholson thought 'unfit for this class of work' and who had 'tried to create a deal of trouble at that time'. Later Brooks was fined five shillings when he left his post in Swanston Street after he saw his replacement, who was fifteen minutes late, walking towards him, instead of waiting for his actual arrival. Although he was married and living in Prahran, Brooks was then transferred to Geelong. Another officer, James Dunn, who queried his own transfer, was promptly charged with a disciplinary offence and fined. The fine was later overturned, but he received no explanation for the move.

Brooks was then transferred to the licensing branch in rural Colac and refused to go on duty. He was promptly charged with insubordination but obtained a public hearing for his appeal. He argued that he was 'under the impression that the Chief Commissioner had given instructions that he was not to be employed on licensing duty'. He was acquitted.

On 31 October 1923, Derby Day in Victoria, with Melbourne packed for the racing, Brooks persuaded the 10p.m. night shift at Russell Street to refuse to go on duty. Their sole aim, at this stage, was to have the spook system withdrawn. Nicholson did have the sense to declare that the supervisory system would be discontinued, but unfortunately no one told Brooks and the other officers. Why has never been satisfactorily explained. It was possibly because Nicholson did not wish to be seen to give in to a small group of firebrands. Instead Brooks had a meeting with Nicholson and Premier Harry Lawson and was told that, in effect, officers could like it or lump it. Brooks persuaded them to choose the latter.

When on the night of 1 November Brooks and twenty-eight men, later dubbed the Famous Twenty-Nine, refused to go on duty, Lawson told them to return to their posts. They refused; Brooks and another were dismissed from the force, and the remainder were discharged. Dismissal meant not receiving a 'certificate of character', not being allowed to associate with officers, and not being allowed in a police station. Despite his ban, Brooks toured police stations in an effort to bring the force out on strike, telling them, quite wrongly, that all officers at Russell Street were 'out'. By noon he had persuaded over 600 officers to strike, or at least not to report for duty until the situation was clearer.

The news spread like wildfire, and as a result the heart of the city was in the hands of criminals, who mugged and robbed, with the remaining officers unable to stop them. Shop windows were smashed, trams were set on fire and a massive two-up game was played on the streets. Stores such as Myer were looted and the proceeds taken back to the suburbs for sale to the likes of Squizzy Taylor. *Round Table* commented:

> In the police strike riots seventy-eight shops were smashed. Police on strike marched around the city in ordered formation, hooting the constables who were still on duty and in particular abusing those who were still attempting to control the traffic at busy city intersections.

The hapless Nicholson was left isolated and Lawson now looked to the military in the form of Lieutenant General Sir John Monash, who had been knighted after distinguished and decisive action in the First World

War, to restore order. In a matter of hours he rounded up a special constabulary force with batons, brassards and a hat with the letters SCF. After four hours of fighting, the streets were once again under control. But by then three people had been killed and £78,000 in damage had been done. A shopkeepers' association was formed to claim compensation.

Only two of the protesting officers had a right to a pension. None was allowed back into the force, although one man, James Golding, was admitted to the South Australia Police and a second, William Fellowes, joined the Peace Officer Guard in Sydney and later the Commonwealth Police in the Australian Capital Territory. Eventually most of the men obtained better jobs than they had held in the police force. Some took jobs in the tramways as night watchmen and in the penal department as warders. For a time Bill Winterton, who later became a hotel manager, was a well-known figure spruiking outside the Tivoli Theatre.

Brooks was never called to give evidence at the subsequent royal commission on the police inquiring into the riots and their causes, and he later moved to Hay in country Victoria, where he worked as a contractor and then as a night watchman. In 1943 he became a caretaker in a college in Ballarat and died the following year.

There were two more scandals to come. In the summer of 1925 *The Argus* ran a story about brothel owners purchasing protection from police. It was claimed that a Joseph Nicolte had written letters to the chief secretary and the officer in charge of the plainclothes police, complaining that numerous brothels in Little Lonsdale, La Trobe and Spring streets operated without police hindrance. In March Josephine Ricardo handed a sworn declaration to the chief secretary in which she claimed that prostitution was flourishing in central Melbourne and police were being paid off by a core of brothel keepers known as 'the Combine' to avoid prosecution. It was also hinted that drug taking was rife in the brothels.

Police graft was reported as operating at all levels. Unless they were bribed to go away, policemen on the beat would loiter in front of brothels, scaring away the customers. More senior police were said to receive large payments to ensure that no prosecutions were launched against 'the Combine'. It was also claimed that prostitutes who attempted to operate on their own account were invariably prosecuted. By the standards of the times, the sums of money involved were large. In 1921 one woman is said to have paid £2295 to the police in 'protection' money. Amid calls for his removal Commissioner Nicholson was reported as denying 'any knowledge of these things'.

The last scandal of the Nicholson era was the so-called Callaghan Conspiracy case. Despite *The Argus'* banner headline 'Detectives' Den: Secret Meeting Place. Strange Discoveries', it was a fairly commonplace story except for the money involved. On February 1925 liquor, along with some teas and a woman's coat, stolen from the railways, was delivered by a Patsy Quilter to the Railway Hotel in Wellington Street, Collingwood. Almost the moment Quilter left four officers, Detective Inspector Neil Olholm and detectives Leo O'Sullivan, Donald John McPherson and Walter Rufus Fowler, swooped.

In charge of the hotel was Anne Callaghan, the licensee's daughter. O'Sullivan told her that he 'might be able to do something for her' and when she turned him down her father, Terence, was arrested at his dairy in Easey Street, Collingwood, and taken back to the hotel. He was told that the detectives might overlook the matter if he paid them £10,000, a sum he negotiated down to £6500. The detectives stayed the night at the hotel and drank to their success, during which time O'Sullivan told Miss Callaghan that he was a wealthy man—a fine achievement when his annual salary would have been about £500. Next morning O'Sullivan went with Callaghan to the bank and received an initial payment of £1000 in £100 notes. Graciously, O'Sullivan then gave Callaghan sixpence for the tram fare home.

However, Callaghan made a complaint, and Superintendent Potter interviewed McPherson and Fowler. They admitted to being at the hotel with Olholm and O'Sullivan, who in addition to his other duties performed special inquiries for the railways department, but claimed that no one from the hotel had been charged because the goods had been found in the back lane and not actually on the premises. The detectives said they had waited at the scene because they had information that the thieves were returning to collect the goods. When they did not, the property was taken back to the railway lost-property office. Olholm and O'Sullivan backed them up.

Initially it was proposed that an internal inquiry be held. Instead, the four officers were charged with conspiracy to obtain money unlawfully. Although O'Sullivan was junior in rank, he was apparently the ringleader, a phenomenon that was to reappear in future corruption cases, —. Before the hearing O'Sullivan, as befitted a man of means, was admitted to a private hospital with a nervous breakdown. He was apparently unable to recognise any of his friends or relatives and was not even sure who his wife was.

Sensibly, Fowler took more direct action and disappeared without trace. Some charitably thought he was wandering in the bush, suffering from loss of memory. Others thought he would surrender when his fellow detectives stood trial in April. He did not and a warrant was issued that month. For the next year-and-a-half there were stories that Fowler was visiting his aged and ill parents; that he was out of the state; that he was out of the country. In the event, Fowler did not surrender until early December 1926.

So then there were two. The jury found both Olholm and McPherson guilty, adding a strong recommendation for mercy due to their long service and previous good character. Judge Dethridge sentenced Olholm to twelve months' imprisonment and McPherson to nine. Their appeals failed. The suddenly recovered O'Sullivan was brought for trial in July 1925 and sentenced to three years. It is highly unlikely that the Callaghan incident was the first time these men had acted together.

O'Sullivan's comments about his wealth moved a member of parliament to suggest that officers should be forced to submit to an examination to satisfy the court that they had come by their assets lawfully. If they could not, he proposed that the Crown should confiscate their property. Forward-looking as this comment was, it was not until towards the end of the twentieth century that asset recovery legislation came into force. Disclosure by police of their financial affairs has remained a contentious issue in Victoria.

As is so often the case, until this time the four detectives had all been highly regarded, with excellent work records and numerous commendations. Lack of supervision was blamed for their conduct, and Superintendent Potter said during his evidence, 'In practice, I interfere very little with the railway detectives. They have their own liberties and do not report property recovered to the detective office'.

Olholm died following an attack of pleurisy at the hotel he ran after his release. After he resurfaced, Fowler was more fortunate. Terence Callaghan had what in the trade is called a touch of the second (thoughts) and made an unsatisfactory witness. Since the incident his marriage had broken up, and he had lost 150 head of cattle and his money. He could not remember seeing Fowler before in his life. There was no evidence to show that the detective had received money from him. In December 1926 the magistrate refused to commit Fowler for trial, something that shows the merits of staying out of sight until the initial storms have blown away. Callaghan died the next year.

Chief Commissioner Nicholson was admitted to hospital in May 1925 and never resumed his duties, resigning three months later. He died in March 1928. On Nicholson's retirement the First World War hero Sir Thomas Blamey, a decorated soldier who had distinguished himself at Gallipoli and in France, was appointed chief commissioner. His appointment on 1 September 1925, at the age of fortyone, was generally well received by property owners and police alike, but not everyone was convinced. 'An exceedingly able little man, though by no means a pleasing personality', the commander of the Australian Imperial Force, General Birdwood, said perceptively.

Blamey's appointment also averted the possibility of an inquiry into the now persistent allegations of corruption in the force, particularly the licensing branch. Now that Blamey, with his fine war record, had been appointed, the 'right man' was in the post and things would soon be cleaned up. This 'new broom' approach to freshen up a corrupt force, along with a cleansing name change for a branch under suspicion, have proved to be commonly used tactics.

Indeed Blamey had many suitable qualities. As a military man, he looked on the force as a similar operation and was innovative in such matters as training, people management and organisation. He also obtained an increase in wages for the men. However, he began and ended his police career in scandal. Unfortunately, Blamey held the view that liquor was an adult version of mother's milk and should be available to all with as little let or hindrance as possible. He could be found in smart hotels drinking after hours on a regular basis, something that provided, for the right people, a cast-iron guarantee against police raids.

Worse, on 21 October 1925, within weeks of his appointment, someone who carried the commissioner's police badge, '80', was found in a brothel in Bell Street, Fitzroy, run by former actress Mabel Tracey. (The plaque on the door claimed that she was a teacher of elocution.) When it was raided by three constables from the licensing branch, the holder of the badge had an explanation, 'It's all right, boys. I'm a plainclothes constable. Here is my badge.' All the constables agreed that it was not Blamey who held the badge, although the badge was definitely his. Now anonymous letters were sent to the government:

> Do you know that the Commissioner of Police was found in a sly-grog shop at Fitzroy last month

> naked and in bed with a naked woman and that the police who found him there are in terror as to what he will do to them? How is the cursed drink to be put down if the head of the police is an adulterer and a drunkard? Good men are needed at the top, pure and honest (Romans xiiii XI–XIV).

Blamey maintained the badge must have been removed from his key ring the day before the raid and that he found it three days later in his locker at his club. However, his next in command, Superintendent Daniel Lineham, said quite specifically that he had seen the badge on Blamey's desk only seven hours before the raid. A public inquiry was refused and instead Lineham was accused of disloyalty. Now Blamey produced a witness, an old army friend, who said he had been with Blamey and his family from 9p.m. until just before midnight on the night of the raid.

A reasonably likely explanation is that Blamey lied to protect a married friend who had met him after dinner at the club and asked if he had any grog in his locker. Blamey had handed over his key ring with his badge on it, telling the man to drop it back later. He was rather admired for his refusal to betray his friend, but it was hardly a good example to the lower ranks. Indeed it is a classic example of how corruption spreads downwards in a police force.

Nor was Blamey necessarily a good judge of character. While he restored morale among his officers, his judgement was lacking and, importantly, he dismissed a series of allegations of corruption and brutality—thirty in 1933 alone—against officers. He was deceived into thinking that the swindler James Coates might have reformed and he allowed him to run his horses at Victorian tracks. Worse, against the recommendation of his special adviser Tom Dunn, he appointed John O'Connell Brophy to be a criminal investigation branch (CIB) superintendent. Brophy was highly regarded by the underworld and celebrated in the couplet, 'Ashes to ashes and dust to dust; if Brophy don't get you then Piggott [his colleague] must'.

Blamey's career ended with another fudged cover-up. On Saturday 23 May 1936 Brophy was in St Vincent's Hospital suffering a gunshot wound. He had accidentally shot himself in the right arm while handling a pistol. Unfortunately, those who visited him in hospital could see that he had also been shot in the face and the chest. 'Injuries even for the most persistent pistol cleaner it would have been difficult to receive,' said LEB Stretton, counsel at the subsequent inquiry.

It was time for a revision of the facts. Now the heroic officer had been shot while chasing car bandits near the zoo. The press did not give up, and on 5 June County Court Judge Hugh Macindoe was appointed as royal commissioner to investigate the shooting of

Brophy and the subsequent press statements made by Blamey. What was quite clear was that Brophy had been with a chauffeur and two women that night, one of whom was a Madeleine Orr. All sorts of lame explanations—such as meeting with an informer in the dead of night—were offered as to how he came to be chasing dangerous bandits with innocent spectators at risk.

Forty-four witnesses were called, including both Blamey and Brophy, and much of the time was spent trying to refute 'scandalous' allegations that Brophy had been shot by an 'enraged' husband—that is, Mr Orr. Later there were allegations that Brophy was half naked and practising cunnilingus on his companion when the gunman approached. Another version, admittedly third-hand at best, comes from former superintendent HR (Bill) Donnelly, one-time chief of Melbourne's homicide squad, who knew he was going to be quoted by Kevin Morgan in his book *Gun Alley* when he told the writer that he had information from a 'senior source in whom I have the utmost confidence', and that it was Blamey himself on the back seat and Brophy was sacrificed to protect him.

On 2 July Macindoe submitted his report, which many saw as a whitewash. Unfortunately for Blamey, he said:

> Being jealous of the reputation of the force, which he commands, he thought that reputation might be endangered if the whole truth was discovered.

> I was tremendously impressed with Blamey as I saw him in the witness box. I tried my best to steer him to the true story but he was immovable. I couldn't save him from himself.
>
> I cannot accept his evidence that he believed it was an accident ... [he] gave replies which were not in accordance with the truth, with the sole purpose of secreting from the press the fact that women were in the company of Superintendent Brophy.

Blamey was finished. On 9 July he was required to submit his resignation. At first he tried to bluster his way out, although he was told that if he resigned he could have a pension of £260 per annum—but not otherwise. He resigned. The official police history also whitewashes him, 'his only crime being a desire to preserve the reputation of his Force'.

Blamey returned to the army, where he served with great credit in the Second World War, becoming Australia's first field marshall, although General Douglas MacArthur, the Allies' supreme commander in the Pacific, described him as 'sensual, slothful' and a 'doubtful character'.

When it came to it, the Brophy incident had not been the only cause of Blamey's fall. The government had also made the grave mistake of appointing him chief constable for life. The retention of a £1000 philanthropic gift, a running feud with the press and a crusade against newspapermen, active opposition to any form of inquiry into a death during a dockers' strike when police opened fire on the strikers, shootings and the use of batons in 1932 to stop a peaceful march by the unemployed in Flinders Street, and several ineffective police inquiries and open flouting of licensing laws had all counted against him. Apart from the fact that he routinely dismissed any complaints against his force, in 1930, 1933 and again in 1936 there had been allegations that officers were using the 'third degree' to get confessions.

In the wake of the Blamey fiasco the government took drastic action. On 14 July it cabled the Scotland Yard commissioner that it immediately required 'the services of an outstanding Senior Official of Scotland Yard' to report on the organisation of the Victorian police. The first person approached was Sir Trevor Bigham, but he declined within the month and instead the government invited Chief Inspector Alexander Duncan, who had joined the Met in 1910. He was seconded at a fee of £500 and allowances to 'give his views' on the detective and plainclothes branches. His interim findings on the CIB criticised a lack of training and supervision, with a resulting poor work ethic. He was also critical of interrogation methods that favoured the 'hit first and ask questions later' school of thought.

Despite cries from the opposition benches that outsiders were not needed, Duncan was offered the position of chief commissioner in February 1937 and he was appointed at first for a five-year period. His tenure was, by previous standards at least, a conspicuous success.

Duncan's personal commitment to dealing with corrupt behaviour shows in his treatment of the notorious Fred 'Bluey' Adam, then detective first constable, later charged with conspiracy after the 1969 abortion inquiry. In 1945, when he and a detective sergeant charged a known thief with unlawful possession, a complaint was received that they were vying with each other for the best bargain in purchasing the offender's car for their own use.

When questioned, both men freely admitted their actions. Neither they, nor others who were involved in the matter, could see anything wrong with their conduct. Duncan transferred both officers back to uniform duties. As it turned out, it might have been better for the force if the brutal Adam had been retired.

Tasmania also had corruption problems in the 1950s and Duncan was sent to advise on the problems of the police force there. This arose out of a board of inquiry into the bashing of a seaman by Hobart officers at a wharf and then back at a police station. Though suspected of an armed hold-up at the Prince of Wales theatre, the man was later found not to have been involved. The inquiry, conducted by Melbourne barrister DH Little, found against Senior Detective Kaye, who was dismissed, and Chief Superintendent

Mackey, who was demoted to inspector. Little found that Mackey had either participated in the bashing at the wharf or was aware of it but had done nothing to stop it.

When Duncan interviewed officers he found that there was no formal training for the detective division and proposed the immediate introduction of a detective training course. The police were relying far too heavily on a confession to bring about a conviction and, once one was obtained, very often little else was done to find corroborating evidence. Duncan found that there had been a lack of proper supervision and the public had lost confidence in the police. This, he believed, would be restored by 'playing the game'. It also appeared that there was doubt as to whether the police had the power to take fingerprints from suspects in custody.

Notwithstanding Duncan's commitment to developing and maintaining ethical standards of police conduct, corruption did, of course, occur. When interviewed many years later, Victorian chief commissioner from 1963 to 1969 Rupert Arnold, himself a former member of the gaming branch, denied that there had been widespread corruption in the branch during the 1940s. He did, however, admit 'big money was changing hands' and that more than one policeman was taking a payoff of £300 a week to turn a blind eye to the city's gambling schools.

4

CHIEF COMMISSIONER WILLIAM JOHN MACKAY: POLICE REFORMER, CROOKED BULLY OR BOTH?

The man who should take much of the credit for the positives in the New South Wales Police from the 1930s onwards must, unfortunately, also take much of the blame for its disasters of the latter part of the twentieth century. His name, now half-forgotten outside the annals of the police, is William John MacKay, commissioner from 1935 until his death in 1948. Scots-born MacKay has been variously described as 'The best commissioner I ever worked under ... a policeman's man', 'One of the biggest bloody crooks we ever had in the New South Wales police force' and a number of other things in between.

In his unpublished thesis 'William John MacKay and the South Wales Police Force 1910–1948: A Study of Police Power',[1] historian Richard Evans compares

1 Submitted in fulfilment of the degree of Doctor of Philosophy, School of Political and Social Inquiry, Monash

MacKay's career with the much shorter, ill-fated tenure of Peter Ryan, who was appointed in the wake of the 1995 Wood Royal Commission. Both, suggests Evans, were initially welcomed as reformers and modernisers and both later came under attack from politicians, the police union and the media, who conducted long and hostile campaigns against them. Both were autocratic and ambitious and both had a vain streak. Both wanted fundamental changes in the force. Both had their loyal supporters and their bitter enemies. The difference, Evans believes, is that MacKay would never have resigned in the circumstances in which Ryan left the force.

A long-held business precept is never to promote a subordinate who is more intelligent than you are. The police policy of promotion only towards the end of one's career is a good example of this kind of thinking. Until the end of the twentieth century seniority, not ability, was the keyword, and as a result the more able and assertive officers left the force. A wait of over twenty years to reach commissioned rank was the norm, and the biggest hurdle was the jump from senior constable to sergeant. It was also essential to have what the police in the United States call a 'rabbi', who advised and protected a young constable in the early stages of his career. MacKay was fortunate to have one in the form of James Mitchell, 'a

---

University, May 2005. We are most grateful to Dr Evans for giving us a copy of his thesis and generously allowing us to quote extensively from it.

policeman of the best type', who is credited with transforming the New South Wales police from a colonial to a modern force during his time as inspectorgeneral from 1915 and then, when the title was changed in 1926, as commissioner until 1930.

Police officers writing their memoirs have an unfortunate tendency to write themselves a larger role in investigations. The great postwar English detective Robert Fabian wrote how he came home to his wife and said, 'I've solved my first murder', when in fact he had merely drawn a plan of the murder scene. MacKay was no different. He claimed to have been instrumental in solving the 1908 murder of Marion Gilchrist while he was in the Glasgow police force. He maintained that he left the force in protest over what he saw as the paltry sum of £68 reward out of a total of £200, but in fact he does not appear in any of the proceedings. In any event the case is not one with which an officer should be proud to be associated. The evidence against highly unpopular bludger Oscar Slater was a mishmash of fabrication, suppressed exculpatory evidence and prompted misidentification. Slater was sentenced to death but was reprieved. He was awarded £6000 compensation after his conviction was quashed in 1928.

Within three months of arriving in Sydney, MacKay joined the New South Wales Police Force and, unlike the men already there who had to wait twenty years or more for meaningful promotion, his rise was rapid. Unusually for police officers, he knew shorthand and was sent to take notes of the speakers at Industrial Workers of the World (IWW) meetings at the Domain. During the First World War, the IWW was protesting at the conviction of one of its leaders, Tom Barker, for sedition. It was also bitterly opposed to conscription, which was being proposed to assist the war in Europe. The subsequent prosecutions were another example of fudged evidence: *agents provocateurs,* and dubious and lying witnesses gave perjured evidence that led to the men's convictions and long sentences. In a list prepared by Mitchell of officers who had played an important part in the case, MacKay was at the top. He was in line for a reward and also promotion to sergeant. He did not, however, feature in a second list of meritorious officers. Also promoted to third-class sergeant, but this time in the detective division, was Constable George 'Monkey' Fergusson, who had persuaded a witness, McAlister, to give false evidence.

A royal commission headed by Justice NK Ewing in 1920 found a great deal of what was called, through a misprint in the report, 'efictiitiousvidence'. He upheld the convictions of five of the men but, ordering their release, effectively quashed their sentences. Ewing found that there was no evidence MacKay had embroidered his notes, but McAlister, on whose evidence an arson charge rested and whom Fergusson had 'safeguarded and nursed at home', was described as an agent provocateur.

Two years later MacKay was in charge of reorganising the police transport system in the Great Strike and was promoted to sergeant second class. In 1920, after he had successfully organised the Prince of Wales' visit to Sydney, he was promoted to sergeant first class. Three years later he was moved to the detective branch and made officer in charge of the detectives of No 1 Division. By January 1925 he was acting inspector third class. In January 1928, as inspector second class, he was officer in charge of the CIB.

As for Fergusson, his path had not been quite as clear. In 1919 allegations were made that he had been taking money on a regular basis from bookmakers. But, as is often the case, it was the bookmakers who were charged with conspiracy to falsely accuse him of bribery. The first jury disagreed and the attorney-general then dropped the charges against them.

The road to hell is regularly paved with good intentions, and the New South Wales *Vagrancy (Amendment) Act 1929* is a shining example. This law was passed following a time when men such as 'Snowy' Cutmore and Norman Bruhn, self-exiled from Melbourne, were standing over prostitutes and cocaine dealers, and there were fears of a major gang war. Then, in June 1927, Bruhn was shot dead in Darlinghurst and three months later Cutmore was shot and killed when visiting his wife and mother back in Melbourne. By the end of the 1920s the crusading

Truth, never a paper to eschew a few paragraphs of purple prose, reported:

> Razorhurst, Gunhurst, Bottlehurst, Dopehurst—it used to be Darlinghurst, one of the finest quarters of a rich and beautiful city; today it is a plague spot where the spawn of the gutter grow and fatten on official apathy. By day it shelters in its alleys, in its dens, the Underworld's people. At night it looses them to prey on prosperity, decency and virtue, and to fight one another for the division of the spoils ... human beasts that live with no aim, purpose or occupation but crime—bottle men, dope pedlars, razor slashers, sneak thieves, confidence men, spielers, gunmen and every brand of racecourse parasite.

Even the rather more sedate *Sydney Morning Herald* had joined in, with reports of a 'Crime Wave' and suggestions that Cabinet was worried by the current state of affairs. More police were promised and there was an immediate increase in the strength of the CIB.

This was the opportunity for what sociologists call a symbolic crusade conducted by moral entrepreneurs: a situation that arises when, in the guise of reform for the public good, entrepreneurs are able to advance their own causes, which are not necessarily the same as those of the crusade. Good examples of such crusades are those that occur in relation to pornography, drugs and temperance.

The time was ripe for the so-called consorting laws, in practice an amendment to the Vagrancy Act. These would make it an offence to mix with other criminals. While Mitchell and Superintendent Walter Childs were not convinced of the need, MacKay took the opportunity to press for them. For him they would enhance the power of the police. For his then ally *Truth,* the laws would demonstrate the power of the press.

It was during the debate on the proposed legislation that Linda Littlejohn and Jessie Street, both prominent feminists, wrote to the Legislative Assembly presciently pointing out not only that prostitutes would be treated unfairly if the Bill became law but also that, more dangerously, 'It will open the way to bribery and corruption of the police—a very dangerous public consequence'.

In 1962 Lance Hoban, in his official history of the New South Wales Police Force, praised the *Vagrancy (Amendment) Act 1929,* seeing it as a major step forward:

> At the time, the City of Sydney was infested with criminals, undesirables and nefarious groups, better known as the 'razor gang' element. This legislation was imperative ... [and] a Consorting Squad was formed within the Criminal Investigation Branch.
>
> The activities of this new formed squad were largely responsible for the suppression of these

> organised criminal groups and the total extinction of the razor gang adherents ... The Consorting Squad is considered the best training ground of all for aspiring young detectives to acquire knowledge of the 'under-world' and the criminal element generally.

In reality the amendment merely created another class of 'police property', to stand alongside gays, Aboriginals, students, prostitutes and drug takers: men and women regarded by the police as the *untermensch* and sometimes derisorily called 'dingoes', who could be arrested or used for sport at the whim of a police officer without any fear of reprisal.

Thirty-five years on from the praise bestowed by Hoban, the Wood Royal Commission took the opposite view, saying that the consorting laws had been open to abuse and indeed had been abused:

> The special powers conferred later came to be an instrument for ... the establishment of improper relationships ... [which were] a powerful influence in the increased development of corruption.

Back in 1930, one of the principal beneficiaries of the legislation was MacKay, and the next year popular magazine *Smith's Weekly* reported:

> The detectives have now such a firm grip on the underworld that razor slashings are almost a thing of the past and gun play has lost most of its

> charm. But it is generally conceded that the authorities could go very much further by using the Consorting Act to make life really unbearable for the crooks ... the iron hand of Det-Supt. MacKay is something that they really fear in the dark corners of Kings Cross. *Let's Really see it in Action.*

In March 1932, at the age of forty-six, MacKay was assigned to take charge of the Metropolitan Administrative District, so becoming the second most senior man in the New South Wales force. His appointment as commissioner in March 1935 was universally approved, and on 10 February that year *Truth* again led the tributes:

> Mr MacKay will have the powers of a dictator; but it is preferable to have a trained policeman with such powers, rather than a political wirepuller! ... Everyone will be satisfied with this appointment!

The first major scandal of MacKay's career had begun in November 1933, with what was apparently an unremarkable arrest of a shopkeeper for illegal betting. It was one of around 3000 cases a year, of which nearly 100 per cent resulted in a conviction. Although off-course betting had been made illegal in 1906, SP (starting price) bookmakers could be found in almost every hotel in the state standing by the bar and near the telephone.

Bookmaking was one of the so-called victimless crimes—prostitution and sly-grogging were among others—which provided considerable revenue for the court system. MacKay established a specialist squad to deal with SP bookmakers. Each of six areas in Sydney had a special squad devoted to dealing with licensing and bookmaking offences and in addition there was a 'flying squad', based at police headquarters, that could operate throughout the city.

But apart from the requirement of obtaining two witnesses, there were problems with obtaining convictions. For a start, because officers were well known in their own communities, the police had to rely on a system of infiltrators, pimps and informers to obtain the evidence. One of the infiltrators used extensively and patronised by MacKay was Sergeant Joe Chuck, who effectively made a whole career out of disguising himself to gain entry to sly-grogs and hotels where SP bookmaking was thought to be taking place. According to his admiring biographer, Vince Kelly, Chuck made over 15,000 arrests in his twenty-year-long career. There were other problems. Evidence could easily be fabricated and a corrupt officer could establish a form of taxation with one or more bookmakers.

Four plainclothes police officers claimed they saw William Mowlds taking bets in his Marrickville ham and beef shop. They also said that they found lists of horses, which they alleged were proof he was taking bets. Mowlds denied making the calls they claimed and said that the lists were of bets he had legally placed. He was convicted and fined £20, reduced on appeal to £5.

Despite the reduction in his fine, Mowlds would not lie down, and he had certain things in his favour. First, he had no previous convictions and was well thought of in his community. Second, he had high-ranking Masonic friends. Third, one of the officers, Mendelssohn Miller, regularly used by the squads for undercover work, was also a Mason. Fourth, Miller was unhappy about his part in the raid on Mowlds. Through his Masonic connections Mowlds' friend and bailsman Charles Williams approached Inspector Alec Russell, head of the flying squad. Miller was interviewed and convinced Russell that the raid had been a fake.

An internal inquiry was conducted by Monkey Fergusson, by then an inspector. (Fergusson's name, and that of his son Donald, regularly crop up over the years in dark corners of New South Wales Police history.) Fergusson took a different view. Miller was the liar and the other three officers the genuine ones. Mowlds' complaint was dismissed and, as regularly happens to whistleblowers, Miller was recommended for disciplinary charges.

Still Mowlds would not roll over, and on 3 March 1936, three years after the raid, the matter was raised in parliament by Carlo Lazzarini, the Labor member for Marrickville. He put forward a motion to establish a select committee to inquire into accusations against the police, claiming that on race days the police deliberately framed men to obtain convictions. At the time it was almost impossible to defend such a prosecution. In 1936 only 42 out of 5586 prosecutions resulted in an acquittal. Lazzarini did not hold back:

> The whole system in connection with starting price betting prosecutions reeks with injustice ... in many cases the police are rottenly corrupt in their methods of apprehending persons alleged to be guilty of starting price betting. This is a serious statement for a responsible public man to make on the floor of the house. I make it calmly and deliberately, and I say that the police perjure themselves every day of the week.

Even, or perhaps particularly, from a former chief secretary these were fighting words. What Lazzarini wanted was a select committee that could move swiftly and make recommendations. The government thought otherwise and opted for a more cumbersome royal commission. The advantages of this were that the government could be seen to be taking the matter seriously, and by the time the commission made its report the public would have lost interest in the origins. And the government could almost guarantee that the commissioner in charge would be pro-police.

Some years later journalist Sean Padraic wrote:

> First, you narrow the terms of reference as much as you possibly can; secondly you choose your chief investigator who in turn chooses the investigation team; third you choose the legal team; and finally, you choose the judge. Having done all this you know what the answers are going to be.

But just sometimes, as Robert Burns wrote, the best-laid plans of mice and men 'gang aft a-gley' and they nearly did with the appointment of a new judge, Horace Francis Markell, as the royal commissioner. Variously described as a man who would believe the best of the worst of his fellow men and a judge who was 'deeply grounded in the law' and who 'drove through to his conclusions in a manner which never deviates', Markell was no malleable governmental tool. He was not prepared to whitewash the police, although, correctly, he was quite prepared to give them the benefit of any doubt. Where there was overwhelming evidence of guilt he did what he described as 'my unpleasant duty'. He did, however, set a pattern that was followed by successive commissioners throughout Australia: if a witness against the police was of bad character then he could not be believed. Markell, like so many, would not accept that those of bad character were the most likely to suffer at the hands of the police without fear of redress. Although he may not have known it, Markell subscribed to the rotten-apple theory. Sadly, here were corrupt and dishonest officers, but they were individuals. There was no systemic corruption:

> It has been my unpleasant duty to find several members of the Police (including two senior officers) guilty of charges made under the Commission ... This Inquiry has revealed a state of things which is, in my opinion, exceedingly serious and which must have a very disturbing effect upon the mind of the community.

So far, so good, but then:

> Without in any way seeking to minimise the gravity of the position ... the cases which were investigated before this Inquiry go [back] to 1930, thus covering a period of six years, and during that time there have been some 20,000 prosecutions in relation to illegal betting. As the Government paid all expenses in connection to the Inquiry I am bound to assume that the twenty-seven cases actually investigated represent, at any rate, a fair proportion of those in which it was alleged that the Police had acted improperly. Again, it must be kept in mind that the officers who have been found guilty represent a very small proportion of the total number of men engaged in this branch of Police activity. Keeping these facts in mind there would appear to be no reason to believe that the irregular practices are general.

In fact, Markell had received many more complaints than he had investigated and indeed had discouraged would-be complainants. In the report there was also a word of praise for MacKay:

> It is clear the Police Administration has realised the responsibility falling upon it in connection with the suppression of illegal betting ... every endeavour has been made to ensure that the law is properly enforced with a due regard to the rights of private citizens.

Perhaps, after all, the government and MacKay were reasonably well served by Markell.

In the wash-up Markell found against twenty-two officers, and sixteen, including two sergeants, were dismissed from the force. As for poor Mendelssohn Miller, his troubles were far from over. The Mowlds case would produce another two royal commissions, with Miller the focus of both of them.

During the commission Fergusson, his wife and son, Don, had been at the Berlin Olympics, in which Don had been part of the Australian rowing squad. Also on the squad were Merv Wood, later to become police commissioner, and another promising officer, Merv Reilly, later to go to prison for smuggling. On his return the temporarily discredited Fergusson set about retrieving his reputation. The whole thing had been a Masonic conspiracy against him and, letter by letter, he dripped poison about the character and ability of Miller.

In the summer of 1936 the police turned up again at Mowlds' ham and beef shop. This time the raiding party was far more illustrious because in their number were Superintendent Lynch and MacKay himself. This time theirs was a rescue mission, with the aim of proving that, from where the police had been positioned three years earlier, it would have been possible to see and hear Mowlds place his bets. Mowlds had said no and Fergusson had said yes, but crucially in his findings Markell, who had visited the shop during the commission, had said no and that therefore the police were lying: 'I am totally unable to understand either the conclusions at which he [Fergusson] arrived or the reasons he put forward for arriving at them'.

Any police commissioner will want to clad themself with loyal supporters, but MacKay was not always a good judge of character. His support of Joe Chuck was possibly not one of his finest moves and now he supported Fergusson. On 22 December he and the superintendent decided that Mowlds could have been seen and heard placing the bets, and MacKay had himself photographed holding the receiver to his ear. He called for a second commission to vindicate Fergusson. As Dr Evans points out, this may have been a preemptive strike. There were already murmurs about an inquiry into the administration of the police, and MacKay's move might narrow the terms and make them less dangerous to him and his force. He wrote to Attorney-General Frank Chaffney complaining that Markell's findings had been based on the belief that Miller was a man of truth. Every step that could be taken to show the reverse would be taken.

Back in 1934 Miller had already been punished, placed on uniform duties and made to clean out the office. He was then charged with using words 'subversive of discipline' to a sergeant who was drunk at the time and Miller was dismissed from the force. On appeal his punishment was reduced to a fine of ten shillings, but as his reward for speaking out he was sent to Coventry by his fellow officers. Efforts were made to show that he was an adulterer and had accepted bribes from a bookmaker and a sly-grogger. There were also allegations that he had pressured defendants to plead guilty. He was placed on light duties, which effectively meant that he cleaned the station's cars. An inquiry found that the complaints should be dropped, but they continued. Another constable alleged that he had planted false evidence. And there was yet another allegation that he had sold a stolen car. At the age of thirty-three his hair turned completely white.

Miller was fortunate that *Truth* took up his defence, arranging for him to have leading barrister J Shand to represent him and substantially changing its position about MacKay. Initially it had approved of him rather than the force itself. 'Now you have your big chance to clean up the police force in your own way', the paper had written. Gradually it hardened its attitude and became one of MacKay's most vocal critics. A second inquiry, again under Markell, began in March 1937, with the terms of reference limited to an inquiry into the Mowlds case, Fergusson's conduct and an assessment of the various departmental charges that had been levelled against Miller.

If MacKay thought the limitation on the commission would tell against Miller and Mowlds, he was wrong. Fergusson was hammered in cross-examination by lawyer Richard Windeyer, eventually admitting that he was wrong in concluding that Mowlds was an SP bookmaker on the basis of a hearsay report by one of the man's enemies.

There was, however, the question of Miller's harassment and unfair treatment. From the newspaper reports it appears that MacKay was given enormous latitude by Markell, who allowed him to interrupt the cross-examination of other witnesses. *Truth* happily reported:

> Last week was revealed the real MacKay, the Hitler of the New South Wales police force, Mr W.J. MacKay, police commissioner. He has become the great I AM since the State Government created him the omnipotent Csar of the New South Wales police force. Mr MacKay has bared his teeth ... Parliament must deal with the situation, which is reaching an alarming state. Public confidence in the police force is being

> sapped, the police commissioner is defiant and the Chief Secretary a complacent and plastic figurehead.

The commission turned into an attack on MacKay who, clearly suffering from strain, at the end of his evidence offered what amounted to an extraordinary plea in mitigation for both himself and the force, saying that the two commissions had been an 'awful lesson'. If his officers (not including Miller) had made mistakes it was because of their lack of education and sophistication. In his report, however, Markell found that there was no question of unfair treatment of Miller, nor an attempt to discredit or harass him. However, he recommended that no action be taken against him and that he should be treated as having served a number of years without anything against his character. Miller was eventually appointed a senior constable and retired in 1963. In January 1938 MacKay tried to promote Monkey Fergusson to the rank of superintendent. His recommendation was rejected and Fergusson was transferred out of police headquarters to Darlinghurst.

MacKay also worked the squad system. On joining the CIB a recruit was sent around to pick up a payoff. If he declined, his papers were marked 'not suitable for plainclothes work'. It was nearly half a century before Commissioner John Avery began dismantling the CIB in 1987, and by no means everyone agreed with him even then.

But was MacKay financially corrupt? Recent commentators such as journalist Evan Whitton and sociologist Alfred McCoy seem to think there is evidence that he was. Without doubt he must have known about the brothels in Darlinghurst when he worked from that station in the 1920s, and his efforts to shut down the baccarat clubs run by organised-crime figures such as Siddy Kelly, who had once received five years and a whipping for his part in slashing a rival bludger, and Phil 'The Jew' Jeffs in the 1940s were farcical. It was said that Kelly was making in excess of £1000 a night and so well able to pay police protection money that he was only once raided during his career as a club owner. In 1947 the raid on his Mont St Clair club in Kings Cross was not a conspicuous success. Kelly told the officer in charge, 'You have made a fool of yourself. We are only playing rummy—I had a ring from Darlinghurst about 11.30p.m. to say that you were out'. As has been said about subsequent commissioners, 'If he didn't know, he should have done'.

Corrupt detective Ray Kelly flourished on MacKay's watch and so did Kelly's offsider, the standover man Richard Gabriel Reilly, who at the time of his death in 1947 was probably the city's leading criminal. Reilly had long had good police connections before Kelly. When in December 1937 Reilly was charged with the murder of fellow gunman Clarrie Thomas, Inspector William Toole was on hand to give character evidence, telling the jury that Reilly was a 'highly reputable man

... of sober habits, an earnest worker and generally a good citizen'. Evidently the inspector did not read *Truth,* which the year before had labelled Reilly as a man who bashed people in Graham's, a Hunter Street nightclub, and had once pulled a revolver there.

On the plus side, MacKay founded the airborne division and the police pipe band (modestly dressing band members in a MacKay tartan), and, after a visit to Italy and Germany before the Second World War, extolled the benefit of police boys clubs. But he also founded the notorious 21 Division, with Frederick Hanson (soon to be known as Slippery) a founding member. At first it was known as the 'Basher Squad' and it was designed to prevent gangs from robbing wartime servicemen of their pay. But by the 1960s the division had deteriorated into a McCoy class-four corruption operation.

The most damaging thing MacKay did, however, was to promote two wholly unsuitable officers, Frederick Hanson and Norman Allan, to positions from where their move to commissioner was, if not inevitable, at least made much more likely. At the beginning of February 1946 MacKay had even promoted Hanson to sergeant in an *ad hoc* publicity stunt after Hanson piloted the first airplane purchased by the police to a safe landing at Mascot. The reality was, he later admitted, that 'I jumped 1150 men'.

5

RAY 'GUNNER' KELLY AND CO: PRINCES OF THE CITY

One of the best detectives of the New South Wales police during and immediately after the Second World War was Ray 'Gunner' Kelly, whose nickname came after he had shot and killed a suspect in 1930. After his retirement, *The Sydney Morning Herald* thought that 'he [Kelly] deliberately made friends in all walks of life because he knew that was the way to be a successful detective'. Good detective he may have been, but unfortunately Kelly was also probably one of the most corrupt policemen worldwide. He was a good friend of the prostitutes and madams Tilly Devine, Kate Leigh and 'Pretty' Dulcie Markham. Sydney standover man Richard Gabriel Reilly and onetime 'first among equals' in the city's criminal hierarchy Frederick 'Paddles' Anderson were more than just his informants; they were his partners in abortion and other rackets, as was the fashionable Dr Reginald Stuart-Jones.

During the war Bondi was the place for the backstreet abortionist, whose trade had increased substantially with the number of women who had become pregnant by visiting servicemen. The police targeted those abortionists who did not pay them protection money and the women were arrested as they left the clinics. Often there was a police photographer in attendance to complete their humiliation. Obtaining cooperation from the police was therefore a must for the clinic operators. Kelly and fellow officers Fred Krahe and Monkey Fergusson's son Don were part of a ring run by Reilly that demanded 10 per cent of all doctors' fees from abortions.

For a time Kelly, born in New South Wales in 1906, had worked as a jackeroo, but he craved excitement and moved to Sydney in 1929, where he joined the police. He was on bicycle patrol on 24 August 1930 when he saw three men, eighteen-year-old Joseph Lloyd Swan from Marrickville and housebreakers Reginald Farran and William Garton, in a stolen car in King Street, Newtown, and followed them into a dead end. They tried to run him down and he leapt onto the running board, grabbing the steering wheel. The car crashed into a shop window and the driver again tried to shake Kelly off by reversing at high speed. Instead Kelly shot all three, hitting Swan in the back and another in the head (the third man lost part of a finger). Five days later Swan, already a reputed standover man, died in hospital. In a dying deposition he said, 'I did not know the man was a policeman. He did not tell me he was or sing out. If he had said he was he could have saved himself the trouble of shooting me. I thought he was a hold-up man'. At the inquest Kelly told the coroner that Swan had tried to run him down and in fact had then reversed over his bicycle. He had been pushed off the running board by the driver and had fired a shot at the back of the car as it drove off. He then fired a further five shots at the speeding car. Other officers gave evidence that the shots must have been fired from some distance, which, given that all three men were hit, showed what a good or lucky shot Kelly was. On 17 September the coroner exonerated him, returning a verdict that he had intended to shoot at the car rather than the passengers:

> Fortunately the police, in the execution of their duty, very seldom shoot a man. There may be an occasion when to shoot a man is justifiable. In this case, I am not going to find that it was justifiable. I find it was accidental.

On 8 October 1930 Farran and Garton each received a year's imprisonment for having stolen the car.

The next year Kelly worked with the riot squad and his skull was fractured in the eviction riots in Newtown. Recovered from his injuries, Kelly progressed onward and upward in his career. He went into detective work in 1936, equally at home, said his colleagues, with bankers and standover men. Although some of the photographs of him appear to show a small, bespectacled, almost dapper little man, in fact he was over 2 metres tall and weighed nearly 90 kilograms. Described as having 'flat, glossy hair parted in the middle, a slit mouth, and glittering eyes', he was a keen golfer and surfboarder, a non-drinker and non-smoker. He had 'power above his rank', recalled Justice Don Stewart, who had been an officer on the force. 'He told senior officers what to do and what not to do. And he had killed people. He had murdered people, had Ray Kelly'.

On 15 March 1953 Kelly killed another criminal, the well-known safe-blower Lloyd Edward Day, who with four companions had spent a weekend dealing with the safe of Marcus Clark in Central Square. Kelly and others had been on a seventeen-hour stakeout. When the men emerged, two got into a truck, said to have been driven by one of Sydney's Mr Bigs, Lennie McPherson, although he was never charged. The other three got into a car driven by Day. They were chased down College Street, Drummoyne, and Kelly called out for them to stop. When they did not, Kelly leaned out of the window and fired a number of shots, one of which hit Day. The men's car careered out of control and crashed. The other men ran off but halted under what the newspapers described as 'a hail of police bullets'. Others in the squad at the time were both Fergusson and Krahe.

Kelly was also involved in the repeated captures of the gunman and escaper Darcy Dugan, on one occasion in 1958 using his informants to tell him where Dugan was waiting patiently in a 1.3-metre hole in Long Bay prison for the chance to move over the wall. That same year he confronted and disarmed James Hackett, who had shot dead Marlene Harvey in her home and wounded two other men. The next year he was part of the team that tracked down Kevin Simmonds and Leslie Newcombe, who had clubbed an Emu Plains prison warder to death while searching for food following their escape. Kelly was also in the Arthur Street, North Sydney, shoot-out with the cross-dressing Tony Martini and Edward Garland, for which the pair were sentenced to death and later reprieved. That was his public good side, but he was also quite capable of arranging for criminals such as Dugan to take the blame for some robberies he and his colleagues had set up—indeed, that was said to be his speciality.

Promotion to the detective division was an aspiration for most young policemen. It had kudos and it took the young officer out of the quasi-military structure of the force. And for those so inclined it offered the opportunity of undeclared gains. But the detective division of any force was not for the squeamish. In London in the 1960s, when recruits were known as aides to CID, they were dropped off at one side of a mainline railway station and told to make two arrests before they came out the other side.

In Sydney Kelly was one of three senior detectives who, when questioning applicants for the plainclothes division, asked them if they were prepared to load a suspect. If the answer was no they would be rejected, and Kelly was apt to remark derisively, 'Give him back to the Cardinal. He's no good to me.' The Cardinal was the incorruptible Catholic officer Brian Doyle.

Those Kelly took on and groomed included Murray Riley, another Olympic oarsman, whom he seconded in 1954 to moonlight as bodyguard to Lennie McPherson's mate the slot-machine manufacturer Ray Smith, after a bomb attack on his car.

When his relationship with Smith became known, Riley was transferred back to the uniform branch, from which he soon resigned and took up the lucrative, if dangerous, life of a drug dealer. In June 1978 Riley pleaded guilty and received ten years in Adelaide for the importation of 2.7 tonnes of cannabis. He had overloaded his boat the *Anoa,* which had been unable to make port. He had also been importing heroin bought in Thailand at several thousand dollars a pound and selling it, duly cut with sugar, at several thousand dollars an ounce in Australia. In 1980 Riley received a further seven years on charges of possessing an unlicensed pistol and conspiracy to cheat and defraud the American Express Company of $274,000. Shortly before his release in May 1984 he was made bankrupt, owing over $132,000 to the Nugan Hand Bank, which was by this time in liquidation. In 1985 he was named in an inquiry by Justice Bredmeyer of the Papua New Guinea Supreme Court as being part of a ring to import $40 million of heroin from Bangkok.

Kelly's retirement party on 3 February 1960, a £5-a-plate buffet with unlimited drink, was attended by nearly 900 people and included a mix of luminaries such as Premier Robin (who later changed his name to Robert) Askin, Police Commissioner Norman 'The

Foreman' Allen, judges, horse trainers, criminals and the gambler Perce Galea.

Farewell dinners attended by politicians and criminals alike were common at the time. In 1950 James Sweeney, a retiring metropolitan superintendent, was feted by 600 vice traders at Sammy Lee's restaurant, where he received a cheque for over £600. Inspector Noonan, metropolitan licensing inspector, did rather better on his retirement, pocketing £1000 that was presented to him at the Australia Hotel. The 1951 Royal Commission on Liquor Laws in New South Wales found that the practices were simply 'indiscreet' rather than illegal.

Shortly before Premier Askin's funeral in 1981, attention was drawn to the late premier's finances and his relationship with Kelly, who in 1975 had received an MBE in Askin's last New Year's honours list. The journalist Evan Whitton was told:

> If I was investigating Sir Robert Askin, I would search land titles of land bought since 1958 by Detective Sergeant Ray Kelly.
>
> Kelly was his bagman. Such land would have been purchased and then sold promptly to Government departments and then held by those departments for long periods of time as it would be land not required by them. A good place to start looking would be land at Ourimbah.

During his service Kelly approached policeman-turned-reporter Kevin Perkins and offered him $500 a week cash to keep him informed of trends in media views on illegal gambling. At the same time he told Perkins:

> No one can open one (an illegal casino) without the permission of the Premier and the Police Commissioner (Hanson). If anyone opens against our wishes, we just close them down. They pay for protection and the right to operate ... I still collect the money and distribute it. I make sure Bob Askin gets his share and so on down the line.

He also told Perkins that he had controlled the abortion rackets and reported to Norman Allen and later to Hanson. Perkins turned down the offer. Kelly died on 11 August 1977.

It was Kelly and his offsider Fred Krahe who nurtured a young officer with a good pedigree, Don Fergusson—son of Monkey Fergusson and described by Evan Whitton as being much in demand at Masonic lodges for his detailed knowledge of the liturgy—to be their bagman in the abortion rackets. It will be remembered that Monkey was watching his son row in the Berlin Olympics during the Markell bookmaking inquiry of 1936.

Krahe had joined the police as a cadet in 1940 and by the time of his premature retirement was a striking example of the abuse of police power. One fellow officer observed: 'Krahe was known as a scoundrel within the Force' and another described him as 'an evil bloke—a big, brooding bastard with an aura of power and evil about him'. Krahe prided himself on his criminal contacts.

A good detective involved in a number of major cases, such as the first thallium poisoning, like a number of others Krahe organised abortion rackets and armed robberies, as well as standing over prostitutes and bricking criminals. Along with Kelly, he seems to have been particularly set against safebreaker and thief Darcy Dugan, whom he attempted to set up on a number of occasions.

George Freeman, never lower than No 2 in the criminal hierarchy of the period, thought Krahe was a 'deadly and evil' killer who had his own pricing scheme:

> After he'd arrest you, the paying began. You'd pay him to get bail, you'd pay some more later for a reduced sentence, you'd pay more for remands, you'd pay for whether or not he gave verbal evidence against you, and you'd pay again if he decided not to give evidence ... And believe me, everybody paid. It was stupid not to ... Krahe not only stood over crims once he arrested them, he had others working for him, doing everything from stealing cars to house-breakings and armed robberies.

Interviewed for Sydney exhibition *Sin City* at the Police and Justice Museum, Karl Bonnette—known as the Godfather and alleged to have been part of the Double Bay Mob—recalled the Kelly and Krahe era:

> I never had run-ins with them at all. The only thing I knew was that Fred Krahe was known as the Big Till. They said when he knocks at your door, have a handful of money or you're going to jail. I was lucky enough for him never to knock on my door.

An incident that backed up Freeman's assessment took place in February 1972 when Alan Burton, who had been involved in a huge car-stealing racket with the one-legged Reg Varley, vanished. The Varley-Burton combo had stolen cars worth $1.5 million in seven months, the lion's share of which, said Varley, was received by Krahe. In January 1972 a series of raids began on the Varley chop-shops, and on the night of 7 February Burton disappeared. Varley was accused of paying two New South Wales detectives $5000 to dispose of his partner. Much of the evidence against him came from another member of the gang, Paul Hos, who told the Central Criminal Court that Varley said he went to Burton's house with some detectives, one of whom hit Burton with a cosh. Varley allegedly then also hit him and the body was taken 200 miles down the coast and dumped at sea. In his defence Varley told the court that Krahe had called on him that night and told him they were going to give Burton a hiding. He had, it was said, swindled the officers out of $20,000. When Varley protested, he was hit on the ankle of his one leg and his aluminium crutches were smashed. Burton and he were taken for a drive and then Burton was taken from the car and Varley heard shots. However, Varley was convicted of manslaughter and sentenced to fourteen years. He served nine, and after his release constantly tried to have his case reopened, claiming the kidnap had been organised by detective Cyril Edwards.

The case had a curious sequel. The next year Edwards was dismissed from the force and although it was recommended that charges be brought against him, none were. Edwards disappeared from view until March 1986, when 1100 Indian hemp plants were found at his chicken farm. He was charged with cultivating and on 31 October, shortly before he was due to appear in court, his body, with legs and hands trussed, was found in the sea at Mackenzie's Bay near Tamarama. He had been shot in the head. Before he disappeared he told his wife he had information implicating high-ranking officers and was going to see two detectives in Sydney to 'fix' the evidence against him. He had also taken out a life-insurance policy and changed his will. A company director, Peter Collis, claimed he could produce evidence showing who had shot Edwards, but he never did. Despite leaning towards a verdict of suicide, the coroner returned an open verdict.

Journalist and author Richard Hall thought:

> He [Krahe] was a crook all right but he was locking up half the crims in Sydney with the information he was getting from the other half. Krahe had been so close to the Gladesdale Mob, then the dominant group in Sydney, as to be almost a member.

Hall may have been overly generous to him. Krahe was also said to be a senior member, if not the leader, of the Sydney-based Toe-Cutters Gang, named because of their predilection for snipping off the toes and other body parts of criminals to persuade them to share the greater part of their haul. One of his offsiders was criminal and fellow toe-cutter Kevin Gore, who was thought to have been killed in the winter of 1972 by standover man John 'Nano the Magician' Regan. Gore was last seen walking with Regan in Darlinghurst. Krahe was said to have tried unsuccessfully to persuade William Maloney and Linus 'The Pom' Driscoll to kill Regan in retaliation for Gore's murder and that of his friend, another standover man, John Edward 'Ratty Jack' Clarke, who was shot and killed while drinking at the Newington Inn at Petersham in August 1974.

During the last ten years of his career Krahe was involved with Shirley Brifman, a working girl and brothel madam in the Kings Cross area and in Queensland, who said she paid him a regular $100 a week for protection from standover men. He was, she said, always at her brothel, arriving most days about

11a.m. She claimed he had told her that he had organised about eight robberies and collected money from an abortion clinic. She gave him expensive presents and when she was in Queensland he would ring her daily saying how much he missed her.

Following a flat-warming party at Brifman's new brothel, The Reef, in 1968, photos of Krahe and other senior police officers were leaked to *The Sunday Mirror.* Newspaper stories describing her as the 'Kings Cross call-girl queen' followed. Overnight she had become a liability to her police protectors. While it dawned on Brifman that she could be facing some serious prison time, it also occurred to Krahe—and Queensland officers Tony Murphy, Glendon Hallahan and the rest—that she might start to talk. As a form of insurance, Krahe is said to have tortured Brifman twice in Sydney in the latter half of 1970, on one occasion badly burning her feet.

Despite this, talk she did. When Brifman was arrested for allegedly procuring her fourteen-year-old daughter, something she bitterly denied, she went public, maintaining that Krahe had helped organise a theft of bonds from a bank. She also claimed that he and Queensland officer Tony Murphy had 'exchanged' criminals—Donny 'The Glove' Smith, shot dead in 1970 by club owner James Anderson in Abe Saffron's Venus Room, and Donald 'The Hammer' Kelly, bashed to death in a motel near Newcastle in 1988—so that they could work in each other's state without fear of recognition. Given that the police were still getting over a scandal involving massaged crime figures, this was the last thing that was needed.

Under threat from Krahe, Shirley Brifman fled to Queensland and from July to October 1971 she was interviewed by Brian 'The Cardinal' Doyle from New South Wales and Norman Gulbranson in Queensland, both officers of indisputable integrity. She named over fifty officers from both states, the majority in connection with specific crimes—passing forged $10 notes, setting up burglaries—or general corruption such as visiting her brothels and taking money on a regular basis.

Before she talked, Don Fergusson, then in his late fifties, was in serious difficulties on both a personal and a professional level. He believed his memory was failing and that he was going mad. Despite this he had been successful in his application to become metropolitan superintendent, the fifth-highest-ranked officer. He was also at loggerheads with Kelly and Krahe over taking money from drug suppliers. For him, drugs were one step too far. Made of sterner stuff, in turn they thought that his new position meant he was digging out and he might no longer be willing to protect his former tutors.

With the abortion business about to break, on Sunday 15 February 1970, Fergusson's body was found in the lavatory of his personal office at Campbell Street CIB. He had been shot in the right temple and his revolver was nearby. He appears to have left a note indicating that he thought he had a malignant tumour in his brain, but an autopsy found no trace of one. A verdict of suicide while suffering severe depression was returned, but many thought Krahe had held the trembling hand. In turn, Krahe offered a cryptic remark, 'The silly cunt didn't have to do it'. At the funeral service in St Andrew's Cathedral, Bishop FO Hulme-Moir described Fergusson as 'a man who never lost his high sense of duty', which was one way of putting things. The card on one wreath read, 'With deepest sympathy from Lennie'. Now who could have sent that?

Shirley Brifman was found dead in her Brisbane flat in March 1972. Shortly before midnight on the night of her death a man had called on her. She died either of a heart attack or a drug overdose, but over the years there have been persistent rumours among the police that it was Krahe, with or without the active assistance of a Queensland officer, who forced the pills down her throat.

Krahe was allowed to retire that year, at the age of fifty-two, with a thrombosis in the leg. He was later suspected, without any hard evidence to back it up, of involvement in both the murder of Griffith anti-drug campaigner Donald Mackay and the disappearance of Juanita Nielsen, who was campaigning against the development of Potts Point. Krahe had certainly been helpful in evicting protesting squatters from the Potts Point site. He was also involved in the Nugan Hand Bank affair and was charged with conspiracy to defraud the group but acquitted on all counts. He died, aged sixty-one, in December 1981 from the thrombosis, brought on, said one admirer, 'by kicking too many people to death'. Arch villain George Freeman, unsurprisingly, disliked Krahe and in 1988 Krahe's son failed in an attempt to obtain an injunction against Freeman's autobiography, which was heavily critical of his father.

However, Krahe's champion Bill Jenkings wrote, 'Krahe, a CIB legend, had his admirers and his critics. I was among the former. And there wasn't one in the latter group whose achievements came within a bull's roar of Krahe's'.

6

MACKAY'S LEGACY: COPS AND CROOKS IN CAHOOTS

When New South Wales Commissioner William MacKay died following a heart attack in 1948 he was succeeded by his assistant commissioner, James Frederick Scott, who does not even merit a mention in the *Australian Dictionary of Biography.* But, by the time Colin Delaney, the first Catholic appointment, took over four years later in 1952, there were allegations of corruption and brutality in the force, something with which Delaney never came to grips. Instead, since he regarded homosexuals as Australia's 'greatest menace', copious time and resources, which might have been spent on organised crime, were devoted to their entrapment by young, good-looking constables.

There was a precedent for this. MacKay had been involved in two distinctly dubious cases in which gay men were set up for political reasons, and in general over the years homosexuals have been targets for some officers. One former detective has said, 'Sport for some coppers was chasing blokes around toilets and either arresting gays, beating them or both'.

In March 1943 a charge of obscene conduct in a public lavatory against Clarence McNulty, editor-in-chief of Sydney's *DailyTelegraph,* was dismissed by Stipendiary Magistrate McCullough. It was alleged against police officers Thomas Carney and Neville Grigg that, working with bent solicitor Herbert Munro, they had bricked McNulty and other men over the past year. They then pointed them in the direction of Munro who, appearing for them at a fee of £100, usually was able to persuade the magistrate to record a finding of guilt against them but without recording a conviction. The constables were given half Munro's fee, and sometimes other money changed hands so that Munro could bribe the press not to report the case. As a result, in April constables Carney, with fifteen years' service, and Grigg, with five, were dismissed from the force. The officers appealed to a tribunal, which reinstated them in July that year. Backed by the Police Association of New South Wales, Grigg then brought an action against Commissioner MacKay and *The Sunday Telegraph,* claiming damages for libel over an article in the paper. He lost and was later bankrupted over unpaid costs.

Such actions and attitudes were not uncommon. Gay activist Gary Burns recalls Sydney officer Frank 'Bumper' Farrell—a legendary hard man of policing and rugby league, who was alleged to have bitten off an opponent's ear—taking him to the cells under Darlinghurst police station in the 1970s. 'He put a phone book against my stomach and beat the shit out of me. He said, "I don't want poofters in my street".'

And it wasn't always police acting on their own. It was alleged but never quite proved that in 1972 a group of policemen, for evening post-drinking sport, threw gays in the Torrens River near Government Gardens, Adelaide, known as the No.1 Beat, a trysting place for homosexual men. Homosexual acts were illegal in South Australia at the time, and 'a ducking' was considered by some a much easier and certainly more fun form of punishment than the trouble of processing the men through the courts.

On 10 May 1972 Roger James and 42-year-old law lecturer Dr George Duncan, who had been in the country for less than two months after teaching in England, were victims of what was described in a police report as 'a high-spirited frolic gone wrong'. Duncan, who could not swim and had only one lung as a result of contracting tuberculosis as a child, drowned. James, who suffered a broken leg, managed to crawl out and onto a road, where he was found and taken to hospital.

The attackers, whom James failed to identify, were alleged to be three senior vice-squad officers accompanied by a fourth man, a tall civilian, said to have connections in high places, who was never identified. On the grounds of self-incrimination the officers declined to give evidence at the coronial inquest. They were suspended and later resigned.

Scotland Yard sent over Detective Superintendent Bob McGowan and Detective Sergeant Charles O'Hanlon to scrutinise the conduct of the police investigation, but the report was only made public in 2008, when gay activist Malcolm Cowan described it as homophobic and glib. It took fourteen years for a prosecution to be brought against two of the officers. As was their right, they did not give evidence and, amid allegations—which were never proved—that a juror had been got at to return a not guilty verdict, both were acquitted. At the trial a former vice-squad officer gave evidence that it was common for officers to chase homosexuals, fire a couple of shots in the air and then throw their captives in the river. One result of Duncan's death was that in 1975 South Australia became the first state to legalise homosexuality. Over the next twenty years other states followed suit.

Commissioner Delaney did take steps to modernise the New South Wales force at the start of his term in the 1950s, extending the number of four-wheel vehicles and decentralising decision making, but he was another who failed to convince the Crown Employees Appeal Board of the benefits of promotion by merit rather than by seniority.

He retired in 1962 and what followed was an unbroken seventeen years of systemic corruption. It was not surprising that there was corruption in the senior and lower levels of the New South Wales police during those years, as for twelve of those years corruption went straight to the office of the premier, Sir Robert Askin.

Sir Robert, who disliked his given name of Robin and changed it by deed poll in 1971, served in the Second World War, and afterwards managed the travel department for a bank while moonlighting as an SP operator. He joined the Liberal Party in 1947.

For years, particularly after Askin died in September 1981 leaving something over $2 million, the belief was that both Police Commissioner Norman 'The Foreman' Allan and Askin were on the take from illegal casinos, abortion rackets and prostitution. Justice Moffitt, who in 1973 conducted an inquiry into the infiltration of New South Wales clubs by organised crime, viewed the premier with some charity:

> There was no evidence against him in my inquiry, never any solid proof. I always thought he got money by being put in on the Stock Exchange. There was a smell about his selling knighthoods but there was no evidence. It's a false assumption that a person who ends up wealthy has been getting it in a brown paper bag.

However, as the years have gone by, so much evidence to support the systemic-corruption theory has emerged that it would seem Moffitt was being unduly generous.

As for Allan, a former assistant commissioner remembered:

> I was a cadet when Fred Hanson was commissioner; he was an alcoholic and corrupt. So were Norman Allan and Mervyn Wood [corrupt].

MacKay's protégé Norman Allan had been the commissioner's personal assistant and later assistant to both Delaney and Scott, and had designed the police-department crest *Culpam Poena Premit Comes* ('Punishment follows closely upon the crime'). Appointed in 1962 at the age of fifty-two, he was then the youngest ever police commissioner. The always well-groomed Allan, a man who favoured the death penalty and admired J Edgar Hoover, was known as The Foreman because of his undoubted administrative abilities. He had been commended for 'exceptional skill and ability' in the hunt for Stephen Bradley, convicted of the kidnapping and murder of the small boy Graeme Thorne in 1956.

In 1967 Allan, or possibly his then assistant Don Fergusson, had the great idea of solving major crimes by using phone taps as a cheaper and certainly more reliable alternative to the traditional method of paying dobbers. The evidence might not be admissible in court, but very often the evidence of informers could not be used either. Allan called in Sergeant DR Williams and three years later, after tests in the United States, a working group was set up. Evan Whitton believed that the group insisted their tapping should not include allegations of police misconduct, but over the years a number of officers could be heard on tape in unfortunate circumstances. By the time they ceased operations, personnel of the unit had undertaken over 200 separate interceptions and Allan was proud of his illegal activity, telling a police conference, 'There is no reason in the world why every facility, including wire tapping, should not be made available to the police'.

Perhaps Allan simply lacked judgement. On one occasion he proposed to give young constables time off so that they could have dancing lessons before the Police Commissioner's Ball. More seriously, in 1968 he made some extraordinary decisions while in command of the siege that followed after mentally disturbed petty criminal Wally Mellish took his girlfriend Beryl and her twelve-week-old son hostage. There have been suggestions that Allan and Mellish had, in some way, been connected. Negotiating techniques were not as developed then as now, but certainly in the twentieth century the head negotiator would not have agreed that Mellish should be given an Armalite rifle and 200 rounds of ammunition. It is doubtful also if he would have arranged for a clergyman to marry the gunman and his hostage, and be on hand himself to provide the wedding ring. Fortunately, the siege ended without bloodshed, but the Police Association rightly complained about Allan giving Mellish a gun. Apparently it had been doctored by Don Fergusson so that it would only fire one shot. The bride left her husband for good after his surrender.

Allan was another who, despite the efforts of the press to alert him, declined to target SP bookies or gaming in general. In 1981 Fred 'The Cat' Silvester, father of journo John and then the head of the Australian Bureau of Criminal Intelligence, told how he had warned Allan that there were SP links between Sydney and Melbourne, which had a combined turnover of $2800 million, but no action was taken. As for the baccarat clubs, in June 1967 Allan announced that 'Police action is taken at all times and in all cases where evidence of any unlawful gaming and/or wagering is forthcoming'. The announcement was met with derision. *The Sydney Sun,* which could hear the 'screech of the cockatoos down the Cross', began, 'Come off it Norm! ... surely you don't expect us to cop that memorable quote of yours when you're quizzed about baccarat'. *The Sydney Telegraph* more sedately thought, 'Mr Allan seems to be in a state of continual wide-eyed surprise over allegations of illegal gambling'.

As the years went by the corruption of Allan's senior officers became an open scandal, as did the 'cold store' he kept in the Sydney Market, where traders would deliver tributes. The store had been seen as a perk for previous commissioners, but now it became a public outrage.

Allan's career came to an end with the disclosure that the crime figures were being massaged to show a higher clear-up rate than was the case. It had been going on for close to forty years and worked on the principle of one book for the tax inspector and one for the business. In this case it was one book for the public and one, known as Paddy's Book, for the force. Certain crime, regarded as difficult to clear up, appeared only in Paddy's Book. Almost every detective in the force must have been complicit in the cover-up over the years. Allan could have survived, but he chose to ignore the concerns of police computer expert Phillip Arantz who, when he could get no positive response from the commissioner, went instead to *The Sydney Morning Herald.* Also on Allan's debit side were the numerous inquiries he conducted for Askin that took the heat off sensitive issues but the findings for which were never released.

Allan's most disastrous act, however, was to ensure the promotion of Fred Hanson to commissioner in November 1972. Under Frederick John 'Slippery' Hanson, the New South Wales Police became known as 'the best police force money could buy'. Hanson began his working life as a railway porter, joining the force in 1936. Two years earlier he had been rejected as undersized and had gone on a bodybuilding course. After the war he was a founding member of 21 Division, set up to deal with the young bashers who were causing general mayhem in the Sydney suburbs. His nickname was a play on words. Not only was he devious but also he had an unfortunate knack of losing his footing.

But one good turn deserves another. As commissioner, Hanson—who, curiously, disliked his nickname—declined to go after the casino owners, such as highly popular gambler and identity Perce Galea, said to be pushing $5000 a week all the way to the top ranks of police and politicians. Unbelievably, Hanson claimed that the police did not have the authority to go into the clubs. His appointment coincided with the growth of organised crime in New South Wales and, if there is not clear evidence against him, there is the deepest suspicion that he protected identities such as his duck-shooting friend Robert 'Aussie Bob' Trimbole, part of the Mr Asia drug syndicate, who gave him an expensive shotgun. He allowed officers named by prostitute Shirley Brifman as corrupt to retire 'hurt on duty' and so avoid questioning and possible charges. He also cocked a snook at the Moffitt Royal Commission by promoting Sergeant Jack McNeill to inspector when the commission found that he and his colleagues were involved in a 'deliberate or corrupt' cover-up of details relevant to their investigation into organised crime in clubs.

By 1974 Hanson was slacking off, working only 47 per cent of his official hours. In February 1976 he brought and settled an action that implied he had an interest in an illegal casino at West Gosford, but, with that, his days were numbered. He agreed to retire early if he could appoint his successor, and he sat on the three-man committee to select his nominee Mervyn Wood, overlooking Brian 'The Cardinal' Doyle, who would have been a far more suitable appointment and who might just have stemmed corruption in the force.

One perhaps fanciful suggestion is that as a Catholic, Doyle disapproved of the decision five years earlier in the Heatherbrae case, which legalised abortion in New South Wales, and he might have used his influence as commissioner to challenge it.

After Hanson retired it is alleged that he flew drugs down from Cairns in partnership with an Oxford Street, Sydney, brothel owner. He died of carbon-monoxide poisoning in his car in October 1980, a death many believe was suicide. The coroner dispensed with an inquest. It was thought that Hanson's death came shortly after he learned that he was to be the subject of a newspaper exposé.

Overall, the attitude of his successor, Merv Wood, appointed in 1976, was at best one of live and let live—unless and until he was forced to do otherwise. Many, however, thought that this laissez-faire attitude concealed a rather darker side. Son of a police sergeant, Wood—another noted oarsman who was the baby of the Australian Olympic squad in Berlin—later won a gold, a silver and two bronze at successive Olympic Games. There must have been some sort of delayed reaction to the German water, because three of the squad who joined the police went off the rails in a serious way. In 1950 Wood won the double sculls at the Auckland Empire Games with the later even more disgraced Mervyn Riley. Wood took the position of commissioner amid a general round of applause, but he did not last long. On his appointment he said that he hoped the vexed question of gambling would soon be cleared up and, while he had heard of Mr Big and Mr Sin—George Freeman and Abe Saffron—they had been built up by the press to be bigger than they actually were. You could find their equivalents in any major city, he said.

It was during Wood's time as commissioner that Superintendent Merv Beck was invited by Assistant Commissioner Jim Lees to take action against the gaming clubs, which were running unhindered in Sydney and elsewhere in New South Wales. As a result Beck and his family endured years of threats, death threats and harassment. Beck taught his wife how to use a shotgun, and by the end of his stint cleaning up Darlinghurst police station and 21 Division she had taken to sleeping with the shotgun in her bed. During the course of his tours of duty he ran up against the so-called Barbecue Set, a group of politicians, criminals and corrupt police who met on a Sunday afternoon. Doubt has been cast on the existence of the Barbecue Set, but veteran journo Bob Bottom recalls:

> Johnny James organised the meat for the Barbecue Set. Dick Cox, head of the Vice Squad, controlled prostitutes and when his cortege turned up at the cemetery there were 100 girls and madams and a band played 'When the Saints Go Marching In'.

Beck found Darlinghurst police station in 1977 to be in complete disarray; a drinks bar operated from one of the cells, property went unreturned after cases were finished, and an honour system was in place so that items could be borrowed and returned at will. He began to install some sense of discipline and to tighten security, but it was clear that not everyone approved of his purge. Soon he was offered $500 not to take action against the gambling joints and prostitutes. Instead he began Operation Eagle against the clubs, including Thommo's, which far from being the paragon of two-up establishments, lent money at 300 per cent and had bouncers who broke the kneecaps of defaulters. Beck had Lees' full approval to raid the clubs, but Lees warned him to lay off the girls because politicians would not like it. Then Wood removed Beck without notice and he was sent to Central police station. Abe Saffron had upset things.

Two years later, when Wood had gone and Lees was commissioner, Beck was again asked to clean things up—this time in 21 Division. Unfortunately, his new immediate boss was Chief Superintendent Bill Allen, who told him which casinos were to be left untouched. Instead Beck, whose team was known as 'Beck's Raiders', went after both them and SP bookmakers, who were paying $100,000 a week to the police to be left alone. It was now that offers were made to him; when he refused them, they were followed by threats. After he had been in charge for ten months, Allen called him and said that he had done his work. Beck was transferred to the Central Coast. Simply by staying away from Chinatown, 'I could have made a million', he told *The Sun-Herald* on 30 May 1982.

Wood's first clash with Premier Neville Wran came in December 1977. At last, after years of tolerance, illegal casinos were to be closed, but Wood stated publicly, and to a great deal of ridicule, that he did not intend to close them before Christmas because of the hardship it would cause the 300-odd employees who would lose their jobs. The next and more serious blue came in March the next year, when Wood did not pass on to Wran a report linking George Freeman and Lennie McPherson to the upper echelons of the United States' Mafia, saying rather disingenuously that he did not think it was important. The third came at the beginning of May, when Wran appointed Bill Allen to the post of chief superintendent ahead of recommendations by Wood and without informing him.

That winter was not a good one for Wood. In the face of mounting criticism of the police and leaked allegations—which he denied—he resigned in early June. The allegations included an association with casino owner George Ziziros Walker, later charged with conspiracy to murder, although the charges were dropped and Walker was discharged. Wood was also said to be associating with George Freeman and Abe Saffron and, more specifically, it was alleged that one of his senior officers had been at the Wentworth Hotel on 7 November 1977 with a casino operator. Two of the casino's female croupiers were killed by Walter Coman, a nightclub bouncer, two days later.

Coman lived in a flat at beachside Bronte with his wife of two months, the former Joanna de Marco, and his common-law wife, Erica Scott. Mrs Coman and Miss Scott were lovers. The three engaged in group sex and the prosecution's case was that, in the early afternoon of Wednesday 9 November, the women taunted Coman with their lesbian relationship and, when he produced a .45 pistol, said he would not have the guts to pull the trigger. If they did say that, it was imprudent: he shot them both dead. Coman, in prison for life, later offered a different motive: that they had been killed not by him but because they had seen a bribe being passed. There were also allegations, never proved, that Wood was linked to a drug conspiracy case with one-time chief stipendiary magistrate Murray Farquhar, dishonest Sydney solicitor Morgan Ryan and convicted drug trafficker Roy Cessna. It was to this period that Sydney solicitor Chris Murphy referred when he said, 'Lennie McPherson and George Freeman may have been the Mr Bigs of Sydney crime but in truth the real Princes of the City were the police. When they came back after the Second World War the uniform seemed attractive. By the 1960s they had started networking criminals and they got lazy. In the end, by the late 1980s they were using criminals to kill people'.

The Cessna case itself was heard in May 1979, when Farquhar dealt with Cessna most leniently, giving him an eighteen-month good-behaviour bond for importing over 100,000 Buddha sticks. Originally Cessna had been charged with the importation of cannabis valued at $1.5 million. In court the value was more amorphously given as 'some value'. The allegations were that Morgan Ryan had pressed his old friend Wood for help. Wood maintained that the magistrate dealt with the case as he did because the drug content in the police haul was very low.

On 6 June that year Wood resigned, giving five hours' notice, days before Harvey Bates, head of the Federal Bureau of Narcotics (Australia), also resigned amid allegations of corruption in the FBN, which was later subsumed into the Australian Federal Police. Bates later withdrew his resignation. Wood did not. The catalyst for his premature retirement was not only the Cessna affair but also the document prepared by senior officers and sent to Askin the previous month detailing extensive allegations against the police, politicians, lawyers and brewery interests.

On 12 May 1994 Wood told *The Herald:*

> It's a sad state of affairs pervading Sydney at the moment. I wonder what is wrong with the city.
>
> The old hard-nosed copper is finished. You have management experts now—it has been going on for years—and the good, hardened, knockabout policeman has disappeared.
>
> Police are not getting the information. They are not allowed to fraternise with their informants.

> That's how you get your information. After all, you don't get your information at Sunday School.
>
> Without the right information, you are on a desert island. You are lost and you are in trouble. But if you do talk to someone outside a particular area there are all these snide remarks.

In 1996 the not-always-reliable drug dealer and Kings Cross identity Louis Bayeh told the royal commission on the police that Mervyn Wood had been a regular at dinners given by drug dealer and fixer Frank Hakim—known as the Lebanese Godfather, and a man who had corrupted many officers over the years—at his flat near Centennial Park, both before and after Wood became police commissioner.

In 1989 Wood was charged with two counts of acting with intent to pervert the course of justice over the Cessna case, but Justice John Sinclair stayed the proceedings because of the delay in bringing the charges and also because Wood was apparently losing his memory. Wood died aged eighty-nine in 2006. He had been suffering from cancer.

Jim Lees, a devout Christian, was the next to be appointed commissioner, with Brian Doyle once again overlooked. Doyle lasted only three months as Lees' special adviser before he resigned with his head held high, maintaining that there had been 'no row, no blue, no blow-up', but even with, and particularly without, Doyle, Lees was always struggling. In June

1979, after the turbulent term of Merv Wood, the government had made Lees acting commissioner and then in October it confirmed him in the position. Lees simply could not cope and lasted only two years. During his time, however, he had to deal with the corrupt Bill Allen, still clawing his way to the top.

Lees had joined the force in 1936. He headed the internal affairs branch for twelve years and had enjoyed the 'Untouchables' tag given to him and his men. Starting in 1958 with a staff of one, he built up the section under—perhaps despite is a better word—commissioners Norman Allan and Fred Hanson. During that time, 412 policemen were sacked and 402 criminal charges were laid against officers. Lees said that he was putting officers before the courts at an average of one every ten days. He restructured 21 Division, responsible for the policing of gaming, and expanded the crime intelligence unit.

After his fortunate appointment as assistant commissioner ahead of sixteen more senior and, as it transpired, far better candidates, Bill Allen had a second piece of good luck. This time Police Minister William Crabtree ignored the advice of Lees and promoted Allen to deputy commissioner. Lees resigned, to be replaced by Cecil Abbott. In October 1981 Crabtree was sacked; on the face of it this was the result of a Cabinet reshuffle, but in reality Crabtree had proved inadequate in dealing with corruption in the force. In turn, in June 1982 he was cleared of corruption charges by an investigation conducted by

Detective Inspector Joe Parrington. The investigation had arisen after an allegation in parliament that a senior Labor MP had been interviewed by Premier Wran over allegations that he had received thousands of dollars in bribes. Crabtree admitted that he was the MP referred to but denied any wrongdoing.

In 1986 the government was forced to invite Justice Jack Nagle to conduct a special inquiry into police handling of the highly controversial disappearance of anti-drugs campaigner Donald Mackay from outside a Griffith hotel in 1977. The original investigation, also conducted by Parrington, had failed to solve the mystery.

Justice Nagle found no corruption but said in his scathing report that Parrington had withdrawn evidence from the Mackay inquest, allegedly suppressed evidence and misrepresented people involved in the investigation. Nagle found that there was sufficient evidence to prosecute Parrington for attempting to pervert the course of justice in the Mackay case, but no criminal charges were brought against Parrington, with whom the new commissioner, John Avery, said he worshipped as a Christian. Instead he was charged departmentally with neglect of duty and fined a total of $1000 on two charges in 1987. As former Victorian police officer Simon Illingworth commented generally, 'People survived because of being an embarrassment to the force if prosecuted, so they were promoted'.

After Lees came Cecil Abbott, who in his turn shut down various inquiries, including one into Police Minister Rex Jackson. He was helped by officers such as Parrington, who had investigated, usually without success, a number of other matters, including the death of 24-year-old drug dealer and socialite Maria Hission in 1975, and the corrupt Norman Allan, against whom he found no evidence of wrongdoing.

It was in November 1981 that the lid blew off. As was often the case, the problem arose over gambling; the trigger here related to plans for a casino at a time when Bill Allen was assistant commissioner for licensing. There was a separate allegation that on five occasions that year Allen had given Warren Molloy, then chief of the special licensing squad, $500 cash in an envelope. There was also the problem of the regular visits of Abe Saffron to Allen's office.

In May 1981 Allen, his wife and his 23-year-old daughter were in Macau, guests of the Sociedade de Turismo e Diversoes de Macao, run by the Yip family of the Macau Trotting Club. Then came the second freebie in as many months. On 6 June 1981 the three flew first class to Hawaii, where they met another of Allen's daughters and her husband. There they stayed at the home of Lori Yip, the daughter of the chief of the Macau Trotting Club. On 11 June they went on to San Francisco, staying again free of charge at the Holiday Inn in Union Square, courtesy of 'representations' by Sydney bookmaker Bill Waterhouse. Then it was on to Las Vegas, where once again they were in luck because the tab was picked up by Mafia-linked Jack Rooklyn, head of Bally poker machines in Australia, and a man who had come under heavy fire from Justice Moffitt. Not only had the Allens been shouted the trip but also lucky Bill won $1000 on the machines. He was a man who liked cash. He told the subsequent inquiry into his conduct that he was a regular winner at the races. He bought his house for cash, paid off his American Express card in cash and, he said, kept $10,000 in cash at home. In turn the inquiry told him that by accepting hospitality and associating with the likes of Abe Saffron and Rooklyn, he had acted in a manner likely to discredit the police. By offering money to Warren Molloy he had tried to compromise him. Allen resigned.

With men like these at the top, was there any doubt that corruption would pervade the lower ranks?

7

WHISTLEBLOWING V THE BROTHERHOOD: AND THE WINNER IS...

Whistleblowing on one's colleagues is not a sport encouraged by rank-and-file police, and the line of officers who have fallen foul of their fellows when they have tried to point out defects in people or the system is a long one. 'If a senior detective complains about his fellows he is finished when it comes to working with detectives thereafter', New South Wales Deputy Commissioner John Perrin was quoted as saying in the December 1989 *Report on an Investigation Relating to the Raid on Frank Hakim's Office.* But if whistleblowing on your offsiders is dangerous, it is a wholly different game from ratting on your superiors.

One of the perennial problems for senior officers in a police force is the question of crime clear up rates. And, over the years, it has led to allegations by junior officers that these have been massaged. Currently there are minor scandals in both Britain and France that crime statistics are being manipulated on a regular basis. But things are never that simple. For a start how are crime statistics recorded? Is the clear up rate to be decided on arrests, convictions or even the unproveable belief of an investigating officer?

Assuming there has been a series of thefts from, say, twelve different premises in an office block on the same day, is it reasonable to suspect that this is the work of the same person or gang, and so should this be recorded as one incident or twelve? If a person is arrested and admits to these burglaries, should they be recorded as one matter cleared up or twelve? Various forces take different attitudes, but over the years the swing in attitude to these questions has been considerable.

In December 1971 computer expert Philip Neville Arantz, a 42-year-old New South Wales detective working on a computerisation program in the police research branch, found that the New South Wales Police Service had been systematically under-reporting crime statistics by up to 70 per cent for years. He drew the inference that police were trying to conceal both corruption, which allegedly extended up to Norman Allan, the police commissioner at the time, and also widespread police involvement in organised crime. Published crime statistics gave a completely false figure of the existence of crime and its clear-up rate.

Arantz was not the first officer to draw attention to the practice—back in the 1950s Sergeant R Blissett had been transferred back into uniform when he raised questions about the integrity of crime figures—but he was the most vociferous. He took his findings to senior officers, but they were dismissed out of hand, as was an approach to Allan. Eventually Arantz realised that Allan and commissioners for the previous decade, if not directly involved in it, were at least aware of the scheme, and the commissioners wanted to suppress his findings. The frustrated Arantz approached journalist Basil Sweeney, who had both sets of figures published in *The Sydney Morning Herald.*

Arantz's punishment was swift and harsh. He was promptly certified mentally ill and sectioned in a mental hospital for three days. The advice to section him had been supplied by former senior police medical officer Dr Morrie Vane, who told the *7.30 Report* in 1988 that, in retrospect, he believed he had been duped and used in the affair by Allan, and '[I] deeply regret the role I played' in declaring that Arantz was mentally ill.

On 20 January 1972 Arantz was dismissed without pension for misconduct—namely, supplying police secrets to Sydney newspapers. An employment appeal tribunal unanimously upheld the dismissal. Worse was to follow. Premier Askin also indicated that any firm in the computer industry employing Arantz would be looked on with extreme disfavour. It was only after an outcry when, a decade later, disgraced deputy commissioner Bill Allen was granted a detective sergeant's pension, that Arantz was given $250,000 compensation by the Wran government, which, after championing him when in opposition, had effectively abandoned him when in office. His name was eventually cleared by special legislation. He died on 4 March 1998.

Four years before his death Arantz told *The Sydney Morning Herald* that he had not been alone in causing embarrassment, but that:

> I was the odd one but there were so many others (20 years ago) who were in a lot of trouble and, rather than be proceeded with departmentally, it suited them to go out medically unfit and have their pensions for the rest of their lives. And it suited Norman Allan when he was commissioner because he had no further problems and it didn't look bad for his administration ... They would be 'boarded out' (retired through illness).

In November 2009 former Assistant Commissioner Geoff Schuberg, who had resigned after a disagreement with Commissioner Peter Ryan, interviewed by Tim Girling-Butcher for the Sydney exhibition *Sin City,* recalled:

> Well it was a massive cover up. Like I felt sorry for the guy [Arantz]. I've had contact with many, many whistleblowers in my time but I would always speak to them and say 'you sure you want to do this? Because your life will be ruined. Your career will be finished' and a lot of them refused to believe it. They think they're doing the right thing by coming forward and exposing what they

> know. But they do it at a cost. And the cost is to them and their family.

If corroboration is needed, here is a 'working girl' speaking of her life in the 1970s and 1980s:

> There was no way you could work if you didn't 'weighin'. There's a lot of cops' wives whom I've helped to put fur coats on their backs and a lot of cops' kids whom I've helped to educate until the law changed [in 1979] and all of a sudden I had surplus money, heaps of work and I didn't have to close the door for an hour to entertain cops.

Greg Wheadon, son of a chief inspector, was another who fell from brotherly grace when in 1987 he approached New South Wales Internal Affairs alleging corruption by a senior officer at Ballina police station. Over the next ten years he was persecuted by his former colleagues—at one time, a contract was taken out on his life. He was eventually sent to police a one-man station. In 2001 he was awarded $660,000 as compensation for his treatment and the failure of the police service to protect him.

Two other notable whistleblowers who suffered for their sins in New South Wales were officers Kimbal Cook and Deborah Locke. On 13 June 1988 bookmaker Allan Tripp was arrested and detective sergeant Ferrenc Deak and senior constable Eugene Zubrecky wanted to sell him back his gaming ledger. They approached Kimbal Cook for help. Cook not only refused but also dobbed them in. Their cases took five years to come to court, and they received short sentences. During this time Cook was subjected to harassment and was left unsupported by his superiors.

The reaction of the gaming squad, according to ICAC evidence, repeated at the 1995 Wood Royal Commission, was to ostracise him. The harassment, including a break-in at Cook's home, drove him from the service. He did not receive much sympathy from Police Commissioner Tony Lauer, who thought he was trying 'to exit the police service on the highest possible pension'. His application for a discharge was deferred and he was told to supply further independent evidence.

On the other hand, Col Cole, a former New South Wales assistant commissioner who had been criticised by Cook, first took extended sick leave and then supplied medical certificates to ICAC, the police board and the parliamentary committee, excusing himself from giving evidence on the grounds of stress. On 26 October 1993 questions were raised in parliament about Cole's suspension and apparent failure to discharge his duty to inform his commissioner of the full facts about the Frenchs Forest incident. The House was told that he was in fact on sick leave, having reported a stress-related illness on 2 March, and the police board had lifted his suspension as assistant commissioner on 7 October. Cole then applied for a medical discharge and his application was promptly granted.

Officers who have for whatever reason been under a cloud, have regularly found that the 'stress express', as it is known, ensures their generous pensions continue. One former officer says that getting out on stress leave before heads roll is referred to as 'beating the posse'.

Even when there was no corruption, high-ranking officers behaved indiscreetly. In December 1992 Cole, then New South Wales assistant commissioner, lunched with two reported criminals, Tom Domican and Louis Bayeh, along with Tony Day, president of the Police Association, who had arranged the meeting at Domican's request. Later the commissioner was told by an informant that Domican had been boasting he had Assistant Commissioner Cole in his pocket.

Deborah Locke's story, *Watching the Detectives,* is a litany of low-level corruption: taking money from prostitutes and warning of gaming-squad raids. Once when officers broke down the door of a suspected club in Surry Hills there was a table of food, a welcome banner, the solicitor Chris Murphy and a man with a video camera to record the search. There was also sexual harassment and drunkenness, and derelicts moved into another jurisdiction.

Geoff Schuberg found the situation to be similar:

> When I went to 21 Division they would never let me work on illegal gambling there because I had a reputation of being straight. And for that reason I wasn't trusted.

He found that even low-level prostitution was organised:

> Prostitutes were told where they could work, when they could work. If they didn't, well then they'd be arrested and they'd be charged ... Prostitutes when they were charged, they even paid station staff so they could be bailed out quickly so they could get back on the street.

Deborah Locke soon realised:

> If you didn't agree with something you were expected to look the other way. Kim (Cook) had broken the code that said loyalty to the brotherhood was the most important thing.

In fact Locke and Cook may have escaped relatively lightly. Perhaps the worst thing for a whistleblower was to discover that their information had been quickly leaked and they would hardly be back at the station before it was known that he or she had turned dog. Deborah Locke soon found this out, but perhaps the most egregious example is that of

[redacted]

[redacted]

Today, still not all superior officers are sympathetic to whistleblowers. Tony Lauer, who had experienced his own period of exile to the bush, summed up official government and police attitudes as, 'Nobody in Australia much likes whistleblowers, particularly in an organisation like the police or the government'.

In 1988, the year New South Wales Chief Commissioner John Avery publicly stated that whistleblowers would not be the subject of discrimination, 22-year-old recruit Simon Illingworth took the Victoria Police pledge:

> to serve the community without favour or affection, malice or ill-will ... and to discharge ... all the duties legally imposed upon me, faithfully and according to the law.

He was then taken by his superior on duty and he watched, dumb-struck, as the officer walked into the back room of a cafe. There the card tables bore all the signs of illegal gaming. But, rather than make an arrest, Illingworth's senior officer merely helped himself to the cash in the register behind the counter, stuffing it in his pockets, before scraping more cash off the table. The cafe owner apparently took the theft quite calmly.

Illingworth did nothing at the time, later claiming that there were two conflicting trains of thought running through his head. Certainly, the cafe owner was running illegal gaming and everyone seemed to be in on it. Illingworth had already seen evidence of police careers fasttracked for 'mates secretly looking after each other'. The other train of thought came from the shock of realising how many on both sides of the law simply accepted police corruption as normal. He learned that meticulous record keeping was not only to assist prosecutions. Corrupt police kept notes of other members' minor breaches or rule breaking, so that the pot was less likely to call the kettle black. Later Illingworth would learn that one difficulty in getting honest police to come forward against corrupt police was the fear of being targeted for breaking minor rules, put on hellish rosters or given finetooth-comb supervision. He wrote in *Filthy Rat:* 'No police officer can claim that he or she has always followed the strict Victoria Police code of ethics and conduct to the letter, seasoned cops call the manuals

"150 years of fuck ups" because every time someone fucked up a new rule would be made.'

In fact over the years and in various states officers have spied on each other, not always for the good of the force. In New South Wales when Deputy Police Commissioner Bill Allen was under siege over his relationship with organised-crime figures such as Abe Saffron, he produced a tape recording he had made of an interview with Commissioner Jim Lees. In itself the tape produced nothing remarkable—simply Lees saying that it was not he who had investigated Allen—but it raised a number of questions. First: how could Lees be so naïve as to think that Allen would not do something like tape him? Second, and of far greater concern: if Allen had taped Lees, just who else was on tape and in what more sinister circumstances?

Inter-police spying and taping was not that uncommon. In the early 1980s Victorian detectives ran an illegal operation in Sydney to gather evidence on police and political corruption. It ended when New South Wales detectives stole their surveillance gear. In Western Australia in 1985, *The Daily News* revealed that Police Commissioner Bill Bull had spied on his assistant commissioner, Spears, for three months using what was called the 'dog squad'. Unfortunately for Bull and the public image of the force generally, Spears had discovered this and with the help of *The West Australian* had the squad filmed *in flagrante.*

'They have a touch of the martyr', said another senior officer, referring to whistleblowers. He and others believe that an anonymous call to the authorities is better than coming out in the newspapers and so often achieving martyrdom amongst their colleagues. Others see them simply as troublemakers and publicity seekers. It has been suggested that a new recruit, fresh from the academy, will within only a matter of weeks be acclimatised to the corruption or have decided, somehow, to take a stand. Illingworth, called a 'maggot' and a 'filthy rat' for his failure to jump on board, puts it this way: 'Some people get on the corruption bus, some run alongside it, very few have the guts to stand in front of it'.

In the early 1990s in Victoria it was probationary constable Karl Konrad's turn to pay the price. His crime was to dob in fellow officers who were part of a gigantic kickback operation in which windowrepair companies were alerted that a breakage had occurred and a repair or temporary shutter was required. The result was Operation Bart, and 1548 police from eighty-nine stations were investigated. In 1995 alone, payments of $144,000 had been made to police. The investigation revealed that it took less than six weeks for a member new to a particular station to embrace the corruption, put aside ethical considerations and grab a share of the cash. There were also unproved suggestions that it was police themselves who were breaking the windows. In the wash-up, the Director of Public Prosecutions was not confident of securing convictions, as even officers not on the take balked at dobbing in colleagues who were. Ultimately, one senior constable was convicted and fined, along with a shutter company. The remaining 550 were dealt with on disciplinary charges. Nine officers were dismissed, seven resigned before their hearings and eighteen resigned during or after their hearings. Five were demoted and transferred, eighteen were merely transferred and 188 were fined. A further 139 faced in-house disciplinary penalties. In total $239,000 in fines was paid. A decade after the shutters hit the fan, George Brouwer, director of the Office of Police Integrity, would say that Operation Bart had demonstrated that 'one in three police was corruptible'.

When he learned that police were receiving kickbacks, Konrad went to his superiors; ignored, he went to the ombudsman. For his trouble, he was hounded out of the force. Later he told Sally Neighbour on ABC TV's *Four Corners:*

> I went out in the morning and my car was completely vandalised you know, the windscreen was smashed, there were rocks thrown over the top of it, yet no other police, you know, no other private car in the compound was touched. None of them were brave enough to ever say anything to my face, but it was, you know, I got called a dog and a lagger over the PA system throughout the whole building. Matter of fact, one of the sergeants at Moorabbin said to me you know, if I was in the police force 10 years ago I would've

> found myself unconscious in the car park. I had another friend at another station who said, you know, they were openly discussing doing a black balaclava job on me.

For those not personally involved, whistleblower watching is a popular sport:

> partly because of the spectacle of a person being publicly disloyal to the organisation to which he or she belongs and partly too because whistleblowers have often focused public attention on a hidden membrane of popular culture.

Added to this is the voyeurism of watching if and how the whistleblower will be destroyed, rather like the Romans watching to see if a Christian could occasionally evade the lions and at least live to fight another day. Whistleblowers rarely survive within their own organisations and the culture shock and ostracism leave them with deep scars. A very few, such as New York officer Frank Serpico—who was immortalised in the film bearing his name—end up heroes, but it should be remembered that the three other whistleblowers who joined him suffered the usual fate.

The authority challenged has a range of defences and counterattacks at its disposal. As with Arantz, there can be accusations that the whistleblower is emotionally unstable and mentally ill, is an alcoholic, has behaved offensively, or is acting out of malice brought on by a real or perceived slight, perhaps lack of promotion. Whistleblower Simon Illingworth thought:

> Whistleblowers are always accused of being mentally ill. When the leadership of an organisation have been caught out lying, deceiving, thieving and/or incompetent they will inevitably 'go for the man rather than the ball'. The reason for this is because the facts speak for themselves. If the facts point towards incompetence or worse they'll divert attention from them and go for a personal smear of the witness. This is a disgusting trait of Australian people in power that have been caught out being unethical.

Sociologists believe that many whistleblowers come from religious or moral backgrounds and that others may have been isolated as children and grown up 'outside the pack'—and the latter is not an ideal qualification for joining the police. The whole experience may be strengthening to whistleblowers in general.

Geoff Schuberg explained one reason why so many officers remained silent:

> It was well known in those days, if you rocked the boat you'd be transferred to the bush. You'd be just put out of the way. And that's what happened to police. So, there were areas of policing that people didn't want to get involved

> with otherwise they were going to get themselves in trouble.

In the early years of the twenty-first century, widespread corruption in the Victoria Police drug squad was starting to unravel. Within months, dozens of police were investigated by the Ceja Task Force for trafficking in drugs: pseudoephedrine, heroin, cocaine, cannabis. The amounts were substantial—4.5 kilograms of heroin, 2 kilograms of pseudoephedrine. Convictions and jail terms followed.

Illingworth had already given evidence against his corrupt former partner. He had also been bashed and threatened by another officer. At this stage he was working in the professional practices unit. Under the umbrella of the ethical standards department and headed by Superintendent Neil O'Sullivan, the unit fought corruption from the inside. It was O'Sullivan's detectives who located a cache of illegal substances and weapons in the ceiling cavity of the St Kilda CIB complex. But, despite this and other achievements, O'Sullivan's unit was disbanded. It was then that Illingworth came to believe:

> Untangling corruption almost always leads to the disclosure of secrets and the erosion of underground loyalty. To save their own skins, corrupt police and criminals often turn on each other after they've been arrested.

By early 2004 the Ceja Task Force had charged thirteen detectives. Aside from those, Illingworth had given evidence against five of his colleagues. There had been plenty of arrests but ultimately more acquittals than convictions. 'It was the equivalent of a gold miner shoveling through 20 tonnes of shale for one small nugget of pure gold', says Illingworth. Other corruption investigators were also under threat. Two hollow-point bullets were delivered to one of Illingworth's colleagues, with the names of the man and his partner etched on them. Diagnosed with post-traumatic stress and at the end of his tether, Illingworth went to the media. His account appeared on ABC Television's *Australian Story* on 24 May 2004.

After he went public, his vilification increased. The media, however, had latched onto the story of links between criminals and the police and ran with it. A CCTV photograph of 'crim and the cop' showed an accused gangland figure with a suspended detective who was facing criminal charges (of which he was later acquitted). They were filmed together in a pub Illingworth frequented. Another underworld figure with access to Illingworth's address was found in possession of eight guns, night-vision goggles and a silencer. Illingworth, on temporary leave at the time, negotiated to leave Victoria Police. He turned down a payout of $250,000 because the package was coupled with a confidentiality clause. In turn, he told the media about the gagging. *The Herald Sun* ran a front-page story, 'You can't gag me', and later published Illingworth's letter to the police commissioner explaining his decision to refuse the payment. Finally he was offered the payout without restriction. On his retirement he wrote a bestseller about his experiences and became an anti-corruption consultant.

Dr Jean Lennane, consultant psychiatrist and founder of Whistleblowers Australia, defines the act as principled organisational dissent. In a research paper, 'Whistleblowing and the Protected Disclosures Act', delivered to a conference in Sydney in late 2013, she outlined the dangers of dissenting from the accepted culture, internal principles and practises of an organisation.

Her position was based on an early study of Australian whistleblowers in 1998 which showed that 90 per cent lost their jobs or were demoted, 20 per cent got into difficulties with alcohol, 20 per cent had a long-term relationship break up, 20 per cent were threatened with a defamation action, 6 per cent attempted suicide and 9 per cent went bankrupt. Not a good strike rate, as *The Sydney Morning Herald* put it.

Today states and territories have stand-alone acts that provide for the establishment of whistleblowing systems and some form of legal protection against reprisals. It began in South Australia with the *Whistleblowers Protection Act 1993* and was followed by Queensland and New South Wales the next year, Victoria in 2001 and Tasmania the year after. The Northern Territory rather lagged behind, not producing legislation until

2008. Only the Commonwealth remains without protective legislation.

Of course, there is a great deal of difference between theory and practice, as a whistle-blowing Brisbane officer found out when his colleagues handed him a tin of dog food as a secret Santa Christmas present at the office party.

8

VICTORIA FROM THE 1960s: FROM ABORTIONISTS AND BULLY BOYS TO ZEBRA AND ZULU

For twenty years from the 1960s Victorian police were under constant fire from their critics. One of the criticisms, which dated back to the Blamey era of the 1920s and 1930s, related to their method of taking statements from suspects. Alleged by the police to be voluntary, these statements were often challenged as having been extorted from the accused. Police interviews still took place without the presence of independent witnesses, without any attempt to take down proper shorthand or produce a taped record, and without the presence of any person to represent or assist the suspect.

It was not only in Victoria that the problem arose. In Queensland barrister MP Col Bennett, who for decades had his sights on corrupt members of the CIB, thought:

> It is rather amazing that at the CI Branch very few, if any, voluntary confessions are obtained from people who are allegedly invited to enter the CI Branch while in the company of friends ... But not long after they are separated from their companions, out pops a confession, freely and voluntarily admitting every element of the offence in such a fashion that one might believe that the accused was a lawyer who understood how to make admissions acknowledging the truth of every aspect of the charge.

In 1963 at a United Nations seminar in Canberra, during a session discussing human rights being breached by police interview techniques, the judges present were unanimous that the extent to which admissions and confessions seemed to be obtained by intimidation was an 'agonising problem'. They said that tape recording interviews would help solve the problem. But police chiefs attending the seminar argued that 'much police evidence was gleaned during a car trip or while walking down a corridor', policemen 'only hit back spontaneously when provoked by suspects' and 'if police were put in a straitjacket' and denied the 'flexibility' they needed in interrogation, then 'the real job they had to perform would get out of control'. One delegate suggested that the police attitude was 'perturbing'. Too much time was being spent by police chiefs defending existing national practices, and too little on ways to improve them, said Professor Julius Stone, Chalis Professor of Jurisprudence at the University of Sydney.

The next year, during the investigation and questioning of three Italian men for the murder of market gardener Antonio Monaco, two of the men were held for eighteen hours and were, they claimed, kicked, punched and pistol-whipped by police. Dr Macera, an assistant police commissioner from Reggio in Italy, had been flown in to help with the investigation and had advocated 'toughness in handling Italians of this class'. During the trial of two of the suspects, Mr Justice Sholl of the Victorian Supreme Court disallowed the confessions, finding that 'it is impossible to be satisfied that these injuries were not inflicted by the police'. He found that the detectives' contemporaneous notes prompted 'an uneasy suspicion that [they] ... may have been written after the interviews had been completed'.

On 4 June 1965 an exasperated Sholl was quoted in *The Age* as saying, 'After sixteen years on the bench, I have lost confidence in methods used by police in interrogations. The more so since suggestions from the bench to modernise what is done is entirely disregarded'. His comments should have taken no one by surprise: he had been making them since 1961. The acting chief secretary of the day, ER Meagher, was reported as saying that he would discuss the judge's comments with senior police, but no real change resulted from any discussions. It was as though the police and government would simply not take the hint.

Then in September 1965 opposition leader Clive Stoneham announced in parliament that he had obtained and listened to some nine hours' worth of tape recordings containing allegations of misconduct and corruption against a number of police. The man involved, known as Mr X, was a police informer and a convicted criminal. His wife also had allegations to make. Mr X claimed that he had only made the allegations after his wife had been threatened and his police handlers had turned on him. He went directly to a judge who had previously sentenced him and the complaint was referred to the Attorney-General.

From then on discussion of these corruption allegations was frontpage news in *The Age.* Would the officers be named? Who would hear the case? Why was the government taking so long to investigate? Stoneham was persistent, saying in parliament that the government had known of the existence of corruption in the ranks since at least June 1962. As morsels were drip fed to the media, it appeared that the corrupt behaviour related to instances of 'framing' suspects, evidence being 'planted', cooking up false confessions or admissions, rorts with informants, improperly withdrawing charges and good old-fashioned lying.

By the end of 1965 seven policemen were to face disciplinary charges, including one of 'disgraceful and improper conduct' against a senior constable. To an extent there was supporting evidence for Mr X's claims from ex-boxer Robert George Flannery, who alleged that the police had planted a pistol on him. Stipendiary magistrate WN Thompson chaired the Police Disciplinary Board that began on 2 December, and first he determined that the crucial witness, Mr X, could not be named as he and his wife could be in danger from criminal elements. However, Mr X was soon to be outed as housebreaker Brian Donald Latch. Counsel for the policemen was Ray Dunn.

It is not difficult, particularly for a man of Dunn's skills, to crossexamine a man like Latch—prior convictions, especially after pleas of not guilty, can be lovingly put, and motives such as malice and revenge can be examined in detail. Time and again Latch was made to pay for his treachery in turning on his former police friends. He was forced to admit numerous priors, including buying stolen radios up to forty a time from 'dozens of men', as well as two spells in mental hospitals. Finally, he turned to the magistrate, saying, 'I've admitted being an informer against criminals. Now they want me to inform on my own family'. Dunn had already accused him of dobbing in his own solicitor over a procedural matter. Latch's unfortunate wife was forced to admit that the dress she was wearing at the hearing had been stolen.

In March 1966 Thompson dismissed charges against one officer relating to the improper withdrawal of charges against Flannery. Further allegations by Latch dropped by the wayside and a few paltry charges hovered around. In the end only a couple of minor charges stuck. Thompson found that no attack on a sergeant's honesty or integrity had been substantiated: 'We think the error he made was one of judgment'. The penalties were nugatory.

By August that year Latch was living under an assumed name in Rockingham, Western Australia, with his wife and family. He was complaining that he had been recognised by a Victorian criminal and was in fear for his life. Some years later, back in Victoria, Latch wrote his self-serving memoir, *Mr X—Police Informer.*

During the year of Mr X, police morale was said to be at an alltime low. Resignations were flooding in, and so were complaints about 'police brutality' and provocation during demonstrations at the time of US President Lyndon Johnson's visit.

The Police Association was outraged. At a meeting attended by 400 members, police complained that Mr X, who had initially telephoned a judge with his story, had hoodwinked the solicitorgeneral, had brought the police into disgrace and, perhaps worst of all, had jumped the Housing Commission's waiting list. There were also complaints about the way the press had behaved. Significantly, members wanted the association to provide financial aid for legal advice on the possibility of civil action against the solicitor-general, the chief commissioner of police, any of the assistant commissioners or members of the force involved in launching these prosecutions. If the legal advice was favourable, members said that further financial aid should be given to prosecute the matter in the civil court. It was a response that should have demonstrated to the government the strength of the Police Association. It turned out to be a rehearsal for the destruction of the Beach report, which called for extensive police-procedural reform ten years later.

One general problem in any force is that the misdemeanours of an outstanding officer who is also corrupt—Ray Kelly, Fred Krahe and in New South Wales, and later Paul Higgins in Victoria immediately spring to mind—are overlooked because of his arrest and conviction record. And this was the case in Victoria of onetime head of the homicide squad Jack Matthews. He was one of the first to recognise the unchecked and unmonitored rise of organised crime, particularly organised ethnic crime, and he was adroit in solving the murders relating to the Victoria fruit market in which Italian factions fought each other for control. It was Matthews who had persuaded Chief Secretary Arthur Rylah that foreign expertise, including the likes of Dr Macera, was necessary to crack Italian crime circles. That was the plus side of his career. On the debit side were the abortion rackets he ran with other officers.

Medical abortionists had thrived in Melbourne for at least fifty years. One, William Fenton Bowen, had survived a prosecution back in the 1940s. Bowen's offsider Stanley Charles Wyatt, a former homicide chief inspector, had as a detective first constable been ordered out of the CIB by Chief Commissioner Alexander Duncan. He had later been a member of the gaming squad but had resigned from the police in 1948 and set himself up as an SP bookmaker.

Wyatt had two useful friends, solicitor Roy McMennemin and his father, Harry 'Mac' McMennemin, a former CIB officer who had served in the police for forty years and now ran an off-course gambling club above a television-repair shop in Geelong. He also maintained links with unsavoury local abortionist Mario Marchesani, who was known to have roused patients from the anaesthetic to let them know that the fee would be doubled as they were a bit further along than first thought. Marchesani's son-in-law was in charge of the Geelong CIB, having earlier been attached to the sheepstealing squad. When Wyatt was arrested in 1962 by Ronald Jackson of the gaming squad, the pair got him off on a technicality. Wyatt later became an informer for Jackson.

In 1959 Wyatt went to live in Ascot Vale with Elva Isabella Moran, also known as Bella Lewis, who was then the licensee of the Red Lion in Carlton, from where Wyatt ran his business. As a result she lost her licence. In May that year he was sentenced to 3 1/2 months' imprisonment for an assault on her and related charges. Around 1966 he became an abortionist, later working with Fenton Bowen, who had rooms opposite the law courts and who was called over if a defendant was taken ill. The alcoholic Fenton Bowen was unable to perform the abortions because of the shakes, but he saw the patients and then sent them into the back room, where 'Charlie did the business', recalls one lawyer. A ditty was written about the abilities of the pair:

You rape 'em
We scrape 'em
No foetus
Can beat us.

Throughout the latter half of 1969, the Scots-born, Melbournebased abortion-reform advocate Dr Bertram Wainer, described as 'headstrong, erratic, egotistical and self-serving', had been making allegations claiming that police officers were standing over abortionists. On 5 December that year a number of Melbourne doctors who practiced as abortionists, including Bertram Wainer and Fenton Bowen, who had been convicted on an abortion charge in September and had been deregistered, handed in affidavits to *Truth,* which forwarded them to the solicitor-general. They contained allegations that abortionists had to pay some members of the elite homicide squad $150 a week each to avoid raids. Other payments to corrupt officers ranged from $600 to a lump sum of $1200, which would include cover for the 'possible fatality' of a patient. The chief commissioner was directed to investigate the complaints, but five out of six officers named refused to see him. As a result, in January

1970 the government appointed an independent, one-man board of inquiry in the form of William Kaye QC 'to investigate whether members of the Force had demanded or accepted money from persons concerned with abortion in Victoria'. Kaye sat for the next five months.

Unfortunately, when it came to it Bowen, who may well have been in the early stages of dementia, he refused to give evidence before Kaye, so depriving historians of an account of his relationship with Wyatt and his mistress Elva Moran, matriarch of the Moran family later involved in the gangland wars.

Wyatt, however, was a principal witness, standing throughout the five days of his evidence. He told Kaye that ex-CIB officer Harry McMennemin had been for several years the head of 'Crime Incorporated' and he had boasted that he had a direct line to Police Commissioner Reg Jackson, with whom he often lunched. Wyatt said that McMennemin had cashed cheques for him on which he had forged his wife's signature. He also claimed that he had some 'connections' but denied paying police through McMennemin. In turn McMennemin denied the allegations Wyatt had made.

Kaye found that there was evidence against Superintendent John Matthews, inspector Jack Ford, detective Martin Jacobson and retired station officer Frederick 'Bluey' Adam, known also as 'Thumper' for obvious reasons, who was once regarded as the scourge of Melbourne's criminal fraternity but who by then weighed 140 kilograms and was an alcoholic. Lawyer Frank Galbally thought, 'He saw little harm in distorting the truth if he thought that the accused deserved to be convicted for one reason or another'. In 1971 all were charged with conspiring to obstruct the course of justice by accepting bribes to protect the illegal activities of abortionists.

Before their trial Margaret 'Peggy' Berman, receptionist at an East Melbourne clinic—and godmother to a child of standover man Norman Bradshaw, and the one-time lover of Norval Morris, who founded the criminology department at the University of Melbourne—pleaded guilty to abortion-related offences. Released on bond and given an indemnity against prosecution, she later gave evidence claiming that the officers had stood over the abortion clinic where she worked, demanding payment in return for warning the doctors of potential raids. Unemployed in 1953, she had gone to a doctor for an abortion and had left with a £25-a-week job. The doctor was in the process of selling his practice and Bluey Adam took £50 a week from the purchaser.

The doctors had then been the victim of what Berman called a somersault. They had, she maintained, originally been paying Adam, who had passed them on to Ford, Matthews and Jacobson, who demanded even more money. In particular, for two or three years she had been giving Ford, her former lover and then head of the homicide squad, $600 a month retainer from her employers as well as $200 a month of her own money to pay his gaming debts. Matthews thought the money was compensation for being overworked and underappreciated.

At the trial Ford heaped abuse on his former mistress, claiming that he thought she had tried to kill him. She had, he said, put poison into a bottle of whisky by injecting it through the cork with a hypodermic needle. It did none of them any good. When Matthews gave evidence he admitted that in eight years as homicide chief he had not arrested one abortionist.

Adam may have been an alchoholic, but he retained his sense of humour. Asked by prosecuting counsel if he had a nickname, he replied that he had. The prosecutor then made a foolish—possibly even fatal—error, saying, 'Perhaps you'd like to share that nickname with the court'. 'Honest Fred' was the crushing reply.

Matthews and Ford were jailed for five years. They were all smiles after the jury verdict and kept up the front for the media at their appeals, but, before Matthews was sent back to Pentridge after one appearance, he was heard to snarl at reporters 'get back to your brothels, you bastards'.

Both were released after serving rather under half their time. Jacobson served thirteen months. Matthews was later given a job writing on consumer affairs at *Truth,* the newspaper whose campaign had in part led to his destruction. He was assigned the chair of Evan Whitton, the journalist who had exposed him, but he took these humiliations in good part—perhaps he had no alternative. Adam was acquitted and died of stomach cancer on 14 April 1973.

Peggy Berman thought that the only lasting effect of the Kaye inquiry and the case was that the price of abortions leapt to $400. After being told in the 1960s that she had cancer and only had eighteen months to live, Peggy unexpectedly survived until she died, aged seventy-nine after a heart attack in December 2002.

An *Age* editorial reflected on the case:

> It would have been naive to suppose that responsible ministers and officials, and successive police chiefs, had no inkling of what was going on.

It could not be expected that the case would go without reprisals and in 1971 Bowen, Wyatt and Elva Moran were all charged with abortion offences. During Bowen's trial doctors rallied round their colleague, one saying that after Bowen had suffered a stroke on Christmas Day 1967 he had advised him to give up practice. A psychiatrist said that to the layman Bowen was in a 'second childhood' and he would 'take advice from people he would not normally have taken it from'. Bowen was acquitted on fourteen counts on 7 December. Interviewed after the acquittal, he told reporters that he had applied for re-registration that very day.

During the trial Wyatt alleged that not only had inspector Jack Matthews framed men for murder but that when the police raided Fenton Bowen and seized his card records, six of them related to policewomen. 'There are many policemen who would like to see me out of circulation, because of my peculiar knowledge of their activities. Police feeling against me is running very high at the moment because I know a great deal about them,' he told the jury in an unsworn statement from the dock. He said he had twenty-one tapes of officers discussing not only the abortion racket but also robberies and payroll robberies. It did him no good. Wyatt and Moran, described by one witness as a 'marvellous woman', were convicted on a total of twenty-five charges. Wyatt received 4 1/2 years, and Elva Moran, who said she had never held an instrument, merely the hands of the distressed women, went down for twelve months.

Later Wyatt would be portrayed by some as a loveable rogue, but he was also regarded by the cognoscenti as a 'dangerous, incorrigible and self-serving criminal'. Peggy Berman was horrified to hear that he had become an abortionist. When Wyatt heard about her horror, he happily said that he would have her killed.

If the Victorian police thought that after the successful prosecution of Matthews and the others Bertram Wainer would let up they were wrong. He was not nearly finished with them and in 1974 he presented sufficient evidence to the government for it to undertake a preliminary inquiry into his new allegations.

The result was that the very experienced Barry Beach QC was appointed to sit as another one-man board of inquiry to report on whether there was 'any credible evidence raising a strong and probable presumption that any, and if so which, members of the Victoria Police Force' were guilty of criminal offences, breaches of standing orders or 'harassment or intimidation of any member of the public'.

Beach began by advertising in the newspapers for members of the public to come forward. The result was not a trickle or even a flow of complaints but something approaching a deluge. The total number of complaints was 131, but Beach decided to examine only twentyone. The inquiry lasted fifteen months, during which time 290 witnesses were called.

There were, of course, the usual criminal stalwarts giving evidence of brutality, including bank robbers Peter George Gibb, Joseph Power, John Palmer and Barry Quinn. The brother of another bank robber, 'Jockey' James Smith, also gave evidence and so did a man who was bundled through a window after the police raided a room while chasing the Melbourne heavy Laurie Prendergast.

However, some cleanskins also came forward. Among them was a man who was viciously assaulted and his wife abused by officers as she waited to collect him after a dinner he was attending, as well as a solicitor's clerk. These were not the sort of people whom the police could be expected to treat as dingoes.

Beach was unimpressed with much of the police evidence, some from very senior men. He found that certain high-ranking officers 'will lie on oath if occasion suits them and no proper investigation will be made'. Of one senior sergeant, he commented:

> One of the most unimpressive of the police officers who gave evidence before the Board. He is clearly a man who will give false evidence whenever the occasion suits him.

Overall, Beach found that police used high-handed, violent and illegal tactics against both known criminals and members of the public in order to achieve their ends, and that police would conspire and commit perjury as necessary, either in court hearings or when appearing before him. His report also identified instances of inappropriate use of informers and the existence of a 'brotherhood syndrome', whereby police at all levels would do whatever was required to protect workmates. What also came across from the report, which the Rupert Hamer government of the time originally did not want to release, is the sheer helplessness experienced by men and women who find themselves in a police station.

In the final outcome Beach made extensive recommendations for police procedural reform in areas such as the investigation of complaints and the interrogation of people under arrest. He was scathing about the complaint processes and the standard of investigations existing at that time, saying 'the Board's inquiry into [specific incidents] established beyond doubt the undesirability of police investigating complaints against police'. Beach wanted fifty-five officers to be charged with a variety of offences, including perjury, assault, corruptly receiving money and conspiracy. Among them was Paul Higgins, whom Beach thought should be charged with assault, conspiracy and malicious damage. Had he been, hundreds of thousands of dollars might have been saved.

Instead what followed was a triumph for naked aggression by the Police Association. The protests over the Mr X case had indeed merely been a very useful dry run. This time more than 4000 men and women from a force of 6400 met at Festival Hall on 18 October 1976 to formulate a plan of resistance. They had not seen the Beach report; they did not know what his recommendations were, and they did not know which officers he had named and why, but they gathered in what the president of the Police Association, LJ Blogg, described as 'the greatest demonstration of unity in the history of the Association'.

The meeting instituted a 'work to rule' campaign, but there were hints also of a strike threat. In the face of such massive industrial opposition, Premier Hamer backed down and accepted a series of demands from the rank and file. Among these was one specifying that:

> Any change in police procedures was to be the result of a conference involving the police department, the Police Association and the government and not made on any recommendations made by Beach.

Instead of the Beach report being effectively a committal hearing, as had been the case with Kaye, now seventeen officers faced actual committal proceedings—fifteen were found to have no case to answer. No bills were entered against the remaining two. As for Beach's recommendations for change, again the government backed down and set up a new inquiry, this time chaired by J Norris QC and implicitly tasked with watering down the Beach report.

In 1977 Mick Miller became chief commissioner and almost immediately clashed with the association, whose policy, 'My Association right or wrong' did not include the nineteenth-century US senator Carl Schurz's addendum, 'and if wrong, to be set right'. There was no question of members being in the wrong. The Office of Police Integrity's board's report *Past Patterns* gives an example of the tortuous road to be followed if an officer was to be disciplined:

> Once he [Miller] had attended the Dawson Street police complex in Brunswick. By chance, he found a member putting petrol into the tank of his

> private motorbike from the police bowser. In due course, the member was charged and appeared at court where he was convicted by the Magistrate. The member's barrister told the Magistrate the conviction could result in his dismissal from the Force and the Magistrate placed him on a good behaviour bond. He was then arraigned before the Police Discipline Board that also found against him, and dismissed him from the Force. The offender appealed to the Police Service Board, which reinstated him. On his return to the Force, he was posted to the Missing Persons Bureau, where he became a malcontent. He took sick leave and, in due course, was boarded out, medically unfit on the grounds of 'management-induced stress'.

Like Tony Lauer in New South Wales, Miller would not accept that there was entrenched corruption in the force. However, in 1981 it became apparent that all was not well with the licensing, gaming and vice squad, with suggestions that the entire unit had been compromised by longstanding and systemic corruption—in other words, from the top down.

Operation Zebra was set up, and the story of the investigation followed the usual lines, with considerable ingenuity being displayed by suspected officers to avoid questioning—perhaps more than that displayed by the investigators, who were hampered by both lack of expertise and today's technical equipment. Although he had never previously been known to suffer from epilepsy, one man had a 'fit' when interviewed. He then took sick leave, before successfully retiring on a pension, claiming that his early retirement was due to stress brought on by the actions of management. Another, when required to answer a report explaining his actions, fired a number of shots through the document with his service revolver. He then went to a nearby hotel and never returned to the force. In the wash-up there was sufficient evidence to prosecute just one man. However, eighteen members retired, resigned or went on long-term sick leave. Operation Zebra may not have produced convictions, but some 560 offenders were fined nearly a quarter of a million dollars, and it was believed that SP bookmaking was temporarily wiped out in the state and the operators of Chinese card games who were linked to Triads were exposed.

Out of Zebra was born Zulu, when it was alleged that a senior police officer was in a corrupt relationship with former lawyer Mario Condello. Born in 1952 and educated at Fitzroy High before going on to study law at the University of Melbourne, Condello, the son of a painter and decorator from Calabria, was a thoroughly undesirable man with whom any officer, let alone a senior one, should never have become entangled. Almost from the start of his legal career he was involved in laundering and extortion. In December 1982 he was sentenced to six years' imprisonment after a marijuana crop was found on land he leased near Ararat. A fortnight earlier he had been struck off the rolls by the Supreme Court.

After his release from prison he became the owner of a restaurant in Bourke Street and, said one of his former lawyers, 'he also had an interest in the cemetery business'. The next year he was found guilty of two counts of arson. On 5 March 1985 he stood trial for the attempted murder of Richard Jones, a businessman who had upset another. Condello had been called in to deal with the recalcitrant Jones, who was shot in the stomach through a doona as he lay in bed. Amazingly, Jones survived because feathers plugged the wound. Condello was found not guilty after a confession he had made was ruled to be not under caution. In 1986 he received four years for conspiracy to defraud an insurance company. His business bought 120,000 prints for $2.40 each and arranged a sham sale in Italy, which valued them at $1.4 million. The prints were said to have burned in Naples during an earthquake riot.

The senior police officer was exonerated and after 2 1/2 years Operation Zulu was wound up. Condello lived another two decades before he became one of the last men killed in the long-running Melbourne gang war.

As always, where products or services are illegal but wanted or desperately needed by the public, there is the temptation for police officers to look the other way, in exchange for some consideration. Graft will find a way.

9

TWO COPPERS, TWO STATES: PAUL HIGGINS AND

[redacted]

Eight years after the Beach Royal Commission came yet another scandal, this time an extremely expensive one, both emotionally and financially, for the administration and the police union.

Following an internal investigation known as Operation Cobra, the prosecution alleged that Paul William Higgins, a former wrestler and twenty-year veteran of the Victoria Police, had led a ring of corrupt officers from 1978 to 1982. They had been working for the wealthy Geoffrey Lamb, Melbourne's then brothel king, whose empire included an estimated twenty-five illegal massage parlours. Higgins was another upwardly mobile officer with a good list of arrests who had been rewarded by rapid promotion. His record included the encomium, 'keen, tireless, efficient and reliable, energetic, knowledgeable, capable and well conducted'. One former officer recalled him as being 'not tall but very fit, he could be intimidating even hanging upside down from gravity boots at the gym'. He was one of the men who were seconded to the armed robbery squad shortly after it was formed and from there he moved into the CIB in 1972. Four years later he was promoted directly to the rank of detective sergeant, something that reflected the opinion of his superiors. Unusually, instead of being returned to uniform he was moved to the consorting squad. Dubbed 'The Consorters', members were part of another squad that was regarded in some quarters as a law unto themselves.

It was there that Higgins met Lamb, who had two luxury homes in Hawthorn and Kew, as well as a Lamborghini and extremely expensive personal habits. His lavish informal parties involved recreational use of drugs as well as women. When Lamb came to the conclusion in 1977 that he could use a little police protection from his competitors and the vice squad, he contacted someone he knew in the New South Wales Police who, for a fee of $10,000, put him in contact with Higgins. He and other police officers were invited into Lamb's circle, and girls were on the house, a facility of which Higgins and other officers regularly availed themselves.

Lamb would carry up to $10,000 in cash, which came in handy because he was soon paying thousands of dollars to police each month as protection money. In exchange his sex empire flourished, as the police on his payroll would warn him about any raids planned for his various parlours on the city fringes. Money, variously said to be $3000 a week or month, was handed over on the first of the month in the back room in Higgins' squad's office. In return Higgins and others agreed to stop investigations in their tracks, fabricate evidence if necessary and lean on the working girls if they were thought to be taking it too easy.

Higgins would instruct junior officers in his squad to make false entries on running sheets when Lamb was visited. On one occasion an officer was taken by Higgins to one of Lamb's establishments at Rathdowne Street, Carlton, and sent in to pick up a gun from Lamb. Higgins then allegedly told him to record that the .32 revolver had been received from a Drummond Street dobber. Lamb claimed he had been told by Higgins that he was to say he was an informant if questioned by police internal investigators.

At the beginning of August 1978, painter and docker turned brothel owner Joey Hamilton complained that police had planted a bomb at his home. It was the third attack and the second bomb in twelve months. When he was asked by reporters when the violence would stop, he replied, 'When people like you stop getting edited and start exposing organised crime—the police'.

Days after Hamilton's home was bombed, Higgins and another detective, acting on behalf of Lamb, helpfully planted a number of bombs in rival concerns, including the Collingwood home of brothel owner James Robert

Slater. Hours later police raids 'uncovered' gelignite and a tin of detonators in a child's toy box. Higgins did not even attempt to make an appearance of conducting a proper investigation. People who had access to the areas where the explosives were found were not interviewed. Charged with possession of explosives, Slater's watertight alibi was not checked. This time it was a case of the biter bit. At his trial he was able to prove, through a traffic-infringement ticket, that he had been staying in Mildura.

In March 1979 Higgins was brought before the Police Discipline Board, charged with being absent from duty and three lesser charges. There he was supported by senior officers, who gave evidence of his value to the CIB. No penalties were imposed, but he was transferred to uniform duties at Russell Street. In no time he was receiving glowing references and was quickly seconded to the car crime squad.

While there, a younger officer reported that Higgins had been helped by an informer to 'set up' drug dealers. Higgins would arrest the dealer, and the drugs seized would be cut by the informer with another substance. Higgins would save some for use as court exhibits, and the remainder would be sold and the profits shared. The young constable also said that Higgins had ordered him to doctor the official records. He also mentioned a gun Higgins provided to the informer for his own protection.

It was the usual fallout for the whistleblower. The constable was vilified and ostracised by his colleagues, and was transferred to a post where no one knew him. Even though he had the personal support of the chief commissioner, his life and career were seriously damaged.

The constable's allegations were not corroborated, so ultimately police management backed off, leaving Higgins to enjoy a free rein. When Higgins applied for a promotion to Russell Street CIB in 1982 he was knocked back, but he then appealed to the Police Service Board. Again the evidence of the young constable was pitted against Higgins' version of events. Again Higgins seemed to be the Teflon man. Although the board felt that he had perhaps been a little too close to his informers and needed to address this flaw, it was conceded that:

> it needs to be recognised that apparently he had throughout his service been somewhat encouraged to behave in this way by the results which he has achieved and the commendations and approval which the achievement of those results have brought him.

In other words, his misconduct had been condoned, even encouraged, by the force. Higgins began at Russell Street CIB on 30 June 1982. In 1983 Operation Achilles was started, supposedly in secret. However, information was leaked to the media, prompting an article that claimed police corruption existed in the massage-parlour and prostitution industry. It was alleged that payments were being made to a group of detectives to ensure protection from both competitors and prosecution. Senior police were said to be investigating these claims. The inquiry bore little fruit, despite fourteen months of diligent police probing. The force made no official comment.

On 25 April 1984 Higgins moved over to the armed robbery squad, known as 'The Robbers', but by 1986 was back at Russell Street as a senior sergeant. He had not been a shoo-in for this promotion. Some superior officers at the Police Service Board regarded him unfavourably, but his immediate supervisors had sung his praises. The decision tipped his way and he was posted to Prahran station.

However, the newly formed Internal Investigations Department (IID) was on the path of police corruption. The IID set up Operation Cobra to inquire into the activities of Higgins and others. During Cobra, investigators interviewed over 800 people and travelled all over Australia. The witness list was narrowed down to 170 people who had been involved in the Melbourne vice industry during the 1970s and 1980s. The list included Lamb's first lieutenant, Sandy MacRae, a serial killer thought to have been involved in up to twenty deaths and whose track record was certainly open to scrutiny. Cobra also accessed new information uncovered by an unrelated drug squad inquiry.

Higgins and Lamb finally fell out over a pre-1984 affair the detective had with Lamb's de facto wife, Lorraine Goyne, who later died following a drug overdose. From this point on Lamb's empire began to crumble. He fell for a gorgeous model turned prostitute who had taken up heroin. He tried to help her break her addiction but instead ended up using himself. Once, in one of the kinder acts of an untidy life, MacRae chained him to a bungalow wall on his Mildura property in an effort to wean him off the drug.

When key witnesses such as Lamb rolled over and made statements implicating Higgins and other officers, prosecutors felt confident they had Higgins, and two others from his old days at The Consorters, in the firing line. On 13 April 1987 Higgins was charged with, among other things, conspiracy to pervert the course of justice and suspended from duty.

The criminal proceedings were an unmitigated forensic disaster. It was, and probably still is, the second-longest case in Victorian legal history. The committal hearing began in October 1987 and lasted ten months. Geoffrey Lamb was in the witness box for seventy days, meekly telling the court he had blown $20,000 a week on heroin and had used up all his brothel profits. Eventually, with little progress being made, the Crown withdrew charges in August 1988, on the grounds that if the case had been allowed to continue, it would have been an 'abuse of court process'.

But then in 1990 one of Higgins' consorting squad associates admitted that a group of police in the squad had accepted bribes from Lamb in exchange for keeping his brothel empire free from prosecution. Later that year Higgins and the others went on trial in the County Court. After 135 days of legal argument, a jury of fifteen—three more than the usual number—was empanelled, in anticipation of some jurors withdrawing from what promised to be an unusually long trial.

And unusually long it was. To Higgins' chagrin and annoyance, much of the supporting evidence of Lamb came from MacRae. MacRae, who owned a massage parlour in Mildura, north-western Victoria, had persuaded an Albert O'Hara that he could make a profit from buying and selling marijuana. Instead, on 21 December 1984 he killed him, shooting him in the head and then cutting up his car so it could be dropped into the Merbein tip.

The list of MacRae's other victims included standover man Michael Ebert, killed outside a Carlton brothel in April 1980. Apparently Ebert had beaten MacRae badly the previous fortnight, and this slight, balding man was out for permanent revenge. In July 1980 police found the remains of a woman buried in the backyard of a home owned by an underworld figure's mother. The dead woman was thought to be a South Australian prostitute, also killed by MacRae. In August 1981 his girlfriend Deborah Joy Faher was found dead in a St Kilda motel. She had absorbed a 'hot shot' of almost pure heroin. Then came a prostitute known as Little Lisa. At MacRae's trial for the murder of O'Hara he claimed that it was his former de facto Judith Ip, whom he portrayed as the mastermind, who had killed O'Hara. The jury did not believe it and he was sentenced to life imprisonment. MacRae's appeal was dismissed.

Including the 135 days of preliminary legal argument, the trial lasted a total of 420 days. The prosecutor's final address took from 16 December 1990 to 26 January 1991. That of the defence ran from 27 January to 17 February 1991 and the judge's summing up to the jury from 18 February to 15 March 1991. The transcript of the aborted committal proceedings ran to over 7000 pages and that of the trial itself 32,000 pages. Legal Aid cost $700,000. The Police Association spent an estimated $1.8 million on legal fees, which nearly bankrupted it. The Crown case cost about $6 million, so the estimated total cost of Operation Cobra, which included court, legal and police expenses, ran to between $30 and $33 million, all taxpayers' money. How could a jury believe the word of brothel magnate Lamb and of a criminal like MacRae over that of a respected police officer? But they did.

Higgins was found guilty by the long-suffering jury, and on 6 April 1993 Judge Strong sentenced him to seven years' imprisonment with a minimum of five. He appealed unsuccessfully against his conviction and served his time at Ararat prison. Unsurprisingly, police officers normally have a hard time in prison, but it is said that when Higgins first arrived he 'beat the shit out of a fellow inmate' as a show of strength. In 1993 his consorting squad associates pleaded guilty to one count each of receiving a secret commission. Both received suspended sentences.

The authorities saw the Cobra inquiry as a 'powerful and symbolic attack on corruption within the Force'. At its heart was a struggle for control between senior management and an entrenched power group who thought they were untouchable. It was also a battle for supremacy between the Police Association and force command that management believed it had to win, no matter what the cost. It also proved divisive among the association ranks. With the association haemorraging money, ultimately pragmatism prevailed and after a series of votes it was decided that it was inappropriate to fund a case where an officer was charged with offences that occurred well outside the course of his duty. The association's accounts show that, in the period from 1988 to 1992, $6,948,682 was spent on legal fees.

Lamb died aged sixty-one sitting in an armchair in what was then his modest West Heidelberg home. Higgins, said to be still upset about what he considers his unfair treatment, has applied for a private investigator's licence.

Higgins' case is interesting in three respects. First is the way he managed to keep his nefarious activities hidden from his immediate superiors, who all appear to have thought him to be an outstanding officer. Second is the apparently open secret that over a lengthy period members of the vice squad were available to be bribed. And third are the complexities involved in dismissing a serving officer or denying him the promotion he seeks.

Meanwhile, Higgins' contemporary in the New South Wales Police had his own troubles. By the middle 1980s, on any account, certain police officers were not only out of control but were, as was said of Lord Byron, 'mad, bad and dangerous to know'.

[redacted]

[redacted]

[redacted]

[redacted]

[redacted]

[redacted]

[redacted]

[redacted]

[redacted]

[redacted]

[redacted]

[redacted]

[redacted]

[redacted]

10

NOBLE CAUSE CORRUPTION AND THE ART OF EXTRACTING A CONFESSION

Without a noble cause to begin with there can be no noble cause corruption. In their study of police ethics, US writers Michael A Caldero and John P Crank thought:

> We believe that the noble cause is something of which the police can be proud. The noble cause enables police to celebrate their special craft, to find meaning in the day-to-day activity of their work. Without the noble cause police work would lose its meaning and police officers would lose their sense of humanity, their concern for the innocent, and their dislike of bad people.

And noble cause corruption?

> It is corruption committed in the name of good ends, corruption that happens when police officers care too much about their work. It is corruption

> committed to get the bad guys off the streets, to protect the innocent and the children from the predators that inflict harm and suffering on them. It is the corruption of police power, when officers do bad things because they believe that the outcomes will be good.

But is it that simple? Les Ayton, Western Australian deputy police commissioner from 1994 to 1996, believed, 'There is no way you can effectively catch criminals by sticking strictly to the letter of the law. Good detectives have to take the law to the knife's edge'.

Cases that end in convictions lead to peer-group praise, to press and public acclaim, to advancement in the force. Advancement in the force leads to a higher salary, and a higher salary leads to an enhanced pension and a better position on retirement: head of security instead of merely driving a security van or carrying boxes from the van to a bank vault. Who ever heard of a mere constable being appointed head of security to a major enterprise?

Suspects are rarely caught *in flagrante,* and so other evidence—identification, forensics, being found in possession of the stolen property or the weapon used, a confession by a co-accused, or if all else fails, the evidence of a fellow prisoner who will say that the defendant has unburdened himself in the exercise yard is required. Sometimes, as in the case of Victorian super criminal Squizzy Taylor, accused of the Haines murder in 1914, someone such as a police matron can be recruited to supply the crucial—and, in this case, ambiguous—words. When Taylor was placed in a cell with his fellow accused John Williamson, he was said to have remarked, 'They cannot very well pot us if they do not identify us'. Perhaps unusually, the judge told the jury that the remark might equally be made by a wholly innocent man.

But best of all is a confession by the suspect:

> The work of any investigator ... is made much easier if a suspect can be induced to confess. It saves a lot of legwork. And it can be considered as the most conclusive sort of evidence if the person with the greatest vested interest in opposing the prosecution actually supports it.

The widely read American manual *Criminal Interrogation and Confessions* outlines no fewer than twenty-six specific techniques to be used in obtaining a confession. Commenting on these, Welsh S White, visiting professor of law at the University of Pennsylvania, thought:

> Most of these techniques will inevitably involve some sort of deception because they require an officer to make statements that he knows are untrue or play a role that is inconsistent with his actual feelings.

According to psychologists Gisli Gudjonsson and James MacKeith there are three kinds of confession, the first and best of which is the voluntary confession, in which no pressure of any kind is required. However, this must come with a caveat: these are not necessarily true confessions. In any high-profile murder case the investigating officers have to cope with, and eliminate, a number of spurious confessions. In the celebrated 1947 Black Dahlia killing of Elizabeth Short in Los Angeles, more than sixty people were reported to have confessed, simply for Warhol's 'fifteen minutes of fame'.

In turn, these false confessions can be broken down into two further categories. The first is the voluntary false confession, perhaps made to divert attention from the actual person who committed the crime. For instance, a man might confess to save his wife, parent or child from gaol. The second is the coerced false confession, made to escape a stressful situation such as so-called third-degree questioning, to avoid the possibility of a beating, or to gain a promised or implied reward, such as a lesser sentence, a respite from the questioning or perhaps simply a cup of coffee.

The term 'third degree' seems to have been coined in the 1880s by corrupt New York police officer Thomas Byrne, who was once described by journalist Lincoln Steffens as 'simple, no complications at all—a man who would buy you or beat you, as you might choose, but get you he would'. He sounds very like New South Wales' Fred Krahe a century later.

The third degree could take many forms and over the centuries the procedure for extracting confessions from prisoners has had many variations. In India the suspect often had their hands tied behind them before being hoisted by their wrists to a roof beam. There was also the practice of walking the prisoner about. Police changed every couple of hours, but the prisoner was kept on their feet until they confessed. In Madras in the 1870s a favourite method of obtaining a confession was beating the suspects' ankles and other joints with a soft mallet.

In Germany it was standard practice in the days when women wore long skirts to introduce rats into the cells of female suspects. In post–Second World War France a prisoner could expect the so-called *passage à tabac* (a bad beating) or being made to kneel in the crucifix position on the rim of a bicycle wheel. But there a confession might also be rewarded with a bottle of wine and dinner in a local cafe or even a visit to a prostitute. The latter seems to have winged its way across the world. Queensland's Crime and Misconduct Commission found that between 2001 and 2005 officers had prisoners removed from jail for conjugal visits as inducements to confess to unsolved crimes.

From the 1860s onwards in the United States there was the practice of sweating. The prisoner was kept in a small and increasingly hot cell until they confessed. They would also be given little sleep and meals would always be late. In December 1881 Mike McGloin, from the New York Whyos' street gang, suspected of the murder of tavern owner Louis Hanier, was positioned so that he could not avoid seeing the bloodstained clothing of his victim, and all the people who could connect him to the murder coming into and out of the prison. Another murderer was made to sleep in the bed of his victim and yet another was forced into the coffin in which his victim was to be buried. In 1892, when an Argentinian called Velasquez refused to admit to police that he had killed his girlfriend's children, he was given a thorough beating, bound and laid beside the children's corpses for the night. Fortunately, after another week of beatings during which he still refused to cooperate, fingerprints showed that he was not the killer.

New South Wales police officer in the postwar period and later judge and royal commissioner Don Stewart recalled his days as a young constable on the court staff:

> I can remember witnessing people in the CIB getting full, free and voluntary confessions out of people by hanging them by the ankles over the balcony of the CIB. And saying 'If you don't confess we'll drop you'. And the Station Sergeant would run out of the charge room and I'd run out and say, 'Don't, don't, don't drop him, don't drop him'. 'Get out, get out, it's none of your business!'

The third category, known as internalised false confessions, are those in which, as a result of highly suggestive interrogation techniques, the person has come to genuinely believe that he or she has committed the crime.

To these three may be added the confession invented by police, known as verballing or bricking. This relates to a verbal admission in full, or a partial confession hedged with ambiguous replies, and made without a lawyer or disinterested witness present. The suspect then refuses to sign a written statement. Former police 'bagman' (bribe collector) Jack Herbert turned whistleblower in exchange for indemnity and admitted to the Fitzgerald inquiry in 1988 that verballing had been endemic in the Queensland police force. This resulted in the immediate release of Walter John Anderson, who had served twenty-two years for the 'chicken-coop murder' at Funnel Creek in 1966 (so called because the bodies of the two murdered men had been wrapped in chicken wire). Herbert admitted to the inquiry that Anderson had been 'verballed' in 1966.

Early in its public hearings the Wood Royal Commission of 1995 to 1997 came to hear of 'scrumdowns', in which police would meet to 'refresh' each other's memories and ensure that 'there were no pitfalls' in the prosecution, even if this involved giving evidence that was wholly fabricated.

Former detective sergeant Neville Scullion explained that, on the first occasion he was required to give evidence, another officer prepared a statement for him that contained matters of which he had no knowledge. Yet, as requested, he gave evidence of them. He acknowledged that this was something he learned on the job from others, in the same way that 'an apprentice learns a trade'. Sometimes it was for expediency—for example, to remove the need to call a civilian witness—and sometimes it arose out of frustration with the difficulty of securing a conviction. He also said that inducements were regularly given to a suspect before the interview and denied later, and that any officer who gave a suspect a caution was considered 'a fool'. The interviewing officer and the corroborating officer were expected to be consistent in their evidence if questioned on these matters.

Although he denied direct involvement in any scrumdowns during his service with the armed holdup squad, former detective sergeant John Swan confirmed that the unit had a substantial reputation for this practice, and that he had an 'understanding' junior officers were informed by senior officers of the version of events that would be given in their statements, with the expectation this would be reflected in their evidence.

If it is accepted that noble cause corruption leads to more general corruption, then judges and magistrates, with some honourable exceptions, must take their share of the blame. At trials and inquiries some have almost wilfully refused to contemplate the disagreeable fact that police might be lying, and in this lawyers for the inquiry or commission have often colluded.

In New South Wales, Chief Justice Laurence Street set the tone when in 1978 he spoke of defence challenges to the admissibility of evidence as wasting the court's time in 'tedious and pointless fishing exercises'. Pointless in the sense that he was never going to accept the defence submissions, that is. . On the other hand, some Victorian and Queensland judges from the 1920s onwards did speak out against bashing and bricking, but they might just as well have been speaking in an empty room.

It was not until the 1991 case *McKinney v R* that the High Court made up its mind about the necessity of warning a jury that unsigned confessions might actually have been fabricated. Before that there had been conflicting judgements about what was required, but now the court noted developments in technology that could be used to record interviews and took, by a majority decision, a firm line. Forces were moving on. Audiovisual recording of interviews would soon commence in New South Wales and it was anticipated that every police station in that state would be appropriately equipped within two years. Section 464H amended the *Crimes Act 1958* (Vic) to make a confession inadmissible in Victoria unless it was recorded. In Tasmania it seems that interviews are routinely recorded, unless they occur in a remote part of the state where equipment is not available. Nowadays, where equipment is available any unrecorded confession should be subject to close scrutiny.

Australia's courts have been littered with examples of the last three types of confession. In theory, the use of the third degree in Victoria came to an end after the suicide of Isabella Newman, who in 1908 claimed to be the female champion pedestrian of Australia. Known as Madame Isabel, she had been sentenced to twelve months' imprisonment for perjury after denying that she had ever visited a brothel run by a woman called Stella Cross. She had also been investigated over the disappearance of the young child Winifred Oates. When police arrived in December 1913 to arrest her over allegations of baby farming, she took strychnine. The officers then arrested her husband and children and questioned them from 9p.m. until 11a.m. the next day without a break, a practice that had apparently been in use in Victoria since the force was founded. As a result the chief commissioner was instructed by the secretary of state that:

> The necessary information shall be obtained by the police without resort to all-night interrogations or any proceedings likely to produce physical and mental exhaustion in the person or persons questioned. He will also direct that any person examined shall be fully apprised of his rights and at the same time be afforded every opportunity

of having a friend or adviser present to watch and, if necessary, protect his or her interests.

In practice the third degree did not go away, but in the 1930s Victorian chief commissioner Thomas Blamey routinely dismissed any complaints about misconduct in his force. In 1930, 1933 and again in 1936 there were allegations that officers were using the third degree to get confessions.

The first two complaints were brushed aside, but on the third occasion chief justice Sir Frederick Mann commented publicly on police brutality, saying that it was a 'growing evil', before he began to sum up in a case in which 69-year-old Benjamin Ries claimed that he had been threatened and beaten into making a confession that he had raped his fifty-year-old housekeeper. Ries had been taken to the police station at 2.30p.m. and had initially asked to see a solicitor. He claimed, and there was medical evidence to support this, that he had been struck by an officer. Eventually he made a confession between 7.30p.m. and 9p.m. Although the chief justice said that he was not referring specifically to Ries' case, it must have been on the minds of the jurors, who found him not guilty in ten minutes. The next day a jury retired for only eight minutes before finding a grocery manager not guilty of theft. He too claimed that he had been beaten and produced evidence to support his claim.

Blamey was a good man so far as defending his force was concerned. He said that in the 'past few years' only one allegation of assault had been proved and that the officer had been immediately discharged. 'When a prisoner has a weak defence it frequently happens that he falls back on accusations against the police.'

Victoria was not alone in facing this problem. There were allegations in the 1930s that police officers in Queensland had been resorting to force, as well as taking suspects to Roma Street police station, where 'they would be overwhelmed by the authority of their examiner instead of being examined in their own home', a practice condemned by Justice Henchman of the Supreme Court. Five years later he called for clarification of what was and was not permissible. In its editorial of 7 October 1935 *The Courier-Mail* was firmly on the side of the police:

> It is within the knowledge of the observant layman that the police secure a considerable number of convictions through the confessions, admissions, or compromising statements of wrongdoers. It may be said with equal certainty that if they were compelled to take a suspect before a justice of the peace or a clerk of petty sessions and allow him to consult a solicitor before they put their questions, they would in many instances be met with a wall of silence. Are they entitled, or are they not, to take advantage of the ignorance or maladroitness of an examinee, his reaction to the uncomfortable atmosphere of a police station, or the unease of his conscience? His Honour Mr.

> Justice Henchman thinks that question should be settled by definite rulings. If and when they are given it will be in the public interest if they recognise that the police are called upon to match their wits against unscrupulous and dangerous men, and that any circumscription of their powers which does more than protect the innocent may help the guilty to escape.

Fifty years later, the 1984 confession of Barry Mannix to the murder of his father clearly came into the second category of confessions. Forty-year-old Kevin Mannix, a Tweed Heads, Queensland, sex-shop owner with a string of minor convictions for obscene publications, was found with his throat cut in the early hours of 22 June. He had been bound, gagged and blindfolded, and was carried from his Gold Coast unit, for reasons that were not immediately apparent, to the alleyway where his body was discovered. In the course of his abduction, Mannix managed to free one hand and remove part of the adhesive tape covering his mouth. When he called out for help, he was thrown bodily down the flight of stairs leading from the unit, his head striking a concrete pillar.

His son Barry, who had been working at the sex shop, said he had gone to his father's unit a little after midnight and found the television and lights on, and his father's coin collection scattered on the floor. He told police that he presumed his father had gone out. He watched television and then fell asleep. It was next morning that he found his father's body. On 6 July he was asked to go down to Broadbeach police station and he went voluntarily. During the evening he signed two confessions and was duly charged. He immediately claimed that the confession had been bashed out of him and he had been threatened that, if he did not confess, his whole family would be charged or, in the case of junior members, put in care. Public feeling against him was so great that when he first appeared in the magistrates' court he had to be protected from the crowd.

He was released in early November that year after a stripper, Jan Hurst, told the police that an Anthony Rau was driving a stolen car. When Rau was arrested he confessed that he, Craig Andrew McConnell, Nigel Andrews and Nicholas Abela had committed the Mannix murder. They were also charged on 26 October with the murder of middle-aged high-class call girl Lovena Cunningham. McConnell had killed her in a botched robbery at her Gold Coast apartment on 26 August. New Zealand–born Cunningham, who had continued working to pay for her son's career as a motor-racing driver, was found strangled and with her throat cut in the same manner as that of Kevin Mannix. Bleach had been poured over her mouth and genitals. McConnell was sentenced to life imprisonment.

An inquiry by the Police Complaints Commission headed by judge Eric Pratt examined the circumstances in which Barry Mannix confessed. It produced a report that effectively trashed Mannix but not the police.

Presumably to show how untrustworthy his evidence might be, the commission found that a band in which Mannix had played had been booed at a Sydney hotel.

Pratt's finding was:

> It is clear that we have discovered a large body of convincing evidence that is available to be led by the Defence in the event that any police officer is charged with an offence arising from these allegations.

There was to be no compensation for Mannix for his ordeal. If anything, he was rather fortunate to come out as unscathed as he did:

> The fact is that the system has allowed the incarceration in prison for some four months of a lad innocent of the charge on which he was being held. BARRY MANNIX has been hurt by his incarceration just as the investigating police have been hurt by the subsequent strain of having to undergo our exhaustive investigation.

One positive thing about police perjury, at least from the perjurer's point of view is, as policeman and journalist CH Rolph pointed out:

> Police perjury—unlike some perjuries—carries no risks. Police witnesses are sometimes discredited but rarely prosecuted for perjury in my experience. The profession appears to give immunity from this misfortune.

Perhaps one of the longest-running, most widespread, most flagrant and, for a time, best-kept-secret—from the public at least—examples of noble cause corruption was the illegal tapping of telephones that was eventually exposed by journalist Bob Bottom and became known as *The Age* tapes. It broke in a slightly arcane way. Drug dealer Robert 'Aussie Bob' Trimbole fled the country in May 1981, shortly before he was due to appear before the Stewart Royal Commission. In winter 1983 the Sydney and Melbourne newspapers began to run stories that he had been tipped off, but it was not clear by whom. Pre-eminent journalists Bob Bottom and John Silvester later told the royal commission that they had seen summarised transcripts of telephone conversations between Trimbole and police officers. In November that year *The National Times* published extracts of the tapes, and these were followed by further *Age* reports in February 1984. There followed another helter-skelter effort to destroy incriminating evidence, but some material survived and was passed on to *The Age.*

It was up to Justice Stewart to determine whether it was possible to identify who was conducting the conversations on the tapes, whether they provided evidence of criminality and whether the tapes helped in the Mr Asia drug case, in which heroin in massive quantities was imported into New Zealand, Australia and the United Kingdom in the 1970s, and in which participants thought to be disloyal were ruthlessly killed. Stewart reported that the material had to be authenticated and that could only be done with evidence from those who had done the taping, which, since it was not court approved, had been illegal. To do this, indemnities against prosecution had to be given to the tapers, and some 350 indemnities were granted to members of the New South Wales force and the Australian Federal Police. It also became clear that members of the later disbanded Commonwealth and New South Wales Joint Task Force, set up after the Williams and Woodward royal commissions, had been bugging illegally. What Stewart found particularly cynical was that commencing the phone taps could have been done legally, with a warrant, probably granted by a judge.

Frustrated by the failure of conventional criminal investigations, the upper echelons of the police had readjusted the balance of power. Illegal bugging was first authorised by Norman 'The Foreman' Allan in around 1967 and had been carried on by the New South Wales force with the approval of 'Slippery' Fred Hanson, Mervyn Wood, the squeaky-clean Jim Lees and Cec Abbott. When it became clear that Abbott would succeed Jim Lees as New South Wales police commissioner, Bill Jenkings, the Sydney *Daily Mirror's* chief crime reporter for thirty-five years—who would not hear a word spoken against either Ray Kelly or his cohort Fred Krahe—wrote on 26 November:

> The 1274 detectives in the New South Wales police force would welcome, probably to a man,

> the appointment of Senior Assistant Commissioner Cec Abbott as their new Commissioner.
>
> And if they still had to wear hats they'd throw them into the air and cheer, according to a survey this week ... Mr Abbott admired and learned from those who have been hailed as the 'greats' of the CIB—people like the legendary Detective-Inspector Ray Kelly.

Three years after Abbott's appointment, the publication of the tapes forced the New South Wales Government to pass the *Listening Devices Act 1984.* A 2007 report by the Victorian Office of Police Integrity asserted:

> Noble cause corruption is the nursery of entrenched and systemic corruption. If a police service wants to rid itself of corruption, it must attack noble cause corruption.

In his book *Getting Justice Wrong,* former New South Wales DPP Nicholas Cowdery argues that periodic exposures of police misbehaviour show if there are not strong controls in place over bodies like police forces, there will be improper conduct and corruption. Unprofessional police will always be quick to exploit any loophole in procedures to achieve what they regard as the 'right' result.

For a police force under pressure for results and immune from genuine scrutiny, Machiavellian cynicism must be a constant temptation. Provided that the victims of injustice are unpopular and without means—dingoes—the rewards for solving cases are great and the risks small.

In his essay *Miscarriages of Justice in Serious Cases in Australia,* writer Paul Wilson identifies several factors that contribute to miscarriages of justice. They include over-zealousness by police, police taking 'short cuts' to secure convictions against a 'guilty' person, evidence from experts who are in reality acting as 'propagandists for the prosecution', and confessions that have been either fabricated or extracted through pressure. Often, he argues, there is no conscious decision to convict the innocent; the police simply adopt tunnel vision and will not look at evidence that might exculpate the suspect. Any illegal means is justified by the end result of obtaining a conviction. And once charges are laid prosecutors will collaborate with the police to do everything possible to make those charges stick.

Given this longstanding scenario of noble cause corruption, a change of attitude may be a long time coming.

11

DRUGS: AN IRRESISTIBLE TEMPTATION

Drugs in different forms have always floated around Australia—notably, there were cocaine wars in Sydney in the 1920s—but it was not until the Vietnam war, when Sydney was home to US servicemen on R and R, that the heroin trade really took off. Between 1967 and 1971 over 280,000 Americans visited Sydney. As late as 1966, with only a handful of known addicts in Australia, let alone New South Wales, drug possession and importation was a very low priority for the force. Ironically, a police officer was amongst the first to take advantage of the vacuum.

In 1966 New South Wales special branch detective John Wesley Egan masterminded a high-grade heroin-smuggling ring. He had begun his criminal career while still a serving officer. A fine swimmer and a man commended for his lifesaving, he was a member of the police diving squad that was asked by customs to try to recover some gold ingots thrown overboard by Chinese seamen to pre-empt a search. He duly located them but taped a number to a pylon for later personal recovery. After that he began smuggling watches, transistors and cameras, which

Egan later claimed were mainly sold to police officers. An unfortunate sale to a customs official blew the lid off that particular scheme and five officers resigned. It was then that Egan was introduced to the possibilities of heroin smuggling by a man connected to the painters and dockers, and he determined to make a million dollars inside three months and retire.

He learned of a potential customer, an ex-CIA agent in New York, borrowed money for 'home improvements', obtained compassionate leave to attend the 'funeral of an aunt' in California and booked a flight to New York on Qantas with a kilo of almost pure heroin. He made $6000 from the run and had a taste of future possibilities. Four months later he resigned from the special branch and began a fulltime career organising drug smuggling.

On his first run to his 'aunt's funeral' Egan had a special vest made for himself, and all his couriers—mostly officers on leave from the New South Wales Police who were paid $2000 a run—were similarly kitted out, giving the group the name the Corset Gang. Six months later, with twenty couriers operating, he was netting $80,000 a week. The couriers were sent to Hong Kong to collect the drugs, which were flown to the United States via London, Tokyo and New Delhi. Egan's downfall came after a tip-off that there was to be a raid. He flew to Hong Kong to tell New Zealander Glenn Reid, in charge of buying from Chinese suppliers, to suspend operations. Unfortunately, Reid kept 2 kilograms, and when he was arrested in Honolulu he shelved Egan and arranged to set him up. Egan was arrested and given bail, which he skipped. He went first to England and was arrested in Paris three years later. Extradited to the United States, he served just under four years of an eight-year sentence. Back in Australia, Egan retired to the Gold Coast, where in 1978 he was fined $1500 for illegal gambling.

It was estimated that over a six-month period from 1966 to 1967, Egan and his gang smuggled $22 million worth of heroin into the United States. As American sociologist and author Alfred McCoy points out, the exercise revealed the capacity for corruption within the New South Wales Police. Its tolerance for that corruption paved the way for a level of drug trafficking that would have astounded Egan, who had already expressed the view that 'Organised crime and highly placed policemen are often the same people'.

For a time Egan's good work and philosophy were carried on by New South Wales constables Michael Woodhouse and Philip Briddick, who in 1978 received fifteen years between them for dealing in cocaine and Indian hemp. Their undoing was a wire tap, in which Briddick was recorded as saying:

> It's amazing how many coppers are in this business.
> They've got it by the balls ... It's guaranteed you know...
> Everything's protected from way high up.

Another on the bandwagon was former butcher and truck driver Maxwell Gudgeon, who joined the New South Wales Police in October 1963. From there his career was an upwardly mobile one until he joined the CIB in 1977. Then two years later came a defining moment. In May 1979 a colleague of Gudgeon's made a series of arrests in Double Bay over a quantity of cannabis. Gudgeon interrogated one of the suspects at Flemington police station before the man was charged with supplying, a charge which carried a maximum of fifteen years. Early in 1980 Gudgeon was promoted to detective sergeant, a fortnight before the Double Bay suspect was committed for trial. The next year Gudgeon and a businessman were alleged to have purchased Knightvale, a property near Byrock, 60 kilometres south of Bourke in New South Wales. Whether due to the strain of becoming a property owner or some other reason, Gudgeon was placed under the care of a psychiatrist for a nervous disorder in the winter of that year. The medicinal properties in Indian hemp for relieving stress are well known and perhaps this was the reason he was alleged to have conspired with others to cultivate the drug at Knightvale from October that year. As for the Double Bay matter, in January 1981 a report from Gudgeon's psychiatrist stating that he and the arresting officer in the case were both suffering from nervous disorders and that neither was well enough to attend court was sent to the Crown prosecutor's office. The psychiatrist was unable to say when the pair might be well enough to give evidence and the Attorney-General entered a no bill in November 1982.

Gudgeon resigned from the police in August that year. He later approached a Detective Keenan to ask him to leave the police and become the manager of Knightvale, telling him what the property was to be used for and that the product would have a 'quality better than that at Hay'—a reference to a police raid on a marijuana plantation there. Keenan blew the whistle and in November 1982, after a police raid on Knightvale, Gudgeon, senior constable Andrew Swan and three others were arrested. On the property were two lots, each of up to 6000 marijuana plants, valued at up to $6 million. It was clear that there had been an earlier harvest. In 1986 all were sentenced to ten years in prison, and in Gudgeon's case there was no set pre-parole period.

Judge Anthony Collins told Gudgeon that he regarded him as the lynchpin and that the law made the gamble worth taking for many criminals, adding that, 'Ten years is not ten years. Ten years for a first offender who behaves himself is a little over six years. Given a few Royal tours and a few warders' strikes ... five'. He called for 'urgent legislative action' to correct a situation that was resulting in some drug users receiving heavier penalties than the dealers themselves. A merciful Court of Appeal reduced Gudgeon's sentence and he was released on parole in 1991.

Prison rarely has redemptive qualities. The month after his release Gudgeon set up a conspiracy in Queensland to import cannabis from Thailand. This time when he was caught he received fifteen years.

By then, however, bent officers such as [redacted] had entered into the spirit of things, teaming up with career criminal Neddy Smith in the 1980s Sydney drug wars. During this period of free-for-all it was difficult to tell the difference between the criminals and some of the police.

Down south, drugs were relative latecomers to the vice industry in Victoria. In 1957 the officer in charge of the drug bureau reported that he had yet to find a marijuana smoker, although a few Chinese had been charged with possessing and smoking opium. Cannabis was criminalised in 1963 and, by 1973, 3601 offenders accused of 'nonmedicinal use of drugs' had been detected across the state. The following year the number of offenders had doubled. As drug busts were made there were increased allegations against police of 'misdeeds including brutality and corruption'. Drug squad Chief Inspector Roy Kyte-Powell believed that most allegations could not be substantiated but were time consuming and morale sapping.

It soon became clear, however, that at least some allegations against police had substance. In January 1981, after months of intelligence gathering, Operation Leo resulted in simultaneous raids on fifty properties near Swan Hill, where marijuana was thought to be growing in between grape vines. Nothing was found—a tip-off had prompted an early harvest. The source of the leak was never identified, but it was believed that it could only have come from within the force.

In the 1990s the force's drug squad, rather than being enlarged as was probably necessary to try to stem the tide of heroin flooding the markets, was divided into three units. The first was to investigate the Asian heroin syndicates, the second was primarily responsible for investigating manufacturers and traffickers of amphetamines, and the third investigated heroin traffickers as well as cocaine and marijuana crops.

There were internal problems as well. Drug squad headquarters were still at Russell Street when, in October 1991, 1.3 kilograms of methamphetamine went missing, allegedly stolen from a locked and alarmed storeroom. Poor management and procedural deficiencies were blamed and several officers faced disciplinary measures.

Relatively easy to produce, amphetamines were being cooked in small laboratories. The profits were many and the dangers were few. A conviction for a major trafficking in heroin could earn twenty years and upwards; for a similar amphetamine conviction the penalty was a quarter or a third of that. By 1990 Melbourne had become the amphetamine capital of Australia. Two years later producers, as opposed to distributors, were to be the main police target.

The rise of gang violence in Melbourne in the 1990s stemmed, at least in part, from the high-risk police policy of arranging the manufacture of their own amphetamines in an attempt to break into the city's network of dealers. By the middle of the decade a system had been devised whereby the police would buy precursor chemicals from wholesalers and, using controlled deliveries, they or trustworthy informers—if that is not an oxymoron—would sell on to the producers, which would provide evidence for prosecutions. The drug squad regularly set up buy-bust arrangements using informers and undercover police. The undercovers also occasionally sold, hence the need for supplies around the office. Damian Marrett, a drug squad undercover of the time, explained:

> At that time we were doling out samples of our wares to interested parties ... Victoria Police figured that if their covert operatives were out in the community, prepared to sell as well as buy, the targets would be more inclined to take us seriously. That was the thinking then ... Granted the perception didn't look good. A case could be made that we were dealing the stuff ourselves.

Unit 2 of the drug squad, now at the St Kilda Road police complex, operated what was later quaintly called 'the chemical diversion desk'. The drugs and precurser chemicals were purchased from chemical companies by drug squad officers and, prior to use in buybust operations, were carefully recorded and kept at the out-of-town Attwood storage facility near Tullamarine airport. Unluckily, in 1992 a substantial amount was stolen and cheaper powders substituted. This awkward fact only emerged during the trial of two drug offenders, who insisted that drug exhibits be retested. Again the culprit was 'management procedures', found to be non-existent. Keys were left in unlocked drawers, the facility was never inspected and there was no audit trail or responsibility.

Attwood was ordered to lift its game. Detective Senior Constable Kevin Hicks—a fully fledged graduate of the major crime squad, disbanded for improper dealings with suspects and corrupt activities in the early 1990s—was put in charge to guard and take responsibility for the drugs and chemicals stored there.

Unfortunately, Hicks soon made friends with a drug-trafficking syndicate. When in August 1996 further thefts of chemicals from Attwood were suspected, the ethical standards department sent in Task Force Guardsman. Hicks was found to have supplied the syndicate with drugs, and a fake drug raid was even staged so that it could get its hands on precursor drugs to manufacture speed. He subsequently pleaded guilty to burglary, bribery and drug trafficking, and received a modest six years with a minimum of 4 1/2 years.

In the mid-1990s documents crucial to Operation Phalanx, a massive investigation into amphetamine manufacturers, were stolen from Level 12 of the St

Kilda Road complex. Gone was the brief on the decade-long involvement of the Black Uhlan motorcycle gang and their speed kingpin, John William Samuel Higgs. Gone also were documents identifying informers, only known as numbers, along with those identifying undercover drug cops. Those responsible were never discovered.

Now heading Unit 2 and so responsible for the chemical diversion program was Detective Inspector Reid. Unfortunately for him, a Beretta 9mm pistol disappeared from his safe. Its theft was a mystery but did not reflect well on Reid's leadership and responsibility. Reid was later charged and convicted of disciplinary offences before locating the missing pistol a few months later. Nonetheless he resigned. Even more unfortunately for the force, he was replaced by Detective Sergeant Wayne Strawhorn, described by a former colleague as 'a true professional cop ... set goals and absolutely determined to get the job done ... whatever it took'. He had recently returned from overseas study and was brim full of drug crime-busting ideas. Other Unit 2 chemical diversion members were Detective Senior Constable Steve Paton and Detective Senior Sergeant Malcolm Rosenes.

Among prime targets for the drug squad were the Reading brothers, Lenny, Joe and Jeff, sometimes called the 'Three Stooges', who had been relatively unhindered by police raids for some years. 'If they didn't have a green light to deal drugs in Victoria, they were flat-out revving the car on amber!', recalled Marrett.

In a classic example of the ability of the police to load members of families whom they consider to be criminals, when Malcolm Rosenes joined the drug squad under Wayne Strawhorn, one of his first missions was to head out to the western suburbs to raid Lenny Reading's house. Strawhorn suggested to Rosenes that, as Lenny was apparently cooking with an exciting new recipe, Rosenes was likely to find three different precursor chemicals. Rosenes and his team scoured the house and found nothing. He phoned Strawhorn and was told to search in the backyard. Again Rosenes reported back in the negative. No worries: Strawhorn now directed him to hunt under a pile of rocks close to the back fence. And there Rosenes uncovered purple chemicals in a plastic bag. Now Strawhorn, directing things by remote control to keep a distance, told Rosenes to try between the shed and the fence. Again, Rosenes struck lucky. Two chemicals down and one to go. Finally Strawhorn suggested, off the top of his head, another hiding spot and there Rosenes found the third chemical stash. It was then that Rosenes, according to his biographer, the former lawyer and drug dealer Andrew Fraser, started to smell a rat in the upper ranks. 'He had been used as the bunny to load Lenny.'

Rosenes wasn't alone. Strawhorn sent another young recruit out to search Lenny's house for a drug recipe book, known as 'Uncle Fester's Cookbook'. Inside was a one-page typed recipe for speed utilising precisely the three ingredients Rosenes had found in the backyard.

Reading protested his innocence and claimed that the gear had been planted. When Reading was tried for the three chemicals plus the recipe bust, the judge effectively directed the jury to acquit. The jury disagreed, but the judge had the final say and Reading received an entirely suspended sentence.

In the three years from 1998 nearly sixty clandestine laboratories were discovered. In 1999 a man regarded as Australia's biggest amphetamines manufacturer was arrested, and a Melbourne identity was charged with conspiracy involving a shipping container of chemicals. But then the wheels began to fall off. There were allegations that chemicals were being stockpiled by the police. A secret bank account was opened by them and sometimes chemicals went missing. In December 2001 the drug squad was disbanded and replaced with the major drug investigation division. But the damage had already been done.

Meanwhile, across at Unit 1, the heroin trafficking unit, Detectives Glenn Sadler, Stephen Cox and Ian Ferguson were taking multicultural relations too far. They had as one of their informants Kenneth Lai, whom they supplied with heroin at a bargain price. He then sold it on, and in exchange the officers were to receive 30–40 per cent of his profits. The arrangement also provided for Lai to help them arrest other drug dealers, and the sweetener was that he would be given a portion of the heroin seized in any bust he facilitated. So it was a merry-go-round of heroin: the police could obtain free heroin from busts, they could sell it cheap to trafficker-informers, and the traffickers could on-sell it to dealers and kick back a share of the cash profits to the police. The police, informed by the traffickers, could then bust the dealers and reclaim the heroin. If the new set of dealers could then be persuaded to work with the police and dob in other dealers, it became a beautiful circular enterprise.

Another dealer, Duy Le, a friend of Lai's, was arrested in August 1998 for aggravated burglary, and again in April 1999, this time for trafficking heroin. He pleaded guilty to the burglary and received a suspended sentence. He was then persuaded by Lai to get back into the heroin-trafficking game and began buying from the detectives. By mid-2000 Duy Le was buying a block of heroin from Ferguson every few days. The detectives also kept him informed of the efforts of the Asian squad to arrest him. In turn, he gave the drug squad information about dealers. Cox had by then retired from the force with a substantial gratuity.

It all came undone when Le was finally arrested in New South Wales in 2002 on the 1999 drug charges. He was induced to cooperate with the Ceja Task Force and became a key witness against the detectives on conspiracy charges. Evidence of the hundreds of thousands of dollars they had managed to accumulate was also compiled as corroboration.

Ferguson was additionally convicted of money laundering and in April 2006 received a twelve-year sentence with a minimum of eight to serve. Sadler and Cox were tried jointly, and in November 2006 Sadler was given ten with a six-year minimum, and Cox received seven with a four-year minimum. All appealed in 2009 without success.

The full disaster of the 1990s Victoria Police drugs policy became brutally clear on 18 October 2006. After three years on remand, high-flying Detective Senior Sergeant Wayne Strawhorn—dobbed in by drug-dealing lawyer Andrew Fraser—was convicted of trafficking 2 kilograms of pseudoephedrine to the late gangland leader Mark Moran and sentenced to a maximum seven years' imprisonment. He was acquitted on three of four other charges, including trafficking the chemical to members of the Bandidos motorcycle gang. Strawhorn appealed against conviction and sentence, but in June 2008 these were dismissed. Another officer, Stephen Paton, had entered a guilty plea in June 2003 and was sentenced to six years with a three-year minimum. Rosenes had followed suit in October 2003 and received six with a 3 1/2-year minimum.

Pending the trial and appeal of Strawhorn, the names of Rosenes and Paton were suppressed and a number of other cases were kept on hold. Once Rosenes and

Paton entered guilty pleas, appellants came out of the woodwork, claiming that the detectives' pleas constituted fresh evidence that might have led to the acquittal of those who had been convicted and there was the risk of a miscarriage of justice. Their hopes generally went unrewarded.

After this spate of cases Detective Sergeant Bill Patten, an original member of the Ceja Task Force, claimed that up to two dozen officers had escaped corruption charges and the only proper investigation would have been a royal commission. Other officers in difficulty at the time included Matthew Bunning, a former member of the drug squad, who was sentenced to a minimum of three years for providing information about intercepts, and former Victorian officer James McCabe, on secondment to the National Crime Authority (NCA), who failed to appear in Sydney to answer charges of robbery and drug dealing. He fled to Cambodia, from where he was expelled. On his return to Australia in 2008 he pleaded guilty to stealing 1 kilogram of drugs and served just over a year. On his release he returned to Cambodia and set up a unit to help abused children. Another officer who fell by the wayside was one-time Detective Senior Constable Paul Hatzakortzian, who was jailed for a year after pleading guilty to dealing in drugs. He had been working at Sexpo while on leave from the sexual offence and child abuse unit.

In February 2007 the Office of Police Integrity (ORI) had told Victorian Police Commissioner Christine Nixon that it had evidence against dozens of officers who had been involved in drug dealing, theft and associating with criminals. However, the OPI maintained that another royal commission was not necessary and the office was the best placed to deal with corruption.

Terence Hodson was by no means the first or last Western Australian villain who came to grief in Victoria, and he brought many people down with him. Born in Great Britain in 1947, he started his criminal career by stealing unattended purses at dances before moving to Western Australia in November 1974. On the face of things he was an old-style polite, even charming, crook, but deeper down he was a dobber who came to be regarded as a man who would give up anyone to save himself. In the early 1990s Hodson moved to Melbourne, where his Kew home was well guarded with an array of floodlights, heavy-duty wire grilles, security cameras and a pair of German shepherds.

On 27 September 2003 Hodson, on bail and lined up to give evidence in drugs trials, together with his handler, Detective Senior Constable David Miechel, were caught *in flagrante* stealing drugs from another dealer's house in East Oakleigh. They had hoped to find $700,000 cash but were seen throwing bags over the back fence. In his flight Miechel was badly bitten by a police dog with whom he had a run-in and was bashed by the dog's handler. Within hours of the burglary Hodson's file, showing that he was a long-term informer, was stolen from a police station and released in the underworld. Miechel eventually went down for a minimum of fifteen years, reduced on appeal to twelve, after convictions for burglary, theft and trafficking a commercial quantity of drugs.

Hodson, as was his game, was preparing to give evidence against Miechel and Detective Sergeant Paul 'Killer' Dale—whom he claimed had masterminded the burglary—when, on 16 May 2004 he and his wife, Christine, were found shot dead at their home. There was no sign of a break-in and it is thought that they therefore must have known their killer. After their deaths, charges were dropped against Dale. Dale, who has always maintained his innocence of any wrongdoing whatsoever, was later charged with conspiracy over the death of Hodson, but when, in turn, Melbourne gang leader Carl Williams was killed on 19 April 2010 in the supposedly secure unit in Barwon Prison, that charge was also dropped. In 2013, after he was cleared of lying to the Australian Crime Commission, Dale called for a reinvestigation of the Hodson killings.

In September 2012 a suppression order was lifted and the Victorian public was at last allowed to know who killed the Hodsons—something they could have worked out for themselves with a little time on the internet. The answer was contract killer Rodney Collins, known as 'The Duke', already serving thirty-two years for the 1987 murder of another pair of drug dealers, Raymon and Dorothy Abbey; he will be ninety-eight before he becomes eligible for parole. That, of course, still leaves the all-important question of who took out the contract.

Over the border in South Australia, on 8 October 1981 *The Advertiser* published claims from its *Extra* team of journalists, who had been investigating organised crime in other states, that there was a substantial degree of corruption among members of the South Australian police. The allegations followed the usual pattern: green lighting, bricking, lawyers fixing cases with the police, standing over dealers, thefts of drugs and money, and a certainly amount of brutality. The Attorney-General indicated that he would set up an internal inquiry. This announcement did not generally go down well with those who would have preferred a royal commission. In a case that week a jury had disagreed over allegations that police had found seventeen bags of Indian hemp in the possession of Giuseppe Romeo and William Gray at Norwood back in April 1980. The bags had 'accidentally' been destroyed by the police and so could not be produced in evidence. Would it be possible for the public to be satisfied with an internal inquiry? The opposition wondered how it was that there had been no look at massage parlours and found it puzzling that some were harassed continually while others near the city centre continued to operate openly and apparently unimpeded. The Attorney-General was sure that the public would be happy. 'These allegations need capable detective work and if anyone is to test the veracity of these allegations then this team will do just that.'

Unsurprisingly, the allegations were not well received by the police. The president of the South Australian Police Association, Inspector Barry Morse, was one who was righteously indignant when he spoke up for his members, saying he believed that the allegations were both 'bland' and 'insubstantiated'. He thought that drug dealers were behind the allegations, which were designed to disrupt police investigation into the trade and were 'an obvious attempt by drug dealers to discredit the police force'.

Depending upon one's point of view, the report the following year either cleared the police or was a whitewash. Former Supreme Court judge Sir Charles Bright had been brought in to comment on the investigations and he found that witnesses had either backtracked, refused to cooperate or were untrustworthy. Of the principal witness, who, in fairness, had thirty-one convictions over a 28-year period, including a few for false pretences, Sir Charles wittily wrote:

> What kind of man is Informant 'A'? Many years ago, in one of his stories of the New York underworld, Damon Runyon introduced a character 'Joey Perhaps'. Another character summed him up in these memorable words 'The kindest thing I can consciously say about Joey Perhaps is—you

> can have him'. I adopt these words as a summary of Informant 'A'.

Sir Charles found that in only one case was there real suspicion, but 'Even in that case there is evidence to suggest a deliberate attempt to concoct a case of corruption'. What he did observe was that:

> Once an allegation of corruption has been made against a policeman it is almost impossible for him to prove his innocence, assuming he is innocent.

He did, however, go on to advise that officers working in areas such as betting, liquor and drugs where there was a high risk of corruption should stay in the squad for a relatively short period of time.

Again unsurprisingly, not everyone was pleased with the outcome. The following week, an opposition call for a royal commission was defeated. Adelaide lawyer RC Bleechmore commented:

> Look—this report has not even scraped the surface—what has happened as a result of the April Fool's Day report is that certain officers are now prepared for any further proper inquiry.

Another year, another dollar. In the mid-1980s, on one day a year good citizens could ring a toll-free hotline and dob in a druggie or, better still, dob in a dealer. A number took the opportunity to dob in a neighbour whose dog might be annoying and ex-spouses dobbed in their former loved ones for unspecified bad behaviour, but despite these distractions Operation Noah was something of a success, rather defying the general belief that Australians don't like dobbers. In 1987 there were some 400 calls, which led to fourteen people being charged with offences. The next year, in the first five hours 1300 people called the hotline with nearly 300 'valuable pieces of information'. Unfortunately, in 1989 the callers to Noah named thirteen Adelaide officers.

At the time Barry Moyse, by now chief inspector, was head of the South Australian drug squad, lecturing at schools on the dangers of drugs. He was also a one-time president of the South Australia Police Association and eventually he became Noah's public face.

It was at that time that dealer and user George Octopodelis, for a long time another Mr X, was about to be franchised. Octopodelis claimed to have been introduced to the heroin trade by the Indianborn Essie Mooseek, who had started life in Australia as a hawker in Fremantle. Mooseek, alleged to be one of the top ten drug dealers in the southern hemisphere and who ran the Mr Oceanic ring, said to be bigger than the Mr Asia syndicate, absconded on bail in 1985 after he was charged with importing heroin to the value of $25 million.

Octopodelis had grown up in Adelaide but had started his career selling fake jewellery in Melbourne. After his friends there were named in the Woodward report on drugs he returned to Adelaide, where he built a drug empire. At its height he was controlling five dealers, who each controlled a street network of ten dealers.

It seems that during a drug bust in August 1986, when Octopodelis was busted over pink rock heroin sent from Sydney, Moyse found an opportunity to take him aside to a bathroom. When they had each satisfied themselves that the other was not wired, Moyse offered to supply Octopodelis with confiscated and recycled drugs. To cover himself he falsified police records that the drugs had been destroyed. In early November that year Moyse arranged a police internal affairs inquiry into allegations against himself. Unsurprisingly, he was cleared. The relationship lasted a bare ten months before Octopodelis turned on his supplier. Moyse should have made sure he was not being taped because Octopodelis was able to hand evidence of the deals to the NCA. Moyse was arrested in September 1987.

Over the months Moyse had made more than $100,000. He received a 27-year sentence that was reduced on appeal to twentyone years after he pleaded guilty to seventeen charges of taking part in the supply and sale of heroin. Moyse, described by AFP Commissioner Mick Keelty as 'A rotten egg cut from the bunch', was released in 1999 and lived quietly, umpiring local cricket matches. He died aged sixty-five of a kidney-related cancer in September 2010. Perhaps back in 1981 Sir Charles should have paid closer attention to the views of Informant 'A'.

After the conviction of Moyse, Octopodelis gave evidence to two NCA commissions claiming that two former New South Wales political figures had key roles in a massive interstate operation being run out of Sydney. He also claimed that Moyse's co-defendant Rocco Sergei had Mafia connections. Despite his addiction to the drug, Octopodelis had luxury apartments in both Adelaide and Sydney, as well as a string of expensive cars. On 4 June 1989 the 32-yearold was found dead in his Porsche in Craigend Street, Darlinghurst. Earlier in the evening he and his girlfriend had injected themselves and when she woke she found him dead. He had left the witness-protection scheme the previous October. At the time eleven people were awaiting trial based on transcripts of taped conversations between him and Moyse. Octopodelis himself was awaiting trial on charges of assaulting the police and fraud. Two Kings Cross officers were alleged to have taken $3000 from him, but no charges were brought and suggestions that he had been given a hot shot went unproved.

The belief was that, while Moyse was the only officer to take the fall, he had not been acting alone. Investigative journalist Chris Masters told *The Advertiser* before a *Four Corners* program on the events went out:

> We have interviewed prostitutes, dealers, users, who all say police are supplying them drugs. The drug and brothel trades are franchised by police who, instead of policing properly, limit and regulate by doing deals with these people.

Meanwhile the Moyse case had a serious spin-off. There were questions about how one of the witnesses, drug dealer and brothel keeper Gianni Malvaso, had been given a suspended sentence of three years. Could it be that Attorney-General Chris J Sumner had been blackmailed into it? The story that circulated in Hindley Street and the surrounding area was that Sumner was a regular brothel visitor and he liked being whipped and ridden as a horse by one or more of the girls. Both allegations were something he denied at the first opportunity, but nevertheless it drove him to a minor breakdown. The allegations were repeated by Chris Masters on *Four Corners* in 1988. His argument was that the police had franchised SP bookmaking in the 1960s and prostitution in the 1970s. Now, in the 1980s, they were franchising drugs. Masters claimed that since he had been in Adelaide investigating the program:

> Ranks have closed in the police, people know we're down here and we're getting letters under the door etc.
>
> The program is a big message for all Australia. Things are going on which the people of Adelaide

> should know about. I want them to get angry, just like Queensland did.

But they did not. While NCA inquiry Operation Hydra was opened, the outcome was again inconclusive. Prostitutes and dealers might have been prepared to talk with Masters and his researchers, but they were less forthcoming when interviewed by the police.

In Hydra's report of February 1991 the witnesses were coyly identified as figures in Greek mythology, but there was no Pandora's box. There were few brothels and many escort agencies in the city. Many of the brothel owners had recording equipment on the premises, but none had used it to tape any clients, let alone Mr Sumner. One girl had made the mistake of mixing up Mr Sumner with a client who looked like him and was also called Chris. There was no evidence whatsoever that he had ever been in a brothel or been blackmailed. But what did emerge was that a Patti Walkuski had run an illegal brothel in the city for fourteen years and a Geoffrey Williams had been involved with seventy brothels from 1972. One brothel in the city, the Holdfast Health Clinic, had run unhindered for an astounding twenty-six years.

In 1991 a former senior constable received three years and another a suspended sentence after agreeing to give evidence. They had been part of a gang of up to ten uniformed officers who had been moonlighting as shop and office breakers for several years. It appears the first inkling came from another officer who, said Commissioner David Hunt, had 'discovered something was wrong or amiss'. Although he denied that corruption was 'institutionalised', it was thought that at the time at least five NCA investigations were targeting the Adelaide police.

In Western Australia one of the scandals of the late 1990s was that of the Kalgoorlie Six: police officers who were alleged to have been flying ecstasy into and out of the town, and to be in cahoots with members of the Gypsy Jokers motorcycle gang. In 1992 a sting was planned and Christos Trifon was given $18,000 to buy morphine from the detectives. Unfortunately, instead of playing his part, he absconded with the money, for which he was given an eighteenmonth suspended sentence. Two of the officers were sacked and two resigned. An inquiry into the Six became part of the, again inconclusive, Kennedy Royal Commission of 2002.

Meanwhile, across the continent, Queensland had more than a fair share of problems of its own.

12

SIR TERENCE AND CO: THE LONG AND WINDING ROAD TO FITZGERALD

In 1934 Mr Justice Macrossan, sitting in Brisbane, was suitably prescient when dealing with the talented, although often convicted, safe breaker Harry Terry. Then aged forty-nine, Terry pleaded guilty to yet another charge of warehouse breaking after tobacco and gelignite were found in a room in Union Street, Spring Hill. His story was that he had been asked by three detectives in 1929 to burgle the home of Judge Henchman, who had, they said, unfairly criticised them. They would fence the proceeds for him and he would get all the money. Unsurprisingly, the detectives denied this and Macrossan called his story a pack of lies, adding, 'if it is accepted for one minute [this] would mean that the police force in Queensland needs a good sorting out'. Terry received five years and was declared a habitual criminal. He was carried fighting from the dock. His appeal against the declaration was dismissed.

Fast forward nearly four decades and the newspaper headline for 25 April 1970 ran, 'Graft paid to police said to run into millions'. It actually referred to the New York City police and appeared in *The New York Times,* but it could just as easily have appeared in Brisbane's *Courier-Mail* a decade later. Similarly, if Alfred McCoy had written his 1980 book *Drug Traffic,* setting out the five stages of corruption, ten years later he would probably have changed his opinion that no level-five corruption existed among the police in Australia to rank with the behaviour of Hong Kong police in the 1970s. Justice Macrossan's disregard for Harry Terry's claims was an early milepost along the road to the 1987–89 Fitzgerald Royal Commission, which exposed systemic corruption in Queensland from the premier down. Long and winding, the road trailed through the factional divisions of the 1950s, when Masons and Roman Catholics vied for senior police positions. It was, says Professor David Dixon, dean of law at the University of New South Wales, a time when:

> Queensland police were part of a political machine. Brisbane was the equivalent of an old time American city and the police were simply the arm of corrupt state government. New South Wales was never as bad as Queensland.

One pre-condition of corruption is an illegal market, such as in alcohol, gambling, prostitution and drugs, which is widely popular. By the 1970s there was a seam of corruption running through the police, not merely at ground level but to the very top. The cause was the rakeoff from permitting prostitution and illegal gambling. The rewards were high, and politicians—some of whom were beneficiaries—were unwilling to do anything about it.

Queensland had always had something of a laissez-faire attitude to prostitution, but when the talented, if corrupt, detective Frank Erich Bischof—another who set up a police pipe and drum band—was appointed commissioner of Queensland police in 1958, he shut down the brothels in the Brisbane inner city by the simple, expedient of padlocking the doors. The now closed houses included the best known, the Killarney, which was not far from South Brisbane railway station and had been operating since at least the Second World War and possibly for up to fifty years. From time to time it had housed Shirley Brifman, usually known as 'Marge', who had a side line as a police informant. Like so many in the trade, Brifman divided her working life between Queensland and New South Wales. Very quickly an arrangement was made with hotel managers to allow girls to solicit in the lounges, and one who did so was the quick-witted and garrulous Brifman.

From 1957 to 1965 Bischof, who had also set up a juvenile bureau with his protégé Terence Lewis in charge, had been collecting graft from bookmakers on a massive scale. The police minister interviewed him and he was allowed to continue in his position on an undertaking to stop the racket. He never did. Bets by him went into a book under the initial 'B'.

When he won the rest of his name was added and when he lost it was entered as a fictitious name beginning with 'B'.

On 29 October 1963 the Labor member for South Brisbane, Colin Bennett, speaking in parliament, told members, 'many of the (police) force are disillusioned, frustrated and discouraged'. He went on to maintain:

> the Police Commissioner and his colleagues who frequent the National Hotel, encouraging and condoning the call girl service that operates there, would be better occupied in preventing such activities rather than tolerating them.

His allegations were quickly denounced as the product of 'infantile imagination'.

On 3 November 1963 *The Sunday Truth,* a committed supporter of Bischof's, attacked Bennett for having exposed the commissioner. Its front page leader read:

> The campaign Mr Colin Bennett MLA is waging against the Police Commissioner Mr Bischof is now completely out of control and in the public interest the State Government can move in only one way. It must order an immediate Royal Commission.
>
> The facts are that the honour and integrity of the Queensland Police Commissioner have been attacked ... His name has got to be cleared.

Bennett persisted in his attacks and some months later a royal commission was set up under Harry Gibbs QC and witnesses were asked to come forward. The response was limited. At that time Brisbane was still a large country town where anyone who was anyone knew everyone else. The locals could hardly be expected to speak up and damage their standing in the community, so it was left to outsiders. One who did so, to his cost, was David Young, a one-time barman at the National Hotel who also acted as a sort of night manager. Young would tell the commission that he had seen Bischof and other officers drinking in the hotel after hours. He also claimed that he had served the malign detective Tony Murphy and other officers with liquor after hours, and had seen prostitutes such as Brifman, Val Weidinger and Lilly Ryan soliciting at the hotel. He also told Gibbs that shortly before he was due to give evidence he had received a threatening telephone call warning him not to do so.

Much of the inquiry was given over to 'kick Young time', a game played with great enthusiasm and no little skill by the participating barristers and also to a lesser extent by Gibbs. Young's past—the number of jobs he had held and had left in short order—was thoroughly raked over. Contradictions in his evidence were seized on with delight and he was also accused of running the girls himself. John Geza Komlosy, another witness who had also worked in the hotel as a porter, said that some of the girls actually lived in the place. Unfortunately, years earlier he had been convicted over a bounced cheque and his evidence was similarly trashed. There was some evidence that women were regularly sitting into the middle of the night drinking in the hotel. Quite what Gibbs thought they were actually doing there went unrecorded.

The police would have nothing of the allegations. They said they had never drunk there and Murphy, who claimed he had arrested more prostitutes than any other officer, said he did not know Brifman was a prostitute and indeed he had been unable to contact her to attend the commission. Officers who lined up to deny that the National was the late-night home-from-home for Brisbane's working girls included Terence Lewis, Donald 'Shady' Lane, Ron Redmond and the English-born bagman Jack Herbert. All would feature prominently in the later Fitzgerald inquiry.

Detective Glen Hallahan, described by Don 'Shady' Lane as a man with a 'taste for fashion and cologne', didn't recognise Brifman as a prostitute either, but Young identified him as the man who had made the threatening call to him. Gibbs was not told that Hallahan had just been suspended. A Gary William Campbell had pleaded guilty to having insufficient means of support and received six months. He appealed against the severity of the sentence and told the Full Court in September 1963 that he had been taken from his place of employment, a sound lounge, to his flat, where Hallahan had told him he would be loaded with house-breaking implements if he did not plead guilty to the insufficient means. Hallahan's evidence was described as a 'fraud on the court'. He was suspended a week before he was due to appear at the commission.

Later, in a closed disciplinary hearing, Hallahan was cleared of giving inaccurate information. He was fined £3 for not keeping his police diary up to date. The barrister in charge of the proceedings had apparently heard exonerating evidence from another detective and from John Hannay, Campbell's then employer and later the manager of the ill-fated Whiskey Au Go Go nightclub.

There was one officer, however, who did identify Brifman as a prostitute, and so suddenly, on 28 January 1964, she appeared at the inquiry in a demure white suit and picture hat to refute any allegations that she was a working girl. Rehearsed by Murphy, she also took the opportunity of denouncing Young, telling the inquiry, quite falsely, 'He done an abortion on me' at a flat at New Farm. She also claimed that Young had told her about renting rooms and selling liquor at the National. She hadn't heard about the inquiry until her name was mentioned, even though she had been in Brisbane over Christmas. There was nothing about it in the Sydney papers.

In April that year Gibbs wrote in his report:

> Young is a man of poor moral character and unstable temperament and I cannot regard him as a witness whose evidence may be believed or

> acted upon unless corroborated by that of some other witness who is himself reliable.

Young did at least fare better than the even more unfortunate witness Komlosy, who was thought by Gibbs to be 'not sane'. A priest had been called to say that the night porter could not be believed, but he was not allowed to be asked why. Gibbs wrote:

> It is obvious Komlosy was quite unreliable as a witness. His evidence contained violent inconsistencies and a curious compound of fact, hearsay, exaggeration, theory, invention and even hallucination.

In his report Gibbs made a positive finding that:

> No member of the Police Force ... has been guilty of misconduct or neglect or violation of duty since the ninth day of October 1958 in relation to the policing of the National Hotel ... no call-girl service was operated at the said Hotel, and no member of the Police Force encouraged, condoned or sanctioned in any way the practice of prostitution at that Hotel.

Which shows that justice can be blind. Gibbs also ruled that the limited terms of the commission did not require him to consider the policing of prostitution or to examine corruption in the licensing and consorting squads. Unfortunately, the failure of his commission encouraged the escalating corruption of the next twenty years. After the inquiry concluded, the unkind joke was that he was 'the only man in Queensland who could not find a tart in the National Hotel'. It was a classic example of how to run a royal commission and come up with satisfactory answers for the government.

In general, in the twentieth century the judiciary at inquiries into police misconduct were often incapable of accepting, or unwilling to accept, evidence that at a certain stage of corruption officers feel they are quite able to act openly. In the 1982 Western Australian Dixon inquiry into police corruption, one officer alleged wholesale corruption and that payouts were made at a lunch party in the public dining room of a hotel. His whole evidence was trashed, among other things on the basis that it was impossible police would have handed out envelopes containing illicit money in public—rather like the belief that sex can only take place with the lights out. But the evidence worldwide is that corrupt police become impervious to public scrutiny. An example is the activities of the Scotland Yard obscene publications squad in the 1970s:

> Thousands of pounds' worth of pay-offs were changing hands every week in Soho's pubs, coffee bars, clubs and mews often in full view of the public on the street.

Thanks to the machinations of Murphy and others and the nearsightedness of Gibbs, Bischof's reputation survived intact. The compulsive gambler retired in 1970 and four years later was charged with shoplifting. He had actually been committed for trial before the charges were dropped. It was only after his death on 28 August 1979 that allegations began to surface he had been involved in massive graft involving SP bookmakers. In 1982 the state treasurer revealed that as early as 1964 bookmakers paid annual protection to the police ranging from the equivalent of $80,000 in large towns to $20,000 in small country ones. Additionally, and this is what really riled them, top-ups were constantly being demanded. In 1989 Fitzgerald found 'in some respects police corruption had acquired a quaint quasi-legitimacy by the Bischof era'.

Seven years on from the National Hotel inquiry, on 15 June 1971 Shirley Brifman came clean—or reasonably so—when she told *This Day Tonight* on New South Wales television that she had lied to the Gibbs commission. In fact she had been a working girl in Sydney from 1965 to 1969, conducting her business at one of the city's wellknown hotels with the full knowledge of the management, something she said was common in all large hotels. She had run a brothel and paid protection money to the Sydney vice squad. She had given evidence at the Gibbs inquiry at Murphy's request, in return for the promise of protection both in New South Wales and Queensland. She had spoken with Murphy, been drinking with another girl and had picked up a client in the time between her arrival from Sydney and her giving evidence. She also said that Bischof had shut the brothels solely due to a fit of pique because while he was on holiday Murphy, Hallahan and Lewis, whom she knew as the 'Collect Boys', had moved in, picking up protection money due to him. By then, however, her confession was far too little and far too late.

In due course she and MLA Colin Bennett were interviewed by Assistant Police Commissioner Duncan. During the meeting she allegedly claimed that Hallahan had committed perjury: he knew very well that she and Irene Dale, who had over fifty convictions, were prostitutes. She also said that Murphy had lied when he said he did not know where she, Brifman, could be found and that he would be unable to help find her.

In September 1971 she told Superintendent Norman Gulbransen, who had once remarked, 'The rewards for dishonesty are greater than for honesty' and was described at his death as one of 'the last of the honest policemen':

> Murphy was always there. He was at the hotel, everywhere. On duty, when he should have been somewhere he was with me. He would carry on his duty at the office and make me sit on the desk ... Then Glen [Hallahan] came into the picture, and Terry [Lewis] was in the picture too.

On 5 February 1972 Murphy was charged with perjury. As might have been expected, his statement of denial was robust:

> I have been charged because of untrue malicious statements by Shirley Brifman, a drug addict, a self-confessed perjurer, informer and prostitute.

On 4 March 1972 Brifman was found dead in her flat in Clayfield, Brisbane, apparently having committed suicide but leaving no note. She and her husband had been due to appear in Sydney on 17 March charged with procuring under-age girls, including her daughter. Investigation of the death was cursory. Coroner William Laherty thought that there would be no good purpose in holding an inquest, and he ruled that Brifman had taken her own life. Her file was marked 'IDU'—inquest deemed unnecessary. Without Brifman in the witness box, after a four-day hearing the magistrate found that no properly instructed jury would convict and refused to commit Murphy for trial.

But who were these witnesses at the National Hotel inquiry, in particular Murphy, Hallahan and Lewis, who had given what was blatantly false evidence to Gibbs? They were a clearly established triumvirate who were in control of graft in the Queensland police. Two, Anthony 'Tony' Murphy and Glendon Patrick Hallahan, were from the Catholic faction and Terence Lewis had aligned himself with them. Ultimately, he was the highest ranking of them, a man who had been awarded a Churchill fellowship to go to England and whose later promotion from sergeant to commissioner had been meteoric. But firmly in charge of the 'Rat Pack', as they became known, was the then senior detective sergeant Tony Murphy.

Murphy, born in 1927, was 'very corrupt and very sinister, a pivotal player', said one Brisbane lawyer. In the mid-1980s a group of officers calling themselves the Committee of Eight wrote to the police minister and Premier Sir Joh Bjelke-Petersen, alleging that the Rat Pack was controlling crime. They suggested that close attention be paid to a number of incidents, all of which had involved Murphy, beginning with the death of Shirley Brifman and continuing with the death of Detective Sergeant JD Connor in the grounds of the All Nations club in Mareeba on 15 October 1978. The list of incidents included the 1973 Whiskey Au Go Go fire; arson at a tourist development on the Sunshine Coast; the murder of Jack Cooper, manager of the National Hotel, in 1971; TAB and other armed robberies carried out by the so-called Bikie Bandits; arson at a nightclub in Cairns running in opposition to the House on the Hill; drug dealing involving the Mr Asia group in the late 1970s and the use of police planes in drug and fauna smuggling; the disappearance of rub-and-tug madam Simone Vogler; and the 1976 Beerburrum mail and Bookmakers robberies in South Brisbane.

The document concluded:

> If you are a policeman, money is nothing more than a magnet attracting the ugly corollaries of robbery and violent crime.

The reference to the Bikie Bandits related to early 1983, when six police officers attached to the CIB were charged with perjury and four were also charged with providing heroin to two of the men while they were held in the watch house. None of the police was suspended and two were promoted while awaiting trial. Lewis was opposed to suspensions of the police involved because he did not think that the offences would be repeated and they were not 'a very serious offence like going out and engaging in shooting of some sort'. After the Crown decided not to proceed with the prosecutions of the police officers, Lewis, along with politician Sir Edward 'Top-Level Ted' Lyons and other senior officers, attended a celebratory party.

Certainly Murphy had come under some fire in the 1983 Stewart report on drug trafficking. The commissioner thought information he had given journalist Brian Bolton contained sufficient material to confirm to a suspicious and vengeful Terrence Clark, leader of the Mr Asia syndicate, that two of his drug runners, Douglas and Isobel Wilson, had dobbed him in, so leading to their deaths.

Murphy was also alleged to have been involved in the 1979 disappearance of Norman 'The Doorman' Ford, a painters and dockers union hanger-on whom police wanted to interview about extortion and stolen-car rackets. Later a police officer on the Ford investigation said Murphy gave him a list of people to whom he could and could not speak. The list included two police officers who were 'off limits'.

After he retired from the police in 1983, Murphy was controversially awarded the license for a TAB on Stradbroke Island, allegedly as the result of representations by National Party powerbroker Sir Edward Lyons who, curiously, had an apartment in the same block as bagman Jack Herbert.

Glen Hallahan joined the force in February 1952, at the age of twenty. He had first come under public scrutiny in 1958, when as the youngest detective in Queensland, he took part in the arrest at Mount Isa of Raymond John Bailey, who was later hanged for what was known as the Sundown Murders of Sally Bowman, her daughter Wendy and their friend Thomas Whelan in the northern South Australian outback. Much of the evidence against Bailey rested on a highly disputed confession to Hallahan.

According to notes from Superintendant Gulbransen's questioning, in 1971 Shirley Brifman recalled:

> Glen hit the pot over the Sundown murder ... I used to cop it night after night. Hallahan said that the real killer was free. It did really play on his mind and I thought he was going to go off his head over it. At that stage I would say he was not crooked but after that he went bad. I never saw anything eat a man inside like that did.

Terence Lewis would later tell the Williams Royal Commission in 1980 that he had possibly worked with Murphy during an abortion inquiry but that he did not really know him. He certainly knew Hallahan and in most favourable circumstances. On 8 August 1959 the pair had been awarded the George Cross for bravery when they disarmed German-born seaman Gunther Ernst Martin Bahnemann, who had been bashing his wife, Ada. After he threatened her with a gun she telephoned the police, and when Lewis and Hallahan arrived to arrest him he fired at them. Bahnemann was convicted of attempted murder. Over the years doubt has been cast on whether he actually was the dangerous man portrayed by Lewis and Hallahan.

Less worthy was Hallahan's relationship with robber and standover man Donald Ross 'The Hammer' Kelly, who in 1972 had been arrested over the August 1970 raid on the Bank of New South Wales at Kedron. Sentenced to eight years, he then made allegations that he had given Hallahan $900 of the takings of $2750. On 29 June 1972 the stipendiary magistrate ruled that there was no case for Hallahan to answer. Even if he believed Kelly, he was an accomplice, and there was no corroborative evidence. There had also been allegations that Hallahan had dealt in forged banknotes, and on one occasion a man arrested in Townsville with such notes claimed that Hallahan had given them to him.

The third of the trio was Terence Lewis, who before his appointment as commissioner had had a chequered career. On the credit side were the awards to him of the George Cross and a Churchill fellowship for his work in the Juvenile Aid Bureau. In the 1985 *Police Source Book 2* brief histories of the forces were provided and the contributor on Queensland wrote:

> The Lewis period [as Commissioner] has been relatively uneventful except for perhaps one significant change. In 1982 the government established a Police Complaints Tribunal as a result of massive public pressure surrounding allegations of police corruption and cover-ups.

The man who turned police corruption into an art form was the tall, thin Jack Herbert, an English policeman who in 1947 emigrated first to Victoria and then to Queensland, where he joined the force in 1949. It was not until 1959 that he joined the licensing branch, a squad of around two dozen officers, and became involved in taking bribes from SP bookmakers and casino and brothel owners—a process known as 'The Joke'. He maintained that he had first slipped from the path of righteousness when he had to pay heavy medical bills after his wife became ill. He would always deny that he was involved in the drug trade, but there is little doubt that drugs were washing around the Herbert-protected massage parlours in Fortitude Valley owned by Hector Hapeta.

In October 1974 Herbert retired from the force on the grounds of ill health and in December was charged with corruption. Two years later he was acquitted after cleverly turning the hearing into a trial of the officers accusing him. It was a tactic the Rat Pack regularly used, smearing and framing honest officers such as Arthur Potts, Basil Hicks and Alec Jepperson. From then on Herbert was more or less untouchable. In 1977 he began working for Jack Rooklyn of the pokie company Bally Machines and others in the 'in-line' gaming industry, and began making substantial payments on their behalf to senior officers. Four years later he was the Rat Pack's official bagman, taking money from prostitutes, brothel owners, SP bookmakers and gambling and in-line operations. In all, he claimed that he had collected $3 million on behalf of Lewis and the other members of the pack.

The quartet was firmly behind Premier Joh Bjelke-Petersen and equally firmly against undesirables such as homosexuals, Aboriginals, and demonstrating students and hippies, not necessarily in that order.

Bischof's successor was South Australia's Ray Whitrod, another sometimes described as 'The Last of the Honest Cops', but also as a 'fence sitter' and a 'quitter' by disgruntled officers. He became Queensland's police commissioner in 1970 and immediately set out to eradicate corruption. At the time the standard of education of the force was abysmal. Whitrod tried to improve things, bringing women into all fields of policing and arguing that officers should be educated to at least the standard of an apprentice carpenter or bricklayer. He arranged for the Queensland education department to provide officers with classes in literacy and basic arithmetic, and as an inducement to attend, he offered an extra week's leave for every subject they sat. The Police Union objected so strongly that they bypassed both Whitrod and the police minister, Max Hodges, and complained directly to the premier. Bjelke-Petersen, himself a former police minister, endorsed the union's stand and publicly declared that 'the Queensland people do not require their police to be Rhodes scholars'.

As an outsider, Whitrod did not realise that Brisbane was not as sophisticated as Melbourne and he got off to a bad start, something that told against him throughout his time as commissioner. He arranged a showing of the film *Ryan's Daughter* on behalf of the Queensland Police Citizens Youth Welfare Association, but the bedroom scenes were too strong for the provincial Queensland audience and he was heavily criticised.

He found a complete culture of corruption in the city, so much so that he would be approached by members of his luncheon club and asked to cancel their traffic tickets. At the other end of the spectrum, he found that candidates did well in police promotion examinations—mainly because the questions were sent to police stations the night before the exams and handed to the applicants.

Even his efforts to remove malign influences failed. In 1973 he sent Terence Lewis to work in Charleville, over 700 kilometres from Brisbane, for what was described as 'the good of the force'. It was a strategic mistake, stemming from his lack of knowledge of Queensland's geography. Not only did Lewis obtain kudos through his handling of a flood disaster there but also he charmed politicians when Charleville was the first halt on their whistle-stop tours of the state.

Over a period of time Whitrod was undermined and defeated by the very strong Police Union. In July 1976, after student demonstrations, he announced that there would be an internal investigation over complaints that a young girl had been struck by a police baton. The police opposed the inquiry and the announcement was countermanded by Bjelke-Petersen. Police Minister Max Hodges, who had supported Whitrod, lost his portfolio. The police had now not simply been policing, they had identified with the interests they were protecting, for example, the Springboks rugby union team. The demonstrators had become the deviants.

Throughout his term Whitrod and his wife were subjected to harassment and intimidation. Unordered taxis turned up, sometimes three or four times a night, to take him to the airport; although he had an unlisted number he would receive calls from strangers enquiring about his health; a specialist came to his house at three o'clock in the morning because he had been told by police headquarters that Whitrod was having a heart attack; he had a large load of gravel he had not purchased dumped on his front garden.

He became so frightened for his and his wife's safety that he took to sleeping with a revolver under his pillow. A large number of personal files detailing police corruption were mysteriously lost in transit between Brisbane and Canberra.

During his time as commissioner Whitrod charged twenty-three officers with offences related to corruption. The Crown law department advised that the chances of a successful prosecution were excellent, but none of the officers was convicted.

The last straw for Whitrod was the 1976 appointment of Lewis as his assistant commissioner. The position had become vacant, and Whitrod advised Cabinet of his preferred candidate and the names of two others also acceptable to him and to the Police Union. It had always been Cabinet practice to endorse the commissioner's recommendation for his assistant. In this case, however, the Cabinet chose Lewis, still an inspector, who was less qualified for the position than at least sixty other men. Whitrod believed, quite rightly, that all his efforts over the preceding seven years to eradicate corruption would be undermined if the appointment went ahead. Now he told Police Minister Tom Newbery, 'This is pretty shattering to me; it's widely known in the force that Lewis was one of Frank Bischof's bagmen'. Newbery replied, 'That was when he was a sergeant; he wouldn't do that sort of thing now'. When Whitrod asked him if that was Cabinet's thinking, Newbery said that it was. Then Whitrod asked to speak to Bjelke-Petersen. The premier refused an audience, and he wouldn't allow Whitrod to address Cabinet on the matter. That night Whitrod wrote his resignation. The question of Lewis's alleged corruption was again raised in Cabinet, this time by Liberal Fred Campbell, but Lewis was appointed commissioner on 22 November 1976. Consumed by his belief that he had failed to eradicate corruption in Queensland, and believing that police chiefs Sir Robert Mark and Patrick Murphy had succeeded in London and New York respectively, Whitrod returned to South Australia. There he was a leading figure in founding the Victims of Crime Service that followed from the Truro and Family murders. He died at the age of eighty-eight in July 2003.

Another opportunity to clean out corruption was seemingly lost at the 1980 Williams Royal Commission into alleged involvement in the illegal drug trade by Queensland parliamentarians and senior police. Part of the inquiry resulted from the arrest of John Ernest Milligan, a Brisbane district court associate turned drug dealer. Never the most reliable of men, Milligan, when short of money in his court days, was said to have done a little shoplifting at Myer at lunchtime and would hold a shirt sale when the court rose. In September 1979 he was caught following a heroin parachute drop at Jane Table Mountain in Far North Queensland, for which he received ten years.

Cooperation after an arrest is usually rewarded by a lesser sentence, and now Milligan began to make a series of statements incriminating a Brisbane customs officer along with Hallahan, Murphy and Lewis. The three all denied any misconduct, and Hallahan explained that he had borrowed money from Milligan on one occasion and that he had sold the drug dealer a piece of land and cattle. Williams, accepting the evidence of these fine officers, ruled that what evidence there was 'falls far short of establishing as even a reasonable possibility that Hallahan has ever been involved in wrong-doing in connection with illegal drugs'. This was unsurprising. Milligan, probably realising on which side his bread was buttered, had backtracked in his allegations to the point where they were worthless.

By then Hallahan had long retired after yet another scrape. In December 1971 he was charged with receiving money from prostitute Dorothy Edith Knight. Later the charge was amended to agreeing to receive money from her. In August 1972 he was discharged after telephone intercepts were ruled inadmissible and the case against him collapsed. Hallahan was reinstated on 10 October that year and minutes later resigned after reading a prepared statement that he 'felt his future and that of his family would best be served in other spheres'.

After his resignation his road was no less rocky. He sued *The Courier-Mail* for defamation after it had reported an unprovable allegation that he had been involved with the Beerburrum mail robbery two years earlier. In 1986 he was employed as chief investigator for government-owned insurance company Suncorp.

That October he petitioned for his own bankruptcy, owing over $180,000 and having cash of $100. He was alleged to have been paid $3000 by bagman Jack Herbert to fix an insurance claim, something he vigorously denied when he appeared before the Fitzgerald inquiry in March 1988. Six months later he was suspended without pay by Suncorp.

Yet another lost opportunity to clean up corruption was in relation to disclosures by a police constable in 1975 that a substantial portion of the evidence in one case had been concocted by police. It gave rise to the wide-ranging Lucas inquiry into police practices, with the Queensland criminal bar seeking once and for all to stamp out the widespread practice of verballing. The inquiry found evidence of assaults on suspects, planting of evidence, forgery of warrants and fabrication of confessions by police. Its most significant recommendation called for the routine mechanical recording of police interrogations in all cases involving indictable offences. The proposal met with resistance from the Queensland police and was not implemented. The government set up a three-man committee comprising Lewis, the solicitor-general and the under-secretary to the Department of Justice to review the report, and for all practical purposes that was the end of the matter for the next ten years.

Gay brothels arrived, or at least were first noticed, in Brisbane in 1984 when Brett's Boys, which operated across the street from a boys school, and The House of Praetorian opened. They were said to be owned by

Hector Hapeta, possibly the king of Brisbane vice. Both offered similarly priced facilities, with a businessmen's lunch halfhour special costing $30, and the first regular hour costing between $70 and $90, reducing after that.

On 10 December 1984 *The Courier-Mail* published 'The men of evil who prey on children', relating to child pornography and male prostitution. It made four allegations: first, the police were taking payoffs to protect pornographers; second, 'Mike' of Inala was being protected by a senior officer; third, a female prostitute had sustained a ruptured stomach after being kicked by an inspector when she refused to sign on for protection with him; and last, the commissioner had failed to act in response to several complaints about PC Darren Moore. Known as 'Constable Dave' on the television program *Wombat,* where he appeared with a puppet called Agro, Moore had been the subject of allegations since April 1982, but they had been ignored. In December 2010 Moore received a wholly suspended fifteen-month sentence after admitting to the possession of child pornography.

The brothels were raided by the police the next day, but by then there had been a fire and the receipts and account books had gone up in smoke. Chief Commissioner Lewis claimed that the raid was the 'culmination of two months' intensive investigation'.

The allegations by *The Courier-Mail* were referred to the Police Complaints Tribunal, chaired by Judge Eric Pratt. Rejecting the complaints, the tribunal found:

> another aspect of the *Courier Mail* article which appears to be either outdated or exaggerated information relates to the operation of brothels by a person known as Hector. It seems possible that the newspaper article is again a distortion of the facts.

In 1985 DPP Desmond Sturgess QC, whose practice had been almost exclusively criminal defence work, conducted a limited inquiry into police corruption in Queensland in connection with male brothels. A preliminary report was said to contain harrowing details, but it was not released. On 28 November that year Sturgess delivered his final report. In it he gave a clear, if coded, indication of just who was running what. He referred to five 'prominent' organisers of Queensland prostitution, to the immunity from prosecution apparently enjoyed by these main offenders, and to the fact that the Lucas inquiry's advice on staffing of the licensing branch had not been implemented. He also referred adversely to Jack Herbert and other key figures in the licensing branch. Sir Terence Lewis did not read the report, which was roundly attacked, in part because the figures relating to prostitution differed from those advanced by the licensing branch, and the vice industry continued unimpeded on its merry way.

Thirteen months after the report twenty-one brothels were still operating. That April there were more illegal casinos—the best known of which was over Bubbles Bath-House in Fortitude Valley, to which losing high rollers were sent to ease their losses free of charge—than there had been the previous year when Police Minister Gunn had ordered their closure.

Other marchers along the road to Fitzgerald were led by Phil Dickie of *The Courier-Mail,* who by 1987 was calling for an investigation into police corruption in Queensland following allegations of money in brown bags. Bob Gordon, his chief of staff on the paper, later wrote of him, 'I must say his courage and thoroughness were such that our society will always be in his debt'. His investigations had apparently begun on what Gordon called 'a slow news day' in December 1986. Dickie, then a relatively junior reporter, was sent out to find why corruption, prostitution and drug dealing were flourishing both in Fortitude Valley and on the Gold Coast, and specifically who owned smart brothel The Top of the Valley (Hector Hapeta again, this time with Ann-Marie Tilley). Other reporters had tried and failed to uncover the ownership, but Dickie decided that a full-frontal approach was the way forward. That afternoon when he went to a brothel and asked who owned it he was obliged to run from the bouncers. During the first months of 1987 *The Courier-Mail* published a number of Dickie's reports as he dug deeper and deeper into who owned Brisbane's brothels and how they survived unmolested by the police, searching *The Yellow Pages* and then making searches of company directorships and car-registration numbers.

Others before Dickie had chipped away at the Lewis regime, and they included Constable Robert Campbell. After Bjelke-Petersen's confidante Ted Lyons was stopped on the South-East Freeway, leading to an alliterative *Courier-Mail* headline: 'Top-level Ted—full as a fowl', within a matter of minutes he had rung Lewis, who ordered his officers to drive him home.

His breath-analysis certificate and charge sheet went into the police-station bin, only to be retrieved and given to Campbell. In early 1982 he went to Labor politician Kev Hooper and together they went to the ABC, whose reporter Alan Hall began to look into things; he produced the first coherent picture of the decline of law enforcement in Queensland. Campbell told all he knew of the bribes, the protection rackets, the gambling, the prostitution and the money.

Hall's investigation soon led to the Rat Pack, but there was a leak and life became extremely difficult for Campbell, for his family and for ABC staff. Campbell and his family were woken late at night with threats and he was called a dog at work; ABC staff members were routinely followed when they left the studio at night. On 17 March 1982 Hall's program was shown across Australia. Police Minister Russell Hinze immediately called a press conference declaring that he would see Hall out of a job, and denouncing

Campbell and all that the report had revealed. Lewis and Tony Murphy, now his assistant commissioner, immediately sued the ABC for defamation, claiming that they had been identified with the Rat Pack. Campbell left the force and the state and went to Tasmania.

The final push, however, came from Chris Masters' 'Moonlight State' on ABC's *Four Corners* on 11 May 1987, which alleged links between organised crime and high-level police corruption. Much of the material in the program had been raised previously in state parliament or published in the Queensland media and ignored. For months, Deputy Premier of the National Party and Minister for Police Bill Gunn had been supplied with evidence of flourishing brothels and illegal casinos, operating in breach of his assurances that either they did not exist or, if by some misfortune they did, they would be closed.

The allegations made in 'Moonlight State' were, naturally, ridiculed. At least Bjelke-Petersen admitted to the rotten-apple theory: 'There may be one or two policemen who are not doing the right thing'. Commissioner Lewis—now Sir Terence Lewis, having been knighted in the last honours list—thought the program 'Disgraceful'. Justice Minister and Attorney-General Paul Clauson described it as 'Airy-fairy'.

But the general reaction to 'Moonlight State' forced Bill Gunn into action. His initial comment had been,

'A series of police ministers have had these types of allegations hanging over their heads. They are not going to hang over mine'. Had Bjelke-Petersen been at home, he would almost certainly have ignored the allegations and refused to hold an inquiry. His sensible, if unhelpful, attitude had always been never to have an inquiry until you knew what the result would be. But, unfortunately for him, at the time he was touring the country in support of his grandiose scheme to become prime minister of Australia, and left holding the parcel was Bill Gunn. The next day Gunn called what governments have always tried, usually successfully, to avoid: an open and public inquiry.

If Gunn had followed the tried and tested rules for setting up a royal commission—narrow the terms of reference as much as you possibly can, choose the chief investigator and the legal team, and finally, choose the judge—all should not have been lost. The terms of reference for this royal commission were initially restricted to allegations raised on the *Four Corners* program. In summary, the questions posed in the initial terms were:

> During the period 1 June 1982 to 26 May 1987:
>
> Were any of Geraldo, Antonio and Vincenzo Bellino, Vittorio Conte, and Hector Brandon Hapeta involved in the use of premises for prostitution, unlawful gambling or unlawful drugs?

> Did the Bellinos, Conte or Hapeta give police financial or other favours in return for non-enforcement of laws in relation to the premises?
>
> Are existing legislation and procedures adequate to ensure that conduct of the above kind is detected and reported?
>
> Did the Bellinos, Conte or Hapeta make a payment of $50,000 to any Queensland political party on or about 8 September 1983?

Lewis and policeman turned politician and powerbroker Don 'Shady' Lane tried to arrange for another former police officer, Judge Eric Pratt of the District Court and chairman of the Police Complaints Tribunal, to head the inquiry. With luck, it might even be held in camera under the aegis of the tribunal. However, there had long been criticism of the tribunal since it had been established in 1982, with observations that it was often a bucket of whitewash—including the particularly egregious example of how Barry Mannix had come to make a false confession to the murder of his father. Lane had also earlier wanted Pratt to chair an inquiry into child pornography.

The chief justice simply refused to make Pratt or any other judge available for the inquiry, originally estimated to run for four to six weeks. That was bad enough. But the next mistake was that, instead of appointing a tame chairman such as Harry Gibbs and despite being threatened by Bjelke-Petersen with removal, Gunn took the advice of Ian Callinan QC to appoint the fiercely independent but then little-known Gerald Edward (Tony) Fitzgerald QC, a one-time federal judge who had returned to private practice.

It was a decision that Bjelke-Petersen and Lewis would come to regret deeply.

13

THE FITZGERALD COMMISSION AND AFTER

When it came to it, the terms approved on 26 May 1987 for Queensland's Commission of Inquiry into Possible Illegal Activities and Associated Police Misconduct were indeed narrow and relatively harmless—the remit only covered the previous five years—but Commissioner Tony Fitzgerald did not want to be tied to looking just at specific allegations against specific people. He wanted the freedom to look into 'any other matter or thing appertaining to the aforesaid matters', and not only at 'related matters' but at any matter whether it related or not. Deputy Premier Bill Gunn undertook to consider changing the terms if Fitzgerald felt it would help his inquiry, and the terms were expanded within the month. Now allegations of corruption would go back as far as January 1977.

Even before the hearings began there were problems with witnesses. One who had given evidence at the Sturgess inquiry into male prostitution thought he'd had enough and was refusing to appear, while bludger Warren Earl Armstrong was charged with threatening a woman with harm if she gave evidence. But two of the most important witnesses who had gone AWOL were prostitute Ann-Marie Tilley, said to be the brains behind brothel owner Hector Hapeta's empire, and bagman Jack Herbert.

Later, former Assistant Commissioner Graeme Parker would say that Terence Lewis told him Don 'Shady' Lane, who had become a Cabinet minister in the Bjelke-Petersen regime, suggested Herbert leave the country. Herbert was not keen to go, thinking—probably correctly—that in his absence he would be a useful scapegoat for his colleagues. Then on 13 June he met up with Jack Rooklyn, from whom he had extorted protection money on behalf of Lewis for nine years over in-line machines. Rooklyn said that he, Rooklyn, should have 'pissed off' from the 1973 Moffitt inquiry, in which he was roundly criticised, 'and suggested I do the same'. Herbert left Australia a week later.

On 27 July sittings began. Appropriately enough, the first witness was Commissioner of Police Sir Terence Murray Lewis, who told Fitzgerald that policing prostitution was a low priority for the Queensland force. Sir Joh and five successive police ministers had instructed him that prostitution should be tolerated. Illegal casinos and bookmakers were the priority. The first instructions he had to go after brothels came on 19 May 1987. After all, there were only fourteen massage parlours in Brisbane, which compared favourably with Melbourne's seventy plus. And no, Sir

Terence had not read the Sturgess report into male prostitution and paedophilia in Queensland.

As the first weeks of the commission passed it became clear that the police had indeed done very little to act against the bosses of prostitution and gambling in the city. Deputy Commissioner Ron Redmond added fuel to the fire by telling Fitzgerald that Police Minister Bill Gunn had told him massage parlours served a useful purpose, acting as a preferable alternative to rape.

By 25 August Fitzgerald had managed to have the goalposts widened again and the terms of reference once more expanded. By now there was more than a whiff in the air that it was not going to be the usual whitewash and there were suggestions that indemnities might be on offer to those willing to give evidence of corruption. That week Fitzgerald made a call for honest officers to come forward to give evidence. Few did, but the first of the brave was Aboriginal sergeant Col Dillon, who told the commission how he had been approached by Detective Senior Sergeant Harry Burgess from the licensing branch and offered $400 a month to keep his eyes and mouth shut.

The alleged brothel keepers and gambling-school owners were next to give evidence. Gambler Geraldo Bellino, who thought he was being treated as badly as Lindy Chamberlain, and Victor Conte admitted owning casinos but denied any connection with girls or drugs. Hector Hapeta refused to answer 164 questions on the grounds of possible self-incrimination, while Geraldo Bellino's brother Antonio denied any involvement in anything. Ms Tilley was still AWOL.

On 28 August, the day journalist Phil Dickie began his evidence, Burgess admitted corruption and was given immunity. He now implicated Jack Herbert and Assistant Commissioner Graeme Parker, the third highest ranked man in the Queensland force, as well as licensing branch chief Noel Dwyer.

At the beginning of September a prostitute given the pseudonym Katherine James began to recite the litany of corruption within the licensing branch, including bribes and free sex for officers. On 17 September Parker, described as 'a man of high integrity' when he was awarded the Queen's Police Medal the previous year, admitted corruption and, given conditional indemnity, initially retired hurt to a hospital bed. Now calls came for Lewis to stand down until the end of the inquiry. He did not heed them and Gunn wrote requiring him to stand down. Lewis immediately transferred his interest in the family home to his wife, the reporting of which was seen by the then Lady Lewis as a gross breach of her privacy. Already the knives were out for Sir Joh, ensuring that he 'did not slither out of taking responsibility for what happened to the police force'.

On 11 October Lewis, who had been commissioner since Whitrod, bravely said that in his forty years as a policeman he had never known or suspected that there was corruption in the force. It was probably fortunate that Judge Eric Pratt had not headed the inquiry, because he was described by Lewis as his 'special friend'. On 14 October it had been alleged that Pratt had attended meetings with the Bellino brothers at Jack Herbert's house to discuss which police should be transferred and which promoted. He stood down from the District Court on 30 October following a motion put forward by the state opposition for his dismissal. Lewis' diaries showed that Pratt had disclosed police tribunal matters to him. Judge Pratt's solicitors immediately issued a statement to the inquiry denying that he had attended the meetings or was guilty of any misconduct. The allegations against him were later put to a triumvirate of retired judges headed by Sir Harry Gibbs. They duly reported that there was no reason why Judge Pratt should not resume his position on the bench.

In November former Inspector Noel Dwyer admitted to corruption and alleged that Lewis, Herbert and Parker were involved. Parker, now out of his hospital bed, told how Herbert and Lewis were involved and in turn implicated Shady Lane. On 26 November Sir Joh stood down and on 1 December he announced his retirement from politics. The inquiry gathered pace and the now beleaguered Geraldo Bellino sent Christmas cards that read, 'To all my friends I wish them well, and all the rest can go to hell'.

In February 1988 former Inspector William Boulton became the fourth officer to throw in the towel, admitting that he took bribes of up to $1000. At this point the inquiry began to look at the socalled Chinese connection. Allegations were made against Lewis and the then Police Minister Russell Hinze, known as the 'Minister for Everything', and their connection to Malcolm Sue, who owned a kung-fu school and was named as a standover man and brothel owner. A witness, 'Mr Brown', claimed that as a special treat Hinze had been offered the pick of the girls in a Sue house. Hinze denied it.

February also saw Shady Lane broken. He denied, not necessarily wholly convincingly, that he had been involved in corruption, saying most of his unexplained income came from cheating on his ministerial expenses and tax returns. Not that he was alone in this—fourteen other National and Liberal Party ministers did it as well. Worse, he named names.

In March 1988 Herbert and his wife were retrieved from England, to where they had fled, and returned to Queensland. Given indemnity, they were placed under armed guard to await their turns to give evidence. On 20 June Anne-Marie Tilley suddenly reappeared to admit that Hapeta ran a $30-million vice empire paying Herbert $38,000 a month and Burgess another $2000.

On 31 August the star witness, Herbert, appeared. He agreed that over the years he had given Lewis $600,000. He called him 'Big Daddy' or 'The Shark' 'because he took the biggest bite'. He continued his evidence into September, detailing payments made to senior officers that totalled $1.5 million. His evidence caused some resentment. 'Herbert should never have had indemnity; he was a mastermind', said one barrister who watched the hearings.

Lewis was back in the witness box for nearly a month from 11 October, explaining that his wealth came not from corruption but from the old, old story of an 88 per cent success rate in backing horses. Unfortunately, he could not explain hundreds of his diary entries.

And so it went on until 1 December, when Sir Joh became the last witness, valiantly maintaining that he did not suspect police corruption.

In all, the six weeks set aside for the commission turned into two years, and nearly 240 witnesses were called. Fitzgerald released his report on 3 July 1989, making wide-sweeping recommendations but being careful not to make accusations. Instead he said that the commission had not been about the guilt or innocence of any individual, but the concern was the 'pattern, nature and scope of the misconduct that has occurred and the lesson it contains for the future'. He did, however, comment about Commissioner Ron Redmond:

> It reflects no credit on Redmond that, on the most favourable interpretation, he as Assistant Commissioner Operations remained ignorant of the problems within the licensing branch over that period.

His two most significant recommendations were the establishment of the Criminal Justice Commission (CJC) and the Electoral and Administrative Review Commission, which was to review electoral boundaries to stop gerrymandering. The need for freedom-ofinformation legislation in the state was noted, as was the need to review laws relating to public assembly and guidelines for the disclosure of parliamentarians' pecuniary interests. The CJC was to be responsible for investigating specific individuals mentioned during the inquiry. In 1989 Premier Mike Ahern promised to implement the recommendations of the Fitzgerald inquiry, 'lock, stock and barrel'.

As for the police, for the decade after the inquiry Jack Herbert received round-the-clock protection, said to have cost $1 million, at his New Farm home. His book *Confessions of a Bagman* was published shortly before his death from cancer in 2004, at the age of eighty. By then he and his family had done well for themselves in the real-estate business. But, of course, he had received around $3 million in bribes, which would have provided a decent springboard.

It was former commissioner Terence Lewis, Herbert's one-time friend, who crashed the hardest. In 1991 he stood trial on twentythree counts of perjury, forgery and corruption. He was acquitted of the perjury allegations but convicted of accepting $700,000 in bribes, as well as forging the premier's signature on an official document in 1981. Although he had denied that he had ever met poker-machine identity Jack

Rooklyn, there were diary entries to show that he had done so on a number of occasions. Lewis was never charged with this particular lie, something many thought would have been easy to prove. He was sentenced to fourteen years and was stripped of his knighthood, while complaining bitterly that much of the evidence against him came from Herbert. In this respect he was no different in his complaint from Victorian police officer Paul Higgins, who had disliked being convicted on the evidence of murderer Sandy MacRae. Lewis has continued to protest his innocence.

Lewis' wife, Hazel, also always denied that she had received parcels of bribe money from Herbert's wife, Peggy, and in May 1995 she told *The Courier-Mail* that she still loved her husband of forty-two years and believed in his honesty.

Towards the end of his sentence there were rumours that Lewis saw himself as a scapegoat and was planning a tell-all to expose other neglected aspects of corruption in Queensland, something that would hardly fit with his protestations of innocence. He must have thought better of it. He was paroled in 1998 after serving 10 1/2 years. He retained the support of Bjelke-Petersen. 'He was only found to be corrupt', said Sir Joh loyally.

Harry Burgess, the first to roll over, went to work in a metal factory. Graeme Parker, who had there not been indemnities on offer might have brazened things out and become the next commissioner, was stripped of his Queen's Police Medal. He was later acquitted of perjury for not telling the truth to the inquiry and so allegedly breaching his indemnity. He turned to Christianity and dropped from public view. In 2005 he was reported to be selling patchwork quilts made by his wife.

Other officers were prosecuted, including Allen Bulger, who was sentenced to twelve years' gaol in 1990 after pleading guilty to official corruption and perjuring himself at the Fitzgerald inquiry. He was released on parole after less than four years. The Australian Taxation Office ordered Bulger, who became a taxi driver, to pay almost $180,000 in unpaid tax.

Tony Murphy, who for some reason was never called to give evidence and never broke his silence, died in 2010. Time may yet show that he was the most sinister of all players in the inquiry.

And the politicians? The wash-up saw the National Party heavily defeated in the December 1989 election and the Australian Labor Party returned to power for the first time in over twenty years. As for the individual politicians, pride of place must, of course, go to Sir Joh, who resigned as premier in November 1987 and the following year gave evidence that paper bags full of cash had been delivered to his office. When he was prosecuted for perjury over a $100,000 cash payment from a Singapore developer, the jury failed to agree. It was later revealed that the foreman had been a member of the Young Nationals, part of

Sir Joh's political party, and was a member of the 'Friends of Joh' campaign. The commission's special prosecutor, Doug Drummond QC, decided not to seek a retrial. Bjelke-Petersen died in 2005, aged ninety-four.

Former policeman and then minister Don 'Shady' Lane was sentenced to twelve months' imprisonment for falsifying his expense accounts to the tune of around $4500. Before his death in March 1995 he published his autobiography, *Trial and Error.* Geraldo Bellino eventually stood for Lane's old parliamentary seat and lost.

One-time police minister Hinze, who had denied that there were any brothels in Fortitude Valley and for his pains had been cartooned as a bulldog with a white stick and dark glasses standing outside one, resigned from parliament in 1988. The inquiry was told that he had accepted bribes and—far from not accepting that such places existed—had been seen in a Valley brothel. He died, aged seventytwo, in June 1991 before pending charges of corruption against him could be heard.

Brian Austin, who was one of those named by Lane as an abuser of ministerial expenses, was sentenced to fifteen months' jail after being convicted on twenty-five counts of misappropriating public funds, involving $8700 spent on private accommodation, travel and meals. He later sold real estate.

Herbert's old friend and adviser Jack Rooklyn escaped prison. Born in London, possibly in 1908—his date of birth changed to suit the occasion—he was around eighty-two when he was charged with making corrupt payments. He had already had a heart bypass operation and collapsed in the dock. On 25 May 1992 he was fined $35,000. Uncharacteristically, Rooklyn later admitted his guilt, saying, 'I shouldn't have done it'. His Queensland scam alone had earned him millions. He died in 1996.

As Fitzgerald had recommended, the CJC was established and for several years, in addition to investigating police and public-sector misconduct, it worked with police to investigate organised crime. In 1997 the newly formed Queensland Crime Commission (QCC) took over investigations into organised crime and also investigated paedophilia. The Crime and Misconduct Commission was born in January 2002 when the CJC and the QCC were merged under that name.

The idea that the Fitzgerald inquiry would have cleaned out all corruption in Queensland's police force is a triumph of hope over experience. There will always be rotten apples in the barrel. The best that can be hoped for is that the whole barrel is not full of rotten fruit. For a time in the late 1990s it looked as though the latter might be the case.

In February 1998 former Whitsunday officer Damon Kirkpatrick was jailed for eight years for his involvement with a North Queensland drug ring. He pleaded guilty in Mackay to trafficking in a dangerous drug, official corruption, breaking and entering a watch house, and stealing marijuana plants. He had gone into partnership with servicestation operator Peter Crossley, who received six years.

That year Gold Coast detective sergeant John Swift, head of the casino crime and break and enter squads, was another who fell from grace when, caught in a CJC sting, he received 5 1/2 years for corruption and perjury. He had agreed to provide protection to a man he believed to be a major cocaine dealer for an initial $10,000 for six months and then $1000 a month after that. Another officer who found himself in trouble was former Gold Coast detective Carl Gibson, who received four years for passing on information about a police investigation to a drug dealer for a fee of $3500.

In July 2009, in a speech at Griffith University, Fitzgerald told the audience he believed that the Labor government had backslid and that under Peter Beattie it believed 'there were votes to be obtained from Bjelke-Petersen's remaining adherents in glossing over his repressive and corrupt misconduct'. He added:

> Unfortunately, cynical, short-sighted political attitudes adopted for the benefit of particular politicians and their parties commonly have adverse consequences for the general community. The current concerns about political and police misconduct are a predictable result of attitudes

> adopted in Queensland since the mid-1990s. Despite their protestations of high standards of probity, which personally might well be correct, and irrespective of what they intend, political leaders who gloss over corruption risk being perceived by their colleagues and the electorate as regarding it as of little importance. Even if incorrect, that is a disastrous perception. Greed, power and opportunity in combination provide an almost irresistible temptation for many which can only be countered by the near-certainty of exposure and severe punishment.

Unfortunately, errant police officers follow the general underworld doctrine that they will not be found out; if they are, they will not be prosecuted; if they are by mischance prosecuted, they will be acquitted; and if they are convicted, they will not go to prison. But, just sometimes, it doesn't work that way.

14

IN AND OUT OF THE WOOD

What Queensland did in 1979 New South Wales did in 1995, its royal commission not reaching quite so high but perhaps wider than the Fitzgerald inquiry. Throughout the 1980s independent MP John Hatton had been a thorn in the flesh for a series of governments with his repeated allegations of corruption and his calls for a royal commission into the New South Wales Police. In the early 1990s he began to assemble evidence that he hoped would be sufficient to force the government to launch an inquiry. There was never a hope in the years during which there was a Labor majority, but in 1994 the John Fahey Liberal government was in a minority and Hatton saw a window of both opportunity and hope. Working with him were two police officers, Kimbal Cook and Debbie Locke, her detective husband Greg, Cook's sister Jackie Payne, adviser Alan King (who had been kidnapped and locked in the boot of a car during an inner-city anti-development campaign) and journalist Morgan Ogg.

On 11 May 1994, shortly after Hatton began his historic speech calling for a royal commission, which lasted nearly an hour and a half, into the public gallery of the Legislative Assembly marched a phalanx of senior police officers, resplendent in full dress uniform, who formed row upon row of what was described as 'intimidating lines of blue'. Ranking from deputy commissioner, to assistant commissioner, to inspector, the officers were intent on staring down Hatton and his supporters. Nigel Hadgkiss, later appointed chief investigator of the royal commission, thought 'Hatton's performance during that marathon debate was a brave one. After all, he was no spring chicken at the time'.

By a vote of forty-six to forty-five his motion forced the Fahey government to establish a royal commission. And—unlike the one in Adelaide, which many thought to have been a whitewash—a right Pandora's box this turned out to be, with reverberations that continued for the next twenty years. Chaired by Justice James Wood, the commission sat for more than 450 days, heard from 902 public witnesses and cost an estimated $64 million. Even its critics agreed that it was the most thorough and far-reaching of all Australian inquiries into the police. The fascinated public learned a new language—that of corrupt police officers—where a 'giggle' or a 'joke' was a bribe and a 'laugh' a large bribe, a 'whippy' was money stolen by police during a raid, and a 'green light' was given to privileged criminals to carry out crime.

The commission's broad terms of reference were to inquire into the existence of corruption and misconduct within the service and into the efficacy, or otherwise, of its internal affairs branch. In 1993 Police

Commissioner Tony Lauer, who had done a great deal to clear up corruption in the time when his predecessor, the much-respected John Avery, was the commissioner, had gone on the record saying, 'In New South Wales we are at the cutting edge of policing as far as our ability to act on corruption among officers'. The next year there was another statement that would come to haunt him: 'It ought to be my responsibility that this service never again has working among it —.'

At the beginning of the Wood Commission in December 1994 Lauer again held himself hostage to fortune when he said that 'in today's Police Service institutionalised corruption does not exist'. Asked by counsel Gary Crookes QC how he could be so confident that the police culture in New South Wales had changed for the better, he replied that he walked 'among my troops', adding 'I do that extensively and I expose myself to the Police Service Officers', which may have been an unfortunate way of putting things.

The commission's star witness was corrupt former detective Trevor Haken, who had worked in Darlinghurst and for a while had been a member of the Commonwealth/State Joint Task Force into Drug Trafficking. At an early stage in the inquiry he had been selected as a man likely to roll over and, provided with a mini-camera, he was persuaded to tape and film his dealings with his corrupt colleagues. On 12 September 1995 he gave evidence about his dealings, including the 1983 New Year's Eve divvying up of $200,000 taken by officers from drug dealers. One of those receiving officers, he said, was then Assistant Commissioner Ray Donaldson.

Called the next day, unsurprisingly Donaldson denied Haken's allegations, claiming that the junior officer was a drunk and an extortionist. He, Donaldson, had never witnessed and certainly not taken part in any corruption. And it was something he continued to deny, although a number of former officers came forward to give evidence that supported Haken's allegations.

Another officer, Graham 'Chook' Fowler, whom Haken had recorded on film stuffing a $1000 bribe from club owner Steve Hardas down the front of his trousers, at least had an ingenious defence, telling the commission, 'It must have been an actor'. (This was more or less the same defence used by officers from the Victorian armed offenders squad when they were filmed bashing a suspect some ten years later.) The commission found that Fowler had given false evidence about a sham accident, in which he had supposedly slipped on a spilt milkshake, in an effort both to claim compensation and avoid giving evidence. He was also found to have made a series of false entries in his official police notebook, recording his presence on duty in Sydney at a time when he had, in fact, been in the Philippines with another corrupt detective, Larry Churchill.

As the weeks went on it was apparent that, when sufficiently armed, Wood was quite prepared to be ruthless with police officers who initially followed the golden rule that they would be all right provided they all stuck together. They were swiftly disabused of this theory.

It was the cross-examination on 11 December 1995 of Wayne Eade by Virginia Bell, counsel for the commission, that broke their collective resistance. First Eade denied any involvement in criminal or even improper behaviour and then he was shown a film in which he behaved and spoke in quite the reverse manner. After the shock of seeing her husband's secret life exposed, Eade's wife appealed for the incriminating videos to be banned from prime-time television.

Detective Constable Duncan Demol was another who changed his mind over a weekend. On a Friday afternoon he had been staunch, saying that anything he had done had been in the interests of the police. Haken he considered to be a good, decent man. The gallery hooted. On the following Monday Demol told of his first day on the squad in 1986, when other officers took him to a Darlinghurst brothel and told him, 'You're not a cop until you can work pissed'. And things had never looked up from there. He told the commission that officers considered the law to be a joke and that 'scrumdowns', in which police officers fabricate the scenario of an arrest, were common—'you had to do it to get a conviction'. Another officer said that the arrest rate rather the conviction rate was what mattered.

Historically, few investigations had gone further than requiring officers to take long- or short-term sick leave, asking them to resign and, if they did not, dismissing them. The commission was no exception. At the end of 1995 an amnesty was offered to corrupt officers if they agreed to tell all and provide evidence against their colleagues. This was, said Wood, a once-and-for-all amnesty. Those who did not take advantage of it would not get a second chance. They had until 9 February 1996 to come out of the locker room. Resignation would be required, but they would be allowed to keep their superannuation, pension and any ill-gotten gains.

Specialist officers from the Fraud Enforcement Agency, northwest regional crime squad and drug squad were implicated in particularly serious abuses and criminality. A large number of uniform officers also left the service due to the disclosure of misconduct. In the final report a total of 284 police officers were adversely named, 46 briefs of evidence were sent to the DPP and by 2001 nine officers had pleaded guilty to corruption offences. Seven police officers received jail sentences, including Eade and Fowler, who received a two-year minimum sentence in February 2000. Wood found:

> A state of systemic and entrenched corruption which extended throughout certain squads, across whole areas, and reached very senior officers.

The contract of Assistant Commissioner Ray Donaldson, who had gone head to head with Haken, was not renewed and that of Bob Lysaught, the police commissioner's chief of staff, was simply torn up. Charges against fourteen officers were dismissed because of irregularities in search warrants and their execution. There were other casualties, however, and in 2010 Steven Reeves, a 29-year honest police veteran, who had his future ambitions stymied by evidence given at the commission by his corrupt boss, Bob Lysaught, was awarded $2 million for his lost career prospects and his 10-year ordeal at the hands of the force.

By 2007 twelve people involved in the commission had committed suicide. The highest profile of them all had been retired judge David Yeldham, due to face the commission after admitting that he had been questioned by police over alleged indecent behaviour at a railway station some six years earlier. Others had died, their illnesses exacerbated, so their families believed, by their involvement.

With the commission winding down, in mid-January 1996 Lauer, forced to accept that corruption was endemic in certain branches of the force, resigned as police commissioner and a search for a new appointment began. Untouched by the scandal were a number of perfectly good home-grown candidates, including Christine Nixon, who went on to become the police commissioner of Victoria, Clive Small and Jeff Jarrett, who along with around seventy others, all applied. But it was decided that a global search should begin for what Nixon described as 'a new commissioner-cum-saviour' to show that the government was serious about changing police culture.

The position was hawked around senior officers in Great Britain before, in June 1996, Peter Ryan—a lecturer at Bramshill Police College in England—was called in at a salary of rather more than that of the premier to drink from the poisoned chalice. Although he had been chief constable of rural Norfolk, Ryan had never commanded a city force. In interviews shortly after his appointment he was keen to dismiss suggestions that he did not have the depth of experience to deal with city detectives bent on hiding their misdeeds. 'People have overlooked the fact that there is a determination to clean up the act. It rests not only with me but with a widespread group of people.' There was now in place a Police Integrity Commission, established in January 1997, to root out corruption.

Although Ryan brought Jo Hampson, a close colleague from England, with him to act as his chief of staff, from the start he was isolated, fed contradictory advice and information, and by no means *au fait* with the situation on the ground. When at his first press conference on 11 June he asked, 'Who is Roger

Rogerson?' the conference came to a hurried end. The only person he felt he could unreservedly trust was Assistant Commissioner Bev Lawson, but sadly she died from a massive stroke in January 1998. One senior officer remembers him:

> My view is that he had good ideas but he was appalling at implementation. He had outward confidence but internally was insecure. Every time you went to see him there was ten minutes of him telling you he was a more experienced officer than you no matter what department you worked in.

Some 200 officers were known to have criminal records when Ryan took over. It was proposed that he should have power of dismissal without appeal. Unsurprisingly, it was an unpopular move and on 20 November there were demonstrations with calls to 'send the Pommie back'. Seventy per cent of officers sacked for having criminal convictions won reinstatement at industrial tribunals.

On 7 February 1997 Ryan launched a new code of conduct, including the banning of free gifts and drinking on duty, and the threat of dismissal for any criminal offence, including drink driving. It did not go down well, particularly when it was immediately disclosed that he had earlier accepted a ticket for the Grand Final and another for the opening night of *Crazy for You.* Professor David Dixon of the University of New South Wales thinks:

> The Wood Royal Commission actually made recommendations for a much deeper change but Ryan effectively said 'Forget about all that'. Police corruption has to be seen as very closely connected with wider political corruption. Here in the 1980s political corruption was very close to the surface and police corruption was a tool of it. England is a more complex society with more layers of influence to go through in a less transparent way.

On 28 June 1997 disturbed drug dealer Ron Levi was shot by officers Rodney Podesta and Anthony Dilorenzo on Bondi beach. Levi had been seen wading fully clothed in the surf brandishing a knife. In March 1998 the coroner decided that the officers had a case to answer over his death, but no charges were ever laid. Two years later Podesta admitted that he had dealt in cocaine. His father, who ran a coffee shop in Kings Cross, had been named in two royal commissions.

By December officers were still behaving as though Wood had never existed; money was being taken for information about potential drug raids and there was access to police computers. Even some officers in Task Force Bax, set up to eliminate crime networks in Kings Cross, had gone bent. Working with the Police Integrity Commission, with whom he later rather fell out over the scale of his operations, over the past year Ryan had put together a covert operation and with Mal Brammer and set up Operation Gymea. In a series of raids two amphetamine laboratories were closed down and twenty people arrested.

Another problem came when police cadet Kim Hollingsworth, a one-time stripper and $400-an-hour prostitute, and also the daughter of a former officer, was dismissed after eight weeks at the police academy. Some of her stripping performances had been for police smokos. About a month after commencing her studies, Hollingsworth was recognised as a former prostitute by a police officer studying on a detective course at the academy. He approached her to work in a brothel that he was opening in western Sydney, an offer she declined. When her earlier career became known Ryan was quite unwilling to let her stay, but he was overruled. Reinstated, she later dropped out of the course.

In 2001 Ryan announced that his reform mission was now complete. In his earlier years he accepted that he had faced a good deal of sniping on a professional and personal level, but believed he had weathered the storm. In his first months he had dismissed twenty officers and 150 had been suspended. 'When it was seen I was dismissing officers, there was a rush to hand in resignations.' The force was now clean, he said, echoing Tony Lauer.

Unfortunately, at hearings of the Police Integrity Commission that same year, Operation Florida—a three-year sting mounted by the force's internal anti-corruption unit—made it clear that the force was not at all clean. Microphones and cameras had been planted in lavatories in Manly and the police were filmed as they met and dealt with drug dealers. One detective, Senior Constable David Patison, was another filmed pushing banknotes down his trousers. He had found the money while searching the home of a cannabis dealer. Another clip showed three officers taking $40,000 and laughing, saying 'happy days'. Much of the evidence came from a former officer known as M5, who had been trapped and persuaded to roll over. For six months he recorded what he did on a daily basis.

Vince Caccamo, a senior heroin dealer of the North Shore area, claimed that he had paid $92,000 in bribes, including a weekly $1000 to Patison and Senior Constable Matthew Jasper in 2000. He was recorded complaining to an associate, Anthony Markarian, that he was being badly squeezed. 'Every cent I make goes to them.' Rather unsympathetically, Markarian thought it was like having a shop and paying rent. In another traditional police rort, Jasper had arranged for a convicted burglar to rob the home of a man known not to be security conscious in return for a percentage of the proceeds.

Patison, one of six officers convicted of offences, received a sevenyear sentence with a minimum of five to be served, as did Jasper. Caccamo received the same minimum sentence. Forty former officers and three serving officers were said by the commission to have been guilty of a variety of offences, but because of lack of corroboration they were never prosecuted. One Sydney solicitor was acquitted of bribery and acting with intent to pervert the course of justice; nevertheless, the law society cancelled his practicing certificate. It was reissued in 2009.

Ryan, who had just negotiated a new $400,000-a-year contract, was said to be very angry, as well he might be. Putting on a brave face, he told his force to 'Wear your uniform with pride', saying that Operation Florida showed his reforms were working. But drivers stopped for speeding were asking the police, 'How much?' In fairness to Ryan, a good deal of the evidence heard had pre-dated his appointment.

Ryan sometimes also showed appalling lack of judgement. When complaints were made about the head of Special Crime and Internal Affairs Mal Brammer, by Detective Sergeant John Ellund and New South Wales independent MP John Hatton, Ryan sought advice on how to deal with it. This was understandable. Because of his background Ryan did not know the players involved. What was not understandable was that he consulted Brammer on how the complaints should be answered. It is amazing that he was unable to see the conflict of interest this demonstrated. Brammer sensibly wrote:

> Given the history of Mr Hatton's resolute pursuit of myself ... it is my submission that any further inquiry is an absolute waste of time and effort.

Ryan canned the investigation.

It was a long, uphill struggle in which, after the death of his trusted assistant Bev Lawson, Ryan eventually became totally isolated—Jo Hampson had returned to England after eighteen months. The lengths to which his enemies would go are demonstrated by perhaps the most audacious piece of intra-police espionage ever seen. Two undercover officers were stationed in Sydney's upmarket Marriott Hotel, where Ryan and his wife went for drinks, in the hope that the Ryans might make some indiscreet remarks that could later be used in the fight to unhorse him. The fact that the undercover cops were posing as a bodybuilding biker and his girlfriend made the surveillance seem even more ludicrous. Surveillance was also ordered by Assistant Commissioner Mal Brammer on a number of other senior officers, none to any effect. Brammer retired before Ryan could move him.

Ryan resigned on 3 April 2002 amid scenes of mutual recrimination and exited to a lone piper playing a lament. He became the security expert of the International Olympic Committee. The experience makes it unlikely that the experiment of importing a commissioner from abroad will ever be repeated.

15

THE TWENTY-FIRST CENTURY: DANGEROUS LIAISONS

The deaths of two retired officers on 1 September 2001 led to yet another re-examination of a case that had long caused problems for the Western Australian police. The deaths were those of Don Hancock, former officer of the Kalgoorlie gold stealing detective squad and one-time head of Perth CIB, and his friend Louis 'Lou' Lewis. Their deaths followed the fatal shooting of Gypsy Joker biker Billy Grierson. The case that was re-opened was the Perth Mint robbery of 1982, of which the Mickelberg brothers, Peter, Ray and Brian, were convicted.

On 22 June 1982 three couriers, each with false cheques, arrived at the Perth Mint and took away gold bullion weighing 68 kilograms, then worth $653,000. In today's terms it would be valued at around $1.5 million. The couriers delivered the gold to an office several kilometres away and promptly vanished. In many ways it was an attractive crime—daring, well thought through and, best of all, involving no violence. In charge of the investigation was Hancock, then a sergeant and one of many officers worldwide who revelled in the soubriquet 'Grey Fox'. He came from an era of policing when rules were bent to get results. The CIB under Hancock got the job done. 'You know they did it; they know they did it; just make sure the jury knows they did it.' They saw themselves as the bastions of noble cause corruption. 'The last line, the defenders of society.' There might have been pockets of corruption, but the CIB was respected, 'almost revered', said one observer.

Although the Mickelbergs, who worked as abalone divers and pilots, had only one previous conviction between them—Peter had been fined $50 for possessing an unlicensed firearm—they were high on the list of suspects. Ray Mickelberg was a former and wellthought-of SAS commando in Vietnam and, given the military precision with which the rort had been carried out, was regarded as the mastermind.

On 26 July that year Peter Mickelberg was driving home to the northern suburbs when a police car forced him to stop. He was taken to Belmont police station, where he was interviewed by Hancock and another officer, Tony Lewandowski. This was regarded as an odd choice of station, as there was a headquarters in the city that had been specially set up to deal with the robbery. Other odd features of the arrest were that all Belmont officers save one had left the station by the time Mickelberg arrived. The one remaining officer, Bob Kucera, later the Western Australian health minister, left shortly afterwards.

According to Peter Mickelberg—something denied until after Hancock's death—Lewandowski first told him that no one knew where he was and that as far as others were concerned he could be dead. Then Hancock told Lewandowski to make the prisoner strip and he punched Mickelberg in the solar plexus and throat. Years later Lewandowski claimed that he told Hancock they really had no evidence but Hancock had replied, 'Don't worry, it will get better'. According to the policemen, Peter then confessed to his involvement and implicated his brothers. The confession was, as so often in such cases, unsigned. The prosecution also claimed that a fingerprint of Ray Mickelberg's was found on one of the fraudulent cheques. The defence claimed that, since one of his hobbies was casting hands—about twenty casts were found when his home at Marmion Beach was raided—it would have been easy for police to obtain a mould of Mickelberg's finger and plant it on a cheque. In 1983 Peter received six years and Ray a massive twenty; Brian served nine months before his conviction was quashed.

The brothers' other problem was that they had also been involved in the high-profile case of the second-largest gold nugget ever found in Western Australia, said to have been discovered near Kalgoorlie by their mother, Peggy. Wearing a wig and glasses and without her false teeth, said to have been taken out because she felt sick on the flight, Peggy left a light aircraft at Perth's Jandakot airport carrying the nugget, to be photographed by the alerted press. She had, she said, discovered the gold while out prospecting. It became known as the Yellow Rose of Texas—the name suggested by an American seaman who won $200 in a competition run by the brothers' friend Bryan Pozzi. Wrongly authenticated by experts, the nugget was sold in 1980 to businessman and identity Alan Bond for $350,000. During the course of the mint investigation police discovered photographs of the nugget, which, far from originating in the goldfields, was being made at the time by Ray Mickelberg and Pozzi, an engineer.

Arrests followed and all refused to sign what were alleged to be confessions but which were admitted into evidence. On 19 May 1984 Peggy Mickelberg received an eighteen-month sentence, of which she served nine months. Pozzi and Ray were sentenced to thirty months to five years, and Peter and Brian to eighteen to thirty months. The Mickelberg brothers' father, Malcolm, was found not guilty. With his sentence tacked onto the end of the mint swindle sentence, Ray now had the longest sentence of any serving Western Australian prisoner. The rort had, said the Micklebergs, merely been a publicity stunt for an adventure business they were running.

Over the years Peter and Ray Mickelberg made a total of seven appeals over the mint swindle—six to the Western Australian Court of Criminal Appeal—and all were rejected. In 1989 some 55 kilograms of the gold was left in a Perth suburb, which certainly cannot have been done by the brothers. Two were still in prison and the meticulous Brian Mickelberg had been killed on 27 February 1986 when the light aircraft he was flying mysteriously ran out of fuel forty minutes into a three-hour flight. That year a gold bar and two containers, later tested and identified by the Perth Mint, were sent to a local television station together with a note that the Mickelbergs were innocent and had been framed. The note claimed that a prominent Perth businessman was behind the swindle.

A 1995 campaign by journalist Avon Lovell saying that the brothers had been the victims of a miscarriage of justice came to a temporary halt when police officer Tony Lewandowski sued Lovell and put a stop to sales of his book, *The Mickelberg Stitch,* which had sold 17,000 copies in a week. The Police Union imposed a dollar-a-week levy on its members to fund Lewandowski's action. There were also allegations that the union prevented Lovell from getting a job with *The West Australian,* telling the paper that, if he did, no officer would work with it. It was similar to the 'you'll never work again' approach that had been used in Victoria after the Beach report and in New South Wales when Premier Askin wished to shut down whistleblower Philip Arantz.

After a further rejected appeal in November 1989, Police Commissioner Brian Bull told the press that the decision 'totally vindicates the actions of the police in their investigation into the Perth Mint swindle'. Peter Mickelberg was released later that year and Ray two years later.

On the back of the successful prosecution of the brothers, and regarded as a man who knew how to get results, Don Hancock became the head of the Perth CIB. One colleague described him as a 'take no prisoners sort of bloke' and as [redacted] of Western Australia without the criminality'. Shortly before the 1983 trial a recording, which was never played at the hearing, had been made by Ray Mickelberg of a conversation with Hancock at Mickelberg's home:

> Hancock: I'm not a mean person, but I'll tell you what: I've done things in my life that you never did, and harder things, worse things, and if I've got to do them again, well, I'll do them again.
>
> RM: In the line of duty?
>
> Hancock: That is, yes. What I believe is my line of duty—to get the job done.

Of course, this sort of conversation can be interpreted in a number of ways. Hancock may simply have meant he was prepared to associate with informers and general scum to obtain information, but there are other less favourable ways it can be construed.

When he retired in the late 1990s the hair trigger tempered, often kilt-wearing and Banjo Patterson–reciting Hancock went back to the Kalgoorlie goldfields where he had grown up and opened a hotel in the remote town of Ora Banda as well as working a claim. There, on 1 October 2000, he met with trouble from the local branch of the Gypsy Jokers motorcycle gang. Hancock banned one of its members, William Grierson, from his hotel after he and other bikers swore in front of Hancock's daughter, Alison. Hancock then shut the bar down for the evening. Later that night the biker was shot dead at a nearby campfire, hit in the shoulder and his spine severed. By the time the police interviewed him, Hancock, known as a fine shot, had showered and changed. He refused to hand over his clothing and he ate an orange, something that would mask gunshot residue. He then returned to Perth, where he took legal advice, declining to assist with police inquiries. Over the next few weeks Hancock's home was firebombed, as was a store he owned, and the hotel was blown up.

In the spring of 2001 the police heard that some Jokers were mounting surveillance on Hancock's home and that there was a plot to kill him at a Kalgoorlie race meeting—he had a horse running in the last race on 1 September. They managed to persuade him not to go and instead, along with his friend Lou Lewis, he went to Belmont racetrack in Perth. Probably while they were at the races, a bomb was placed in Lewis's Holden station wagon. They stayed late at the track because Hancock wanted to listen to the Kalgoorlie race, in which his horse ran third. As Lewis drove them back to Hancock's home the bomb was remotely detonated, killing both men and blowing a large crater in the road.

On 28 March 2002, 38-year-old Sidney John Reid, a full member of the Jokers, pleaded guilty to the murders. After a long police investigation he had been persuaded to roll over and break the bikers' code of silence. Reid, who came from a broken home and was estranged from his children, had come to regard the Jokers as his family. He had come under suspicion because he had been at the campsite on the night Grierson was shot. Now he implicated another Joker, Graeme 'Slim' Slater, as being with him when the bomb was planted. In return for his cooperation Reid was given fifteen years, a reduction of ten in the sentence he might have expected. He also gave evidence in the successful prosecution of Gary White for the murder of Alan Tapley, who had been killed over a debt and barbecued. He later gave evidence against other bikers who, on 27 August 2004, were all acquitted of the bombing campaign against Hancock. Slater, who had earlier been acquitted of the murders, admitted four charges relating to the earlier bombing campaign and received a three-year sentence, which resulted in his immediate release.

Ironically, it had been thought that Hancock's death would end any chance the Mickelberg brothers had of clearing their names, but it was then that Tony Lewandowski, now estranged from his wife and son, broke ranks and swore an affidavit admitting that he had lied and had, in fact, taken part in the beating of Peter Mickelberg:

> I have had enough. Now that Don Hancock is dead I can't harm him and I am now telling the truth ... a couple of times I wanted to come clean but there was no way I could go against Don.

While he admitted fabricating evidence, Lewandowski said he still believed the brothers to be responsible for the robbery. 'I do have remorse, of course, but I still believe implicitly that they were guilty of the crime.' Nevertheless, he asked the DPP for immunity but, while it was being considered, he left the country. He returned to give evidence by video link on 27 September 2002 at a preliminary hearing of a further appeal by the brothers.

On 2 July 2004, by a majority of two to one, the court allowed the appeal, quashed the conviction and indicated that there would be no retrial. It is difficult to see how there could have been. Hancock was dead and so was Lewandowski, who had committed suicide in May that year. The Western Australia Police were unwilling to accept the verdict and Assistant Commissioner Neil Hay said there was an abundance of evidence linking the brothers to the crime. In turn they claimed compensation, which was eventually settled for $1.6 million.

During this period, under Commissioner Bob Falconer, the Western Australia Police lost the respect of the public. There were continual claims of corruption; unsolved murders, including the Claremont serial killings; and sloppy work in briefs handed to the DPP. The consorting squad had been disbanded.

On 4 November 2001 respected *West Australian* journalist Gary Adshead, in his article 'Cops on take', claimed that detectives in the 1990s had been standing over dealers, stealing drugs and cash from them, and giving the green light to favourites. But no witnesses had come forward and if they did, 'He would say that, wouldn't he?' would be the defence. Who would believe a drug dealer's word against that of a police officer?

In a number of examples presented by Adshead, Dealer 1 said that he sold hydroponically grown cannabis from a house in Lansdale and was raided on average every six weeks. The police would take drugs and cash, and charge him with a 'pissy' offence. Once when they had found him with 2500 marijuana sticks or foils and forty-three 50-gram sachets, along with $4900; he was charged with possessing half a gram of cannabis. Once he had been raided while dealing with the son of a senior police officer, who was just kicked out of the house.

Dealer 2, wrote Adshead, claimed that he had been paying $2000 a week to a detective sergeant from 1991 and that he stole a total of twenty-eight cars for another corrupt detective sergeant who was jailed in 1996 for offering a bribe to a third officer to drop an investigation into a smash repairer. A third dealer said that the police had taken well over $100,000 from him over a period of years and that it was not a financial arrangement as in New South Wales but was simply a standover.

The next year Geoffrey Kennedy QC was appointed to head a royal commission 'Into whether there has been any corrupt or criminal conduct by any Western Australian police officer'. During the commission one former officer told of a twenty-year corrupt career and named forty officers whom he said were also involved in corruption, which he listed as stealing cash from a man shot dead by police, forging signatures, and using and supplying illegal drugs to informants. There was also apparently a videotape of a sergeant trying to steal $1 million. Four years later, in 2006, the final report of the commission concluded that it was 'an organisation of mediocre achievements' and:

> the full range of corrupt or criminal conduct from stealing to assaults, perjury, drug dealing and the improper disclosure of confidential information have been examined. The Western Australian Police force has been ineffective in monitoring those events and modifying its procedures to deal with that conduct and to prevent its repetition ... The fact that there remain in WAPS a number of officers who participated in this conduct, and who not only refused to admit it, but also uniformly denied it with vehemence, is a matter of concern.

One of the high-profile cases the commission had examined was that of the death of Stephen Wardle in the East Perth lock-up in 1988. Allegations of police brutality surrounded the death, and seventeen officers had refused to testify at the coronial inquest. The commission also looked at the Argyle diamonds case, in which one of the defendants alleged he had paid nearly $250,000 to derail an investigation into a series of thefts worth up to $30 million from the Kununurra mine. Overall, however, Commissioner Kennedy found little or no substance in claims of corruption in these cases. In particular, Don Hancock was not on the take, nor had he made money from illegal gold dealings and prostitution, as some had thought and claimed.

The report did not please everybody. One question raised was why the commission had put no time aside for any inquiry into allegations of corrupt relationships with Northbridge identity John Kizon and his offsiders when so much time had been spent finding out so little new about Wardle's death nearly twenty years earlier and the old Argyle case. Why had Operation Red Emperor, an investigation into organised crime and Northbridge identities, been aborted? There were also complaints from an undercover detective who had worked for three years with Kizon's associates. 'West Australia's recent history with corruption fighters does not inspire a deal of confidence.'

Another case from the previous century spilled over into this mystery. On 11 September 1995 heroin addict Andrew Petrelis had been found dead following a drug overdose in the seaside town of Caloundra,

Queensland. Supposedly sent there in a Western Australian witness protection program, he was waiting to give evidence against Kizon, for whom he had worked as a driver. His body, hunched over a CD player on repeat, was discovered after he failed to turn up for a flying lesson.

In 1994 Petrelis had been instructed—by whom it was never wholly clear—to dig up some bags, expected to contain cannabis, in Perth's Kings Park and take them to a self-storage unit he had rented, padlocking the door behind him. The owners of the unit became suspicious, broke open the door, discovered $150,000 worth of drugs and called the police. When questioned, Petrelis rolled over. Grass cuttings were substituted for the cannabis. Petrelis was used as bait for a trap and John Kizon's offsider Michael Rippingale picked up the bags on 22 November that year. Following surveillance and phone taps, he and Kizon were arrested. Unfortunately, even before he left Western Australia Petrelis' cover had been blown. A police constable, apparently looking on the web for information about Elvis Presley's manager Colonel Parker, had accidentally stumbled on confidential details of Petrelis' new identity. Worse still, a second officer also came across the details and passed them on to Western Australian criminals. The second officer later resigned. One of the officers who accessed Petrelis' file was Murray John Shadgett and, at best, his record showed a total laxity of supervision by his superiors. As at June 1994 Shadgett had more disciplinary charges against him than any other Western Australian officer and was on a final written warning. In 1995, seventeen days before the Colonel Parker search, information was received that a man on work release from Albany prison was living with Shadgett. He eventually retired on medical grounds on 6 July 2000, shortly before the completion of an internal affairs unit investigation.

A report tabled in parliament on 9 August 2000 showed that Petrelis' supposedly secret identity had been accessed seventeen times on the police database. Despite these breaches he was still moved to Caloundra.

In November 1999 Kizon and Rippingale were acquitted of the drug offences. Kizon, who was in hospital at the time of Petrelis' death, complained bitterly, suggesting that the drugs charge was a slur on his character and that he had only been arrested because of his associates.

In 2006 Queensland coroner Michael Halliday, inquiring into Petrelis' death, found that 'there was no evidence which would reasonably suggest that the cause of death was other than self-administration'. There are, however, believable suggestions, backed by evidence—there was no tourniquet, spoon or needle and the injection was in Petrelis' right arm although he was right-handed—that the overdose was a result of forced feeding.

Coleen Thomas, one witness due to appear at the inquest, simply disappeared, saying she did not wish to have a 'fucking pair of concrete boots'. The inquest was followed by a 2007 Corruption and Crime Commission of Western Australia report, which confirmed the suicide verdict. When it was suggested that Tony Lewandowski should be given police protection after confessing to his part in verballing the Mickelsons, Avon Lovell had commented, 'Put him in the Petrelis memorial protection program? No.'

Sometimes, even in these more sophisticated days, police can be lured into traps by unlikely bedfellows, often with disastrous consequences. In Western Australia one such culprit was police groupie Pasquale Minniti, who came to prominence in 2006 when the Corruption and Crime Commission investigated allegations he was able to have speeding tickets cancelled for his friends.

Throughout the early noughties Minniti, a panel beater known as 'Inspector Minniti', had assiduously cultivated police contacts and obtained confidential information via the police computer, including some for a prisoner on remand. He was taken along by officers on patrol and had errands run for him and his friends. The police would target and harass people who had offended him, and he was given police hats and ties to wear.

In 2009 Minniti was found guilty of corruption, making a false statutory declaration and attempting to induce a witness to give false evidence to the Crime and Corruption Commission. He was jailed for eighteen months, while former police officer Arduino Silvestri, who provided a false statutory declaration for Minniti, was jailed for twelve. Another sergeant received a twelve-month suspended sentence and a $6000 fine for witnessing a forged document. He also received a ten-month suspended sentence and a $5000 fine when he pleaded guilty to unlawfully using a restricted-access computer.

Minniti's downfall was also that of one-time police minister John D'Orazio, whom he assisted in trying to get his traffic fines quashed. Caught on tape, D'Orazio later appeared before the Crime and Corruption Commission to try to explain his relationship with Minniti. Far more serious was the Queensland case of Lee Owen Henderson, who had raped Tracey Dovey on 21 November 1988 in her Burleigh Heads home and then killed her by injecting her with a hot shot of heroin. He was sentenced to life imprisonment and after killing a fellow prisoner received a second life sentence. From his cell, and using elaborately headed notepaper, somehow Henderson scammed the Rockhampton police into thinking he could help with their crime clear-up rate. In June 2002 he became a registered confidential police informant and as result a Sergeant Dalton, who acted as his handler, was alleged to have set up a joint phone-betting account, with Henderson accepting almost $8000 from him—but never asking where the money came from. Henderson was also given his own locker in the police station and was allowed to go out on unsupervised visits for lunch. Under magistrates' orders obtained by police, Henderson was allowed out of prison nine times over three years and once was taken to Brett's Wharf restaurant on the Brisbane River to meet a female associate. He was photographed wearing an armed robbery unit tie. On 28 July 2004 it was arranged for Henderson to have a day's release from prison and attend the Villa Mar Colina Motel at Yeppoon so that he could have face-to-face contact with targets suspected of being involved in the importation of a large quantity of cannabis from Papua New Guinea. Unfortunately, Henderson took a dominant role in the conversations that took place and actually attempted to procure the commission of the offence of importation and/or supply of dangerous drugs.

One officer also arranged for Henderson to be given a $5000 reward for providing information on a crime, but $1000 of it ended up in a police officer's own bank account. A telephone-diversion arrangement was put in place at Cleveland police station, which allowed Henderson to make nearly 1250 redirected, unmonitored phone calls from jail between 2003 and 2006. In yet another damaging revelation, the 2009 Crime and Misconduct Commission report *Dangerous Liaisons* said that Henderson orchestrated the theft of more than $250,000 in drug money during a police raid on a property.

It was not as though the police had not been warned. When Henderson was first used the far northern regional crime coordinator had told them that Henderson, who took the nickname 'The General', was 'not a person to be trusted'. Well before that warning, in 1993 career criminal turned journalist Bernie Matthews had already written an article, 'Superliar', in *The Gold Coast Bulletin* about the dangers of employing informants in general and Henderson in particular.

[redacted]

Operation Capri followed and its report was not well received. Police unions are right to be protective of their members, but sometimes, as with the Beach inquiry in Victoria, they are protective even in indefensible circumstances. Now the Queensland Police Union of Employees was not pleased. On 22 July 2009, the day of the tabling of the Capri report, the union issued a media release:

> This is nothing more than a media stunt by the CMC ... If there was substance to all of the

> allegations in this report there would be 20 or 30 police facing the courts not just three.
>
> The timing of the report today has much more to do with a conference hosted by the CMC next week where Russell Pearce ... is scheduled to do a presentation regarding *Operation Capri.*

Police Union president Ian Leavers said that everyone had the right to innocence until proven guilty, especially when the report comprised 'wild' allegations relying on the word of convicted criminals.

> It is for the courts to decide someone's guilt or innocence, not the CMC, not the media and not the police commissioner. I believe the only reason the CMC was in such a hurry to publish the allegations is so they could grandstand at an anti-corruption conference next week.

Dangerous Liaisons warned of the dangers of the improper dealings between law-enforcement officers and Henderson. Two officers faced criminal charges of perjury and falsifying evidence and were acquitted when the judge stopped the case. One retired and the other was reinstated but due to his 'procedural breaches' lost some pay for his time off work. Eleven others who faced disciplinary action resigned. Leavers was extremely upset about the Crime and Misconduct Commission's handling of the case. 'The CMC should hang their heads in shame', he said.

> There was insufficient evidence to even put to a jury. The two police officers involved ... have been through hell over many years, this has destroyed careers and destroyed families.

In 2009 the CMC began Operation Tesco, an inquiry into allegations that three officers on the Gold Coast were involved in inappropriate associations with criminals, drug use, misuse of confidential police information and accepting gratuities. It soon emerged that there were long-term problems in an environment where there was drug and alcohol abuse by some police officers and a marked reluctance to report suspected police misconduct. Whistleblowers could expect to be punished by their fellow officers. One was sent bullets at his family's home.

The eighteen-month investigation found that free drink cards were given out to police in nightclubs frequented by members of outlaw motorcycle gangs, and police were leaking information to them. One officer had given a reference to an ex-stripper, and yet another had lied as a cadet about her medical history of depression and shock treatment for mental-health problems. But in the end only one serving and one former officer faced criminal charges, and six others were disciplined. There was, said John Allen, counsel assisting the commission, no evidence of endemic corruption.

However, in 2010–11 thirty Gold Coast officers were subject to internal discipline. One was dismissed for theft from a social club and eight others resigned. They had been charged with a variety of offences including fraud, perjury, supplying drugs, sexual misconduct with a witness and forgery.

Criminal lawyer Michael McMillan said that following the CMC investigation the police had lost a lot of their power and were no longer feared by the underworld.

> They're not nabbing the crooks as swiftly as they used to and many are getting away with all their crimes. The courtrooms are empty, we used to go until 5p.m. every day, now it's a busy day if we are there until midday. Temporary helicopters and taskforces won't fix this, permanent resources and more power will.

The Police Union complained that so much money had been spent and so many officers harassed to so little effect. Why, if there was so much corruption, were there no arrests and prosecutions? One answer is that evidence obtained from a suspect in a CMC investigation cannot necessarily be used in a prosecution.

One outcome was the Queensland Police Service gifts and benefits policy, which came into effect on 1 January 2012 and which prohibited free or discounted entry into licensed premises and free or discounted alcohol. Officers were also required to report on the acquisition and disposal of gifts and benefits.

In the year 2012–13 the CMC conducted forty-three inquiries into 192 allegations of misconduct. The most common types of allegations investigated related to official conduct (duty failures), the unlawful possession (use) and supply of dangerous drugs by police officers, the unauthorised release of information from the Queensland Police Service database, and assaults by police officers on members of the public. In other words, a good deal of what Operation Tesco had looked at in 2009.

By September 2013 there were, however, fears that an increase in crime and the escalation of outlaw motorcycle gangs on the Gold Coast were due, at least in part, to the clearing out of experienced officers.

The noughties were damaging for Victoria Police as well. The Melbourne gang wars were at their height. On 13 December 2001 newly appointed Chief Commissioner Christine Nixon announced the immediate disbanding of the drug squad. In its place would be established a new, clean, accountable body, the major drug investigation division. As one former officer remarked, 'Nothing like a cleansing and refreshing name change'.

Unfortunately, members of the disbanded, discredited drug squad were invited to apply to join the new division. While at Harvard, Nixon had studied techniques to create a police force with the capacity to resist corruption. Her hero Patrick V Murphy had been charged with the task of cleaning out the New York police after the 1971 Knapp Commission, and the first thing he did was replace 90 per cent of its senior ranks. Nixon may have regretted not following her hero more closely.

One of the most egregious examples of collective noble cause corruption is that of Victoria's armed offenders squad. In 1979 the Beach inquiry found that the armed robbery squad had committed 'abuses ... so grave as to warrant the most prompt institution of safeguarding reforms'. However, it was not until 1999 that the squad was amalgamated with the special response and prison squads to form the armed offenders squad, with a brief to investigate nonfatal violent crime. The new squad lasted seven years. By then it had, so its critics said, become an uncontrolled law unto itself. Its thirty-five detectives, including the one female member, wore a uniform based on that of the jewel thieves in the film *Reservoir Dogs:* black suit, white shirt and a tie with a logo of crossed revolvers. The logo was superimposed on top of the Victoria Police badge symbol and used on official documents. There were allegations of beatings, bashings and brickings. Supervision was lacking, and in 2003 when a newly appointed inspector drew up detailed proposals to improve the day-to-day working of the squad, these were ignored until he was transferred out and the proposals were shelved. An Office of Police Integrity (OPI) report found that:

> Informal squad culture ... gained such strength and impenetrability that the chain of command was effectively reversed, to the point where some squad members considered themselves immune from managerial accountability or authority.

The lessons from the Wood Royal Commission in New South Wales had, again, drowned in the Murray. Despite the fact that the squad was warned television cameras were being installed in its headquarters at St Kilda in September 2006, one officer was caught on tape punching a suspect and threatening him that his ear would 'come off' by the end of the interview and, when another suspect asked to be allowed to make a telephone call, a second detective beat him with the telephone saying, 'Here it is; here's your fucking phone call ... piece of shit'.

On 13 September Chief Commissioner Christine Nixon told the squad it was being disbanded. She was taped, and the tape was leaked to *The Herald Sun.* A little poem was written that summed up the squad's attitude:

> So long as there's bad crooks, they'll need us around, If they're rid of us then crime will abound.

On 19 September 2006 three detectives were shown videotapes of themselves beating a suspect. All claimed not to recognise themselves on the video but were suspended the same day. The disbanding of the squad was followed by a reprise of the protests about the

Beach report. This time around 300 police and former members of the squad, including the suspended detectives, rallied in the appropriately named Batman Park. Motions calling for the reinstatement of the squad and the resignation of Christine Nixon were passed. Police Association secretary Paul Mullett told the meeting that the result of disbanding the squad would be 'what's currently occurring in New South Wales: drive-by shootings, ethnic gangs, race gangs, youth gangs, street gangs, gang rapes by the day'.

After negotiations Victoria Police agreed that those officers not charged would be guaranteed positions on the newly formed armed crime task force set up to replace the squad. In the wash-up, two of the three officers received community service orders of ten weeks and the third five weeks. Charges against a detective inspector, of counselling and procuring the assault, were dropped.

As the decade went on, public focus was shifting from rooting out crooked, drug-dealing cops, to the top brass and the institutions there were intended to be anti-corruption watchdogs. It was a case of cleaning up the cleaner-uppers.

Much of the trouble for the senior hierarchy arose from the death of Shane Chartres-Abbott, a 28-year-old bisexual prostitute who specialised in rough sex. He was shot in Howard Street, Reservoir, in July 2003 on his way to court to stand trial for the rape of a thirtyyear-old Thai woman in a St Kilda motel.

Her tongue had been bitten in half and Chartres-Abbott, who claimed to be a 200-year-old vampire, was running the defence that he had been lured into a snuff movie in which he himself would be killed. As he left his home with his pregnant girlfriend and her father, he was shot in the neck in what was believed to be a contract killing in revenge for the woman's death or possibly to prevent Chartres-Abbott from naming his other clients in court. Operation Briars was later set up to establish whether police officers were connected with the killing. It was suggested that one had given Chartres-Abbott's address to the hitman. On 27 March a career criminal identified only as 'JP' and known by the pseudonym 'Jack Price' agreed to give evidence against senior officers allegedly linked to the case.

In 2009 there was another twist to this story when former police media director Stephen Linnell was sentenced to eight months' imprisonment, wholly suspended, and fined $5000 on perjury charges. He had agreed to testify against Deputy Police Commissioner Noel Ashby, admitting that he leaked to him information on Operation Briars.

In February 2010 charges of perjury against Ashby were dropped. He had been accused of lying when questioned at an OPI hearing, saying that he had not received information about a serving detective who was being investigated for murder. Justice Robert Osborn ruled that the charges could not be sustained because the hearing at which he was alleged to have lied was not conducted within the law: the OPI deputy commissioner who heard the case had not been formally authorised to do so. As a result DPP Jeremy Rapke withdrew the charges.

In June 2010 Linnell's convictions were quashed. The OPI alleged that Ashby had passed on the information to former Police Association boss Paul Mullett and that, as a result, the suspected detective was tipped off. Charges against Mullett were dismissed by committal magistrate Peter Couzens, who described the evidence against him as 'more chaff than wheat'. Linnell later wrote a book entitled *Don't Tell the Chief: The Untold Story of Police, Politics and Power.*

In November 2010 the OPI admitted that it was incapable of dealing with an allegedly corrupt officer, [redacted] and also to have been the victim of a robbery while guarding $4 million worth of cigarettes in the 1990s. It appeared that files on [redacted] had vanished.

In the late summer of 2009 Christine Nixon, the first woman to become a chief commissioner and who had already been considering retirement, announced that she was standing down not long after a story broke that she had been part of a freebie package that involved travelling to the United States with her husband. And so the baton passed to Purina Task Force head honcho Simon Overland, a former Federal Police officer with 'an impressive resume'. Deputy to Christine Nixon from mid-2006, he replaced her as the new Victorian chief commissioner on 2 March

2009. Four months later the United Kingdom's Sir Ken Jones, with an equally impressive police pedigree, became one of Overland's deputy commissioners.

Within a year there were apparent rifts in the relationship between the chief and his deputies. Sir Ken was not afraid to speak his mind, even when he was out of step with his colleagues and his boss. In 2010 suspicions were raised by a whistleblower that, before the state election, Overland had allowed inaccurate and misleading crime statistics to be published. The stats, which showed a 27.5-percent reduction in CBD assaults, were thought likely to bolster Labor in the elections, and to some it appeared that Overland's relationship with the Brumby government was a little too close. An ombudsman investigation ensued.

Next, Overland drew negative media attention when the police computer system had a cost blow-out of $100 million. Even worse, Sir Ken sent Overland an email regarding a sensitive report he was about to turn in on murders committed by parolees. The report stated that up to four murders could have been prevented had police databases kept better track of parolees, because officers dealing with criminals had not been alerted to their status.

Suspicion for the unfavourable leaks against Overland fell on Sir Ken Jones, who had resigned from his post three months earlier than he had intended on 6 May 2011 amid suggestions that Overland had precipitated his departure. Another investigation was ordered, this time to be run by the OPI.

Meanwhile the press, in particular *The Herald Sun,* ran what some unkindly termed a 'get Baldy' campaign, in reference to Overland's shaved head. In 2011 almost 2980 police members, a quarter of the force, voted in a Police Association online poll, which found that 92 per cent did not have confidence in Overland continuing as their boss.

On 16 June 2011 ombudsman George Brouwer's annual report found that, while Overland had been inadequately briefed by senior police as to the validity of the crime statistics, he had allowed them to be rushed through to the media, despite warnings that the data was not 'settled'. Overland, with dignity intact and denying any improper conduct, resigned the same day.

But the slate was not yet clean. Now Ashby and Mullett complained that Overland, his Assistant Commissioner Luke Cornelius and former Deputy Commissioner Graham Ashton had breached federal communications laws when they accessed OPI phone-tap information. Ashby and Mullett also claimed that Overland had conducted a vendetta against them, instigating a joint OPI and Victoria Police investigation during which they had been humiliated in public hearings.

Even the OPI itself was firmly in the firing line. Critics, including a retired judge, had already accused it of being incompetent in dealing with a police force riddled with corruption. It was thought to be heavy handed, using secret internal investigations, phone tapping and other star-chamber tactics. Not unexpectedly, the OPI was disbanded and replaced in early 2013 by the Independent Broad-Based Anti-Corruption Commission (IBAC). The name and constitution may have changed, but sadly the complaints were carried over.

In November 2013 the new watchdog announced that it was not empowered to investigate anything short of 'serious corruption'. As Graham Ashton had not intended to breach the federal telecommunications law when he provided OPI telephone tapes to Overland and Cornelius, his behaviour had fallen short of corruption and so was outside IBAC jurisdiction. IBAC also cleared Overland and Cornelius of any wrongdoing and found that Mullett and Ashby's allegations were either not made out on the evidence or were outside IBAC jurisdiction. It resolved to hand the Simon Overland–Sir Ken Jones stoush to an outsider: retired judge Murray Kellam. There was immediate press criticism of the watchdog, saying that it needed wider powers and the 'serious corruption' threshold was too restrictive.

It is difficult not to draw the conclusion that the only anticorruption investigations that worked at least in part were ones where, instead of confining the ambit of the investigator, the boundaries were stretched beyond what was initially thought appropriate. By accepting or putting itself in a strait jacket, IBAC risks being thought to be simply pussy footing.

Kellam's report, tabled in the Victorian Parliament on Wednesday 19 February 2014, cleared Sir Ken of serious misconduct. Kellam found that there was no evidence Jones leaked sensitive information directly to the media and, while he may have divulged confidential information to others, he had no intention that the information be passed on to the media. While there certainly were leaks of material confidential to Victoria Police, the OPI and the Victorian ombudsman between 2009 and early 2013, the sources of the leaks were not identified. However, Kellam found that the facts demonstrated there was a 'serious level of dysfunction' in the relationship between Overland and Jones. He was highly critical of the OPI investigation and found sympathy for Sir Ken's argument that the report demonstrated a 'methodology adopted by the OPI of pre-judging Jones' guilt and then conducting an investigation to support that conclusion'. Which is, of course, how many believe the police regularly conduct their investigations.

But the biggest disaster for Australian police was in relation to Mark Standen, former assistant director of investigations for the New South Wales Crime Commission. The highest-ranking officer to fall in recent years, Standen was another in the Kelly, Krahe and [redacted] mould:

> Like the Roman god, a mythological gatekeeper, Standen had two personas: one was the competitive, effective and highly decorated investigator; the other was the shadowy alter-ego of an addicted gambler, who managed to evade paying the debts for his sometimes questionable professional methods and friends.

His questionable friends included Sydney identity John David Anderson and his son Michael, who were convicted in 2008 of the attempted importation of 27 kilograms of cocaine in watertight containers strapped to the hull of the *Tampa* and another vessel. The haul, worth around $11 million, was discovered by New Zealand officers and substituted. The *Tampa* was then tracked and Michael Anderson was seen diving in to try to retrieve the drugs. John Anderson received eighteen years and his son, who was said to have acted out of misguided loyalty, received ten.

Curiously, in Standen's case none of the lessons of earlier decades appear to have been learned. He had been under suspicion for a great deal of his career but, despite this, continued his inexorable rise, lasting a full thirty-three years in law enforcement. Along the way he had been adversely named in royal commissions, faced accusations of destroying evidence and, as Paul Higgins had done in Melbourne years earlier, managed to overturn adverse rulings—in Standen's case over his entry into the Australian Federal Police (AFP).

In 1982 the Stewart Royal Commission into drug trafficking heard that Standen had worked for the Federal Narcotics Bureau, then an arm of customs that later amalgamated with the AFP. In May 1979 Standen and two other narcotics agents had raided the Bondi house of a man called Udy, where they found eighteen silver foils of hashish. Standen later told Stewart that he and his colleagues had, weeks later, flushed the hash down a toilet, falsified entries into the bureau's log book to show that nothing was found in the raid and then destroyed a signed statement from Udy confessing to his ownership of the drugs, thus effectively removing any trace of the bust.

'I do not actually specifically remember the incident—I feel fairly certain I would have destroyed it by shredding', Standen told the commission about this confession. Asked by Stewart if the men were 'really trying to obliterate all traces of this incident', Standen responded, 'That is correct'. The reason they destroyed the hashish and paperwork was that the amount of drugs was less than 500 grams and so charges could not be brought under federal laws.

But AFP Chief Superintendent John Reilly, who investigated the matter after a complaint was made by New South Wales Police, offered a different version of how the agents had explained their actions. According to Reilly, the agents claimed that there had been problems with charging Udy because of lack of cooperation by local police and they then became embarrassed about having held onto the hashish for more than two weeks. Stewart said that Standen's answers during the investigation 'reflected on either his honesty or his quality as an investigator'.

Standen was charged under the *Public Service Act* and recommendations were made that he and another agent be barred from joining the AFP when the Narcotics Bureau merged into the new Commonwealth force later that year. The charge and the AFP ban were dropped because of 'indecision by members of the Department of Administrative Services and what was then Business and Consumer Affairs'. So Standen moved into the AFP, along with Allan Gregory McLean, later convicted for importing heroin into Australia.

Two of Standen's colleagues in the Udy bust, Stephen Innsley and Frank Ramaccia, came to notice again later. Ramaccia joined the New South Wales Police and was investigated by the Police Integrity Commission, though no charges were brought. Innsley was jailed for four charges of perjury at the 1982 Stewart Royal Commission.

In 1979 Standen went to work in the AFP's Sydney office, where by all accounts his gambling escalated. Federal agents who were his workmates said it was widely known that he had a problem and he was a regular punter on the horses, racking up a debt of about $70,000 at his favourite hotel near AFP headquarters.

During those years the AFP was riddled with corruption. In 1990 AFP drug-registry officer Michael Anthony Wallace was convicted of stealing $20 million worth of drugs, some of which he had hidden at his parents' home, and cash and exhibits. He was jailed for twelve years. After his release he was convicted of the manslaughter of Zoe Zou, with whom he said he was in a relationship. He had dumped her body in the Blue Mountains. In 2007 an appeal against his sentence of fourteen years was dismissed. AFP officer Allan Gregory McLean was sentenced to sixteen years' jail for helping to import millions of dollars worth of heroin from India hidden inside a consignment of soccer balls in 1988. In 2001 Cliff Foster, Standen's former boss at the Sydney drugs unit, committed suicide while under investigation for supplying heroin and possible links to a crime syndicate importing hashish from New Zealand.

In 1995 Standen's colleague Alan Taciak rolled over in the New South Wales Wood Royal Commission and alleged that seventyeight AFP officers—15 per cent of the force—were corrupt. Taciak's allegations prompted a 1996 inquiry headed by Ian Harrison, who later became a Supreme Court judge.

Harrison's final report, which is understood to have found widespread corruption in the AFP, was never released. However, in April 1997 the Attorney-General gave parliament limited details of the inquiry, which had investigated eighty-nine allegations in respect of fifty-four current members of the AFP. His statement contained the exculpatory sentence, 'It is worth noting that the AFP currently comprises approximately 2700 persons'.

According to the statement, Harrison had found that many of Taciak's allegations related to times long ago and were to some extent based on gossip and rumour for which no supporting evidence was found. Those matters that Taciak witnessed or in which he was directly involved, where his allegations might be more soundly based, were thoroughly investigated by the inquiry and recommendations were made where appropriate. Every serving AFP officer invited to attend or otherwise cooperate with the inquiry did so, without exception. However, the statement did not add that many agents escaped investigation simply by quitting the AFP.

Harrison made no adverse findings in respect of forty-six of the fifty-four officers. In each instance he found that there was no reliable basis on which to recommend any further steps be taken. He also examined twenty allegations involving seven of the remaining eight officers. While he found that many could not be substantiated, he did recommend that some allegations against seven officers be referred to the AFP commissioner in order to determine, in light of the material available, whether the commissioner retained confidence in those officers. In respect of the eighth officer, Harrison recommended that one issue, going back some fifteen years, be referred to the DPP for consideration as to whether any charges should be laid. Many thought the whole thing was a whitewash.

Standen met Diane James in the AFP drug-targeting unit in 1995. She later married Bakhos 'Bill' Jalalaty, left the AFP and went to work with him in their smallgoods company. Standen and Diane Jalalaty kept in touch, but he became closer to her husband than to her.

That year, 1995, was also the year Standen took voluntary redundancy from the AFP and joined the New South Wales Crime Commission. There he was in charge of what was known as the Gymea Team, which had responsibility for investigating organised crime, drug importation and the manufacture and distribution of drugs.

In 2005 Michael Nicholas Hurley, variously described as a criminal 'head honcho' of a new east-coast milieu or the Coogee Mob, was arrested following a five-month investigation known as Operation Mocha. This related to the alleged cooperation of baggage handlers in smuggling drugs through Sydney airport. The October 2004 haul that ended Hurley's career had been the last thing loaded onto an Aerolíneas Argentinas flight from Chile. As a result it would be unloaded first, so that it could be removed before it reached the baggage hall in Sydney and put into a designated bin for subsequent collection. Hurley died before his trial could take place.

In 2004 Standen was involved in the authorised sale of 7 kilograms of cocaine seized from the Hurley syndicate to an authorised informant codenamed 'Tom', on the curious grounds that it could not seriously endanger anyone's health. A single kilogram was later retrieved, but Tom had either sold the remainder or buried it in bushland near Wahroonga. In any event, 6 kilograms was never recovered.

In late 2004 the Crime Commission received information from an informer that Englishman James Kinch, who was overseas, was a 'big mover' of drugs. In early 2006 Australian police were tipped off by their Dutch counterparts to the plan, which was allegedly being masterminded by Kinch and involving Bakhos Jalalaty, who now had a food-importing and-distribution business in Blacktown.

On 19 December 2005, $47,192 was transferred by Kinch into a bank account belonging to Jalalaty's company. Payments totalling $47,000 were made from the bank account to Standen in December 2005, and in January and February 2006. These transactions amounted to a gift from Kinch to Standen. The gift was not made directly, because Standen did not want the Crime Commission to know that he was receiving money from the Englishman, who was later giving evidence at his trial, or that Kinch had offered to send him as a Christmas present—as one does—the amount of money required for an operation on his eyes. However, the cost of the operation would have been only $5000 or at most $10,000. From May 2006, police and investigators, including Standen's colleagues, intercepted thousands of conversations between Standen, Kinch and Jalalaty. Standen's role in the massive importation plan would be to advise on the movements of customs officers and so pinpoint a time when it would be safe to import drugs.

On 15 September 2007 Jalalaty and Standen met at a Sydney cafe, where they discussed the incongruity of rice being sent by a company named Elegant Hosiery and whether such a name would attract the authorities' attention. Standen gave advice to Jalalaty about how he should answer in the event of his being arrested, and also spoke about customs procedures for inspecting imported containers and the profit that could be made from the venture. He said, 'They will probably make from 100 to 120 a kilo'. Jalalaty then said, 'So if they bring in 100 kilos it makes 12 million profit and he goes half with ... the biggest mule and we go thirds'.

Unaware of the around-the-clock surveillance, Standen and Jalalaty pressed on. In their communications the three of them adopted pseudonyms, including female names. Jalalaty was usually referred to as 'Myrtle'. Kinch was referred to by a variety of female names, including 'Jo-Jo'. Standen was usually referred to as 'Maurice'.

In May 2010 Jalalaty pleaded guilty to conspiring to import a commercial quantity of pseudoephedrine. He received ten years with a minimum of six to be served. Standen fought to the end. On 11 August 2011, after a five-month trial, a jury found him guilty of conspiring to import and supply 300 kilograms of pseudoephedrine, which could be used to produce $60 million worth of 'ice' or crystal meth. He was also found guilty of perverting the course of justice and sentenced to twenty-two years in jail with a minimum of sixteen to be served. In sentencing Standen the judge said he found 'that by his acceptance of this [initial] substantial sum of money Mr Standen was irretrievably corruptly compromised, so far as Kinch was concerned'. Many might think he had compromised himself years earlier.

In 2011 former New South Wales Police Integrity Commissioner and Australian Crime Commissioner John Pritchard resigned from his $417,000-a-year job and began working as a salesman at a Ray's Outdoors store in Caringbah. Since the report on his conduct was embargoed not everything is crystal clear, but it appears that Pritchard had leaked confidential information to the media in an effort to make the Police Integrity Commission (PIC) look better. He had left the PIC for a top job with the Australian Crime Commission in January the previous year, nine months before his five-year term was due to expire. Six months into his new job he was obliged to offer his resignation.

One increasing worry for all states has been the potential infiltration of its officers by a new breed of outlaw motorcycle gang members, in particular those of the Comancheros and Bandidos. In March 2013 there were allegations that Victorian and other states' officers were taking drugs supplied by bikers, using biker-owned tattoo parlours and getting free entry into strip clubs run by gang members. As far back as 2004 a potential AFP raid on multimillionaire drug dealer Amad 'Jay' Malkoun, then president of the Comancheros, had been compromised by leaked information. In February 2011 the multi-agency trafficking investigation Operation Corsair was aborted when Malkoun received a tip-off that he was on its list and being targeted by police. Investigations by the now disbanded OPI and other agencies identified several Victoria Police officers associating with Malkoun or members of his criminal syndicate over several years.

In April 2013 Victorian Police Commissioner Kenneth Lay admitted that the force was investigating breaches of its LEAP computer system dating back three years, with sensitive files allegedly having been sold to motorcycle-gang members. Task Force Eagle was established to tackle the problem. 'It is not just about compromising Victoria Police now; it is about compromising the organisation in five, 10 or 15 years' time', said Lay.

Recent reports of police officers hobnobbing with bikie-gang members in rural Victoria and at high-end city functions suggest that the lines between the gang in blue and those they pursue may be blurring. Just as organised crime has put moles in place in both business and government, it will be interesting to see when, rather than if, the first motorcycle-gang mole planted in a force is unearthed.

16

CONTROLLING CORRUPTION: WHERE TO FROM HERE?

Whether it is possible to safeguard officers from corruption will be the big question for the twenty-first century. An officer at the 1972 Knapp Commission on the New York police made the definitive statement:

> There are three kinds of men in the department ... I call them the birds, the grass eaters and the meat eaters. The birds just fly up. They don't eat anything, either because they are honest or because they don't have any good opportunities. The grass eaters, well they'll accept a cup of coffee or a free meal or a television set wholesale from a merchant but they draw a line. The meat eaters are different. They're out looking. They're on a pad with gamblers, they deal in junk, or they'll compromise a homicide investigation for money.

So how and why does a young constable become bent? If you assume there is any scanning process on entry to eliminate potentially corrupt officers, corruption can be seen to begin after the recruit has signed on. Obviously there will be exceptions, such as the children of previously corrupt officers—Monkey Fergusson and his son Don are a fine example—who already know the ropes. But it seems clear that officers are generally corrupted after they join the force.

Nearly 150 years ago barrister Howard Vincent, assisting the 1877 inquiry into Scotland Yard's CID, wrote:

> I am also of the opinion that it is impossible for the majority of men to be in contact for any length of time with all the worst features of human nature, in its most repulsive aspects, without incurring the most enormous danger of moral contagion. Proofs of this are unfortunately not wanting.

More recently, about forty years ago sociologist William Ker Muir Jr argued that all police officers faced a basic conflict. No matter what, sooner or later a recruit would find themself in a situation from which they could not exit without corrupting themself. A former New Scotland Yard detective puts the situation rather sourly. He is, of course, speaking specifically of England, but it might just as well be Victoria, Queensland, South Australia, Western Australia or New South Wales—or Detroit or Paris, for that matter:

If Bill Bloggs joins the Met and goes to Hendon [training school] even at the early stage he may see that the Job is very much a closed shop; there may be hints that minor forms of impropriety will be overlooked, that what was referred to as being 'institutionally racial' is in real terms nothing but the harmless canteen culture and that the lily can always be gilded—so long as it is not over-embellished.

Arriving at his first station, this will come home to him even more and in those first weeks he has the choice to stay (and forcibly become part or it) or go. There is no middle ground: if he decides to stay but to be aloof, he will be so unpopular and shunned that life will be misery and, without doubt, the day will come when he will be required to play some part in something which will offend his principles—'noble cause' stuff.

So he stays. There will be a few 'noble cause' matters perhaps, but he will be one of the lads, part of the great spectrum. Time passes and he is promoted, perhaps even to high rank—but those who remain beneath him back at the station will know that he is far from white and in the event of problems he can be relied on to help. And those above him (who have done it all before) will also know that he is 'to be trusted'.

> You ask how it can be stopped: in a word, it can't. Power corrupts, doesn't it, in no matter what field! Many [policemen] feel that Mark [the commissioner who took over the Met police after the scandals of the flying, porn and vice squads in the 1960s and 1970s] did irreparable damage. Okay, the CID was bent to some extent, but they did the job. The villains went to gaol, serious crime was sorted out, the gangs sent away—probably screaming 'fit-up' as they went—but all was seen to be in order; the price for what was excellent policing being turning a blind eye to a degree of naughtiness along the way. That, many feel, is better than today where no-one does anything, the copper is scared of being sued, political correctness rules over all and if the WPC is referred to (in jest) as 'the station bike' she can sue for God knows how much.
>
> Did not the public have a better crack of the whip pre-Mark? Today, do not the public have the policing they richly deserve?

He could have added the fear that when the non-cooperator is in a dangerous situation his calls for aid will not be answered as swiftly as calls from those whose feet are under the canteen table.

One former Victorian officer thinks that the induction into corruption is not so swift but that when it occurs it is deadly. 'For the first two years, your head goes up with power. That's when they decide to go one way or another. It's about power rather than the money. But once a copper puts a wad in his pocket he's gone forever.'

So a senior officer who is now trying to eradicate corruption is highly likely to have experienced it at first hand in their younger days and at the time they may have participated or turned a blind eye. If the former, they are at the mercy of their colleagues. If they lean on them too heavily they have a perfect response and the officer, because of their senior position, has more to lose. They may be able to cut a plea bargain by naming the officer. In turn he or she may not have an officer senior to them to name.

It is the whole police culture that lends itself to corruption. For a start the possibility of serious injury promotes a high degree of solidarity within the work group—as it does in other professions where there is a similarly high risk of injury; for example, among fire fighters and steeplechase jockeys—and encourages bonding. For the most part loyalty is to the group rather than to the wider entity. In a paper for the Queensland police department in relation to the Fitzgerald inquiry, Harrison, Hohenhaus and Pitman set out the characteristics that supported a belief in 'solidarity through secrecy'. In turn, that bonding can lead to a willingness to cover up. 'Straight' detectives may well know of incidents of dishonesty or violence, but because of the close links they have with the offending officer they are less likely to dob them in than are people faced with dishonesty in other occupations, say a supermarket manager who discovers that a cashier has been stealing. 'Secrecy is loyalty: secrecy is solidarity.'

One sociological explanation that has worldwide support is the sub-culture theory. It runs that a sub-culture is a group inside the host group. So in policing the host group stands for discipline, law and order, integrity and social harmony, while the sub-culture, or canteen culture, stands for drinking, whoring, excitement, fighting, racism and so on. Sociologist Maurice Punch has argued that the police organisation is not a harmonious integrated entity with a comforting consensus but 'is rather characterised by a deeply divided pattern of semi-autonomous and often conflicting units'.

A second explanation is that policing is full of strain and contradiction: police are set very difficult targets to achieve and because of the controls and hurdles they have to jump, bending of the rules is the only way to achieve them. In their paper for the Fitzgerald inquiry, Harrison, Hohenhaus and Pitman wrote, 'The demands made on the police are so diffuse and contradictory that the police task is unworkable and this leads to an atmosphere of "duplicity and hypocrisy" and of methods bordering on "trickery and stealth"'—in other words, the Machiavellian concept of the end justifying the means. In this police are aided by the public's complicity. Provided that someone is arrested and convicted and the streets are, for the time being, safe, the general public does not mind too much if it is not the right person. One example of this is the convictions of Darryl Beamish and John Button in Western Australia when the real culprit who had been terrorising post-Second World War Perth was Edgar Cooke. If the wrong person is convicted the police can justify this internally with the argument that it was the fault of lawyers, juries, judges. If convictions are quashed then it is the fault of appeal judges in allowing these people back on the streets. There is also a tendency within police to close ranks. If a conviction does not follow an arrest, again it is not the fault of police but of corrupt defence lawyers, incompetent prosecutors, fools on the jury and weak judges.

A third suggestion is that of control, which in police work is difficult to establish. More than in any other work, discretion is exercised in the public interest. The officer can take action or not; they might make further inquiries or not. There is no sensible way of reviewing this discretion, but it has the potential for corruption.

In the 1970s in a European conference on policing, London Detective Chief Superintendent John Simmonds advanced six reasons for officers becoming corrupt and they still ring true. The first is frustration with the court, which the officer in the case believes has dealt too leniently with the accused. Next time they will deal with the criminal themselves—perhaps a few biffs, such as those New South Wales' rugby league–playing Bumper Farrell would hand out in the city's Kings Cross area to show who is the boss and to induce a bit of respect. What's so bad about giving a career criminal a bit of a hiding? The result can be mutually beneficial: the officer feels good that they have administered summary justice and the 'defendant' does not get another conviction logged against them. However, the drowning of Dr Duncan, who was thrown into Adelaide's Torrens River, is another—extreme—example of this kind of thinking. Homophobic officers were punishing gay men because the courts generally did not deal with them in the way the officers wanted. Sections of the public felt that Victoria's armed robbery squad also displayed this sort of attitude when some eleven young men suspected (in one case almost certainly wrongly) of serious crime were shot dead between 1987 and 1989. This led to reprisals and the execution of two young officers, who were ambushed and shot to death on 12 October 1988.

The second is greed—bent for self. There are signs that forces such as Queensland's are looking at officers with problems such as debts, excessive drinking, gambling and so on, and are setting up early-intervention counselling to reduce the temptation to take bribes to feed such habits.

The third is very low-level corruption: chance temptation, such as not handing in all the money found in a lost wallet. Integrity testing is now being used more extensively worldwide to weed out suspect officers. In the United States in one post-Knapp sting in Brooklyn's 77th Precinct a drug dealer who complained that the police were stealing cash and drugs from him was wired and obtained evidence against two officers. In turn they dominoed, dobbing in their colleagues until thirteen officers were suspended. In Los Angeles it turned out that members of the burglar alarm response unit were looting the stores after answering calls. Integrity officers then set up a fake alarm in a store where expensive electronic equipment left a mark on anyone who touched it. The final haul involved a number of officers and a truckful of electronic equipment.

In one of New South Wales' first integrity tests after the Wood Royal Commission, Senior Constable Gregory Joseph Sweeney stole cash in a pre-arranged trap. In a scenario reminiscent of the 'long' con in which a variety of players act out a pre-arranged script, a Nissan car was reported stolen to Sweeney, who was told that there was a missing vanity bag in the car. Sweeney found the car and in turn was filmed pocketing $270 from the bag. He received a twoyear good-behaviour bond. In 1997 more than twenty officers in New South Wales failed various other integrity tests set up by Deputy Commissioner Mal Brammer. These often involved fellow officers, disguised as members of the public, putting temptation in the way of the targeted high-risk officer. Commissioner Peter Ryan bravely explained that since the men being tested were suspect anyway it was likely that there would be a high percentage of failures.

The fourth of Simmonds' reasons was coercion, which he rightly considered the most insidious form of police corruption. Officers are placed by their peer group in a position where they are suborned into corrupt practices. Often it takes a basic test to establish the strength of the individual and find out how far they will go. If the officer shows strong character, the matter will be laughed off and the corrupt core of officers will ensure that he or she is not in a position to inform on them. An example of this is straight officers who are not used in raids on gaming clubs when cash will be swept into the raiding officers' pockets. Coupled with coercion is the fifth explanation—misguided loyalty to the group, and not the force and the public.

The last occurs because of mistakes that have to be covered up. One example is where a murder takes place, but before the body is discovered a beat officer finds a hammer in a hedge nearby and takes it home. He later realises what has happened and tells his sergeant, who tells him to put the hammer back where he found it, to be discovered later by detectives.

It is common to think that police corruption is a thing of the past—that, surely, with all the safeguards in place, all these alphabet committees and boards such as PIC, NIC, ACC, CMC and so on, things really are back to rotten apples rather than rotten orchards. If so, good: this book will then serve simply as a historical document. But, as humourist Damon Runyan wrote, 'It is not the way to bet'. In March 2013 it was announced that there would be an inquiry into corruption and cover-ups in London's Met police going back over the last twenty years. Asked how he thought deviance could be contained, journalist and former policeman CH Rolph said:

> I don't think it can. It's universal and endemic. It invades every level of administration and government in every country. If ever 'social ethics' became an educational subject which had a firmer basis than mythological religions, which themselves eat away at the communal importance of truth, I mean simply telling the truth, the chances would begin to improve.

The key words in eliminating corruption are education and supervision. Professor David Dixon of the University of New South Wales said that, though things had improved substantially:

> Police corruption also has to be seen not as deviance but as the way things used to be done. There has been a broader change in police culture. Formerly the recruits were young men in a working class job that wasn't very different from any other working class occupation. The influence of women in the police is significant and Christine Nixon must be thanked for that. Now effectively in New South Wales a degree is required for entry

> and there are links between Charles Sturt University and police college.

Of course there will be resistance. Old timers, seen as dinosaurs by reformers, resent seeing what was once their force—now service—turned into what they see as something resembling the Salvos. They may change, but it will be in the Marxist way of maintaining the status quo.

The general, if perhaps optimistic, view is that Australia will never again see the systematic corruption of the Askin and Bjelke-Petersen years. 'The massive corruption of whole sections couldn't happen now. There are too many whistleblowers. You couldn't have it where a man like Krahe could run for years', as journalist Richard Hall wrote in 1986. Much will also depend on the press. In the past journalists were protective of their sources, whom they would praise to the skies. Bill Jenkings, who worshipped Fred Krahe, is an example. The Sydney and Melbourne editions of *Truth* were at least critical of the police, but Queensland's edition was protective of the corrupt Bischof. What will not help is the courts' current attitude to suppression orders, which can last for years. 'Secrecy is solidarity.'

Report after report to a large extent lays the blame for police misconduct on lack of management supervision. Of course, a chief commissioner cannot be expected to know if a constable breaks wind in the bush, but his superior ought to know, and in turn that man's superior should know and so on.

Whistleblower Simon Illingworth believes that a three-pronged preventative campaign against police corruption must be maintained:

> Ethical decision-making must be taught and reinforced until it becomes second nature. Focus should be on ensuring the culture is correct across all ranks from senior officers down to new recruits so they can 'buy in'. That way corrupt employees will fear the honest employees, not vice versa. This will increase the risk of reporting and sanctioning less than honourable conduct.

While Professor David Dixon believes:

> If there is to be further corruption it will not be the kind of corruption of the past. We have a more politically sophisticated society today. The corruption will no longer be the brown bag variety but harder to define as criminality.

And Queensland lawyer, writer and lecturer Chris Nyst thinks:

> At the moment, all is quiet on the Western front. But politicians of all persuasions know getting tough on crime is good politics. And unfortunately unqualified support for 'our boys in blue' historically has meant turning a blind eye to police misbehaviour. Once the rules go out the window

for the sake of political expedience, it's only a matter of time before corruption takes a foot-hold.

The days of corruption on the heroic scale of Queensland in the 1980s, New South Wales from the 1960s and Victoria over the decades are probably gone, but that does not mean that the plethora of integrity boards and intervention schemes to help officers with drink, gambling and other problems have won outright. No one will be foolish enough to say that corruption in the police or any other public service can be eradicated. At best it can be managed. But there are again signs that there are troubles at the top. On 4 May 2014 constitutional lawyer and commentator Eric Dyrenfurth, writing in *The Age,* slammed Victoria's new Independent Broad-Based Anti-Corruption Commission as a 'puny toothless tiger' shackled by 'chicken hearted legislation'. In 2014 in New South Wales the police minister stood down over allegations of non-police related corruption. There have also been allegations that Operation Mascot, which investigated over 100 New South Wales officers in 1999, was founded on false information and a perjured affidavit. It is alleged that its flawed basis was covered up for over a decade. Whether a full inquiry will follow remains to be seen.

Philosopher George Santayana wrote, 'Those who cannot remember the past are condemned to repeat it'. New York's Knapp Commission found that cycles of corruption occur every twenty years or so, the cycle being discovery, publicity, nominal reform and gradual loss of public interest in the reform process. If the pattern continues, and Santayana's words are ignored, another cycle is due shortly. Watch this space.

In fact we did not have to watch this space for long. In the autumn of 2014 a new and extremely dangerous scandal broke out in Victoria. It is one which will have serious repercussions throughout Australia. Over ten years ago the Victoria police recruited a lawyer, known only as Lawyer X to the public but well known by lawyers, police and other cognoscenti who handled major defence cases to act as a registered informer who gave them information on drug barons, hitmen, and the gangland wars.

As a result it is possible that cases were compromised and convictions may be overturned. There could also be misconduct or criminal claims against police—some senior—and further allegations of corruption, which will need to be tested.

In April 2014 the Victoria Police were granted an injunction preventing *The Herald Sun* from publishing any information at all about Lawyer X. *The Herald Sun* editor Damon Johnston said that Victorians deserved to know the full truth, 'The police last night moved to prevent us from publishing important details that go to the heart of the public interest.'

There were immediate calls for a Royal Commission but these were pre-empted when in July the Independent Broad-based Anti-Corruption Commission

(IBAC) appointed the former Justice of Appeal The Hon Murray Kellam AO QC to 'examine the conduct of Victoria Police in relation to the management of human sources, and in particular the issue of whether or not such management has complied with appropriate ethical and legal obligations'. The IBAC Commissioner Stephen O'Bryan QC delegated all of his duties, functions and powers to Mr Kellam under section 32(5) of the *IBAC Act 2011.*

NOTES

1. From 'Bent for the Job' to Downright Criminal

In 2006 he was ordered to pay in excess of $286,000: *R v Eade* [2002] NSWCCA 257; *State of NSW v Eade* [2006] NSWSC 84; *O'Sullivan v The Queen* [2002] NSWCCA 98.

As a result the police downed tools: Nat Arch (UK) MEPO 2/7012.

Don 'Shady' Lane: Don Lane, *Trial and Error.*

The rotten-apple theory won't work any longer: T Newburn, *Criminology,* p.625.

The rotten apple theory of police corruption that it is one of individual moral failure: K Bryett and A Harrison, *Policing in the Community,* p.74.

The question of free food: Cathy Alexander, 'Is Macca's supersizing our cops?'

I think his model is a bit simplistic: Richard Evans, conversation with James Morton, 4 September 2012.

American sociologist ER Stoddard: Alfred W McCoy, *Drug Traffic,* pp.32–3. See ER Stoddard, 'The informal code of police deviancy: a group approach to blue coat crime', in *Journal of Criminal Law, Criminology and Police Science* (1968), 59 [2].

He certainly should have been caught in Queensland: 'Police let wanted man off the hook', *Sydney Morning Herald,* 13 January 1982.

By the spring of 1983 the hunt for him stepped up: *Advertiser,* 12 September 1983.

Throughout his sentence Creed's behaviour was exemplary: Nigel Hunt, *The First Police Union;* John Silvester and Andrew Rule, *Tough;* Patrick McDonald, 'Life and crimes of Colin Creed'.

2. Doomed to Be Bad

Damper was all there was to mark the celebrations: John White, *Journal of a Voyage to New South Wales,* p.141.

In 1789 he was forced to resign: Andrew Keenan, 'It began with the first constable'.

The New South Wales Corps, known as the Rum Corps: The colony, like many British territories at the time, was short of coins and rum, mainly from Bengal, soon became the medium of trade. The officers of the corps were able to use their position and wealth to buy all the imported rum and then exchange it for goods and labour at very favourable rates.

Hannibal Hawkins Macarthur: David Philips, *William Augustus Miles,* pp.118–19.

When Wilson's authorship was revealed: *Sydney Herald,* 18 June 1841.

about one of the most thorough knaves: *Bell's Life in Sydney and Sporting Review,* 31 October 1846.

A select committee on police was formed in 1847: WA Miles, *Evidence before the Select Committee on Police 1847,* pp.17–24, in New South Wales Parliamentary Papers 1847, vol.2, pp.55–64.

***Bell's Life* thought him 'about as queer and as funny...':** *Bell's Life,* 19 December 1844.

Here lies the remains of William Augustus Miles: David Philips, *William Augustus Miles.*

Evidence given by Mr Keck and Captain Innes: *Sydney Morning Herald,* 24 August 1849.

That burglaries should be fearfully on the increase: *Sydney Morning Herald,* 27 August 1849.

Keck, his wife, Innes and the turnkey Hibbs were dismissed: James Morton and Susanna Lobez, *Kings of Stings; Sydney Morning Herald,* 24 August 1849.

However, on the Queen's Birthday holiday in 1848: Peter N Grabosky, *Sydney in Ferment,* pp.75–6; Terry Irving and Rowan J Cahill, *Radical Sydney; Sydney Morning Herald,* 12 January 1850.

In the 1850s CGB Lockhart: *Archives of New South Wales,* 2/674.15, p.6.

A peaceful traveller, or even an armed escort: *Sydney Morning Herald,* 2 July 1919.

With reference to the charges of bribery generally: Royal Commission on Alleged Chinese Gambling, 1892.

No less than six cases of police misconduct: *Argus,* 8 February 1853.

The select committee on police in 1852 was told: George Brouwer, *Past Patterns—Future Directions.*

However, magistrates were often perceived: Dean Wilson, *The Beat.*

The arrangement under which the police took a share: John O'Sullivan, *Mounted Police of Victoria & Tasmania.*

Fifty officers from the paramilitary Irish Constabulary: Nat Arch (UK) HO 45/4312.

Nothing could be worse than its condition when he took the reins: Cited in Robert Haldane, *The People's Force,* p.39.

After his retirement as chief: John O'Sullivan, *Mounted Police of Victoria & Tasmania,* pp.79–82.

Standish was not a good choice: Dean Wilson, *The Beat,* pp.162–4.

There were clear examples of favouritism: John Sadleir, *Recollections of a Victorian Police Officer.*

In November 1882 he was nearly thrown through the window of the Melbourne Club: There are various reasons given for his near defenestration in the Melbourne Club. First, that he called the colonel 'Jumbo', and, second, that he had been insulting him all evening. The latter is curious because on five of the six times the colonel was put up for temporary membership Standish was his proposer.

As for Winch and Larner: *Argus,* 16 October and 11 November 1882.

One does not expect the genius of a Sherlock Holmes: John Christie, Private Papers.

3. Spooks, Strikes and Scandals

***Truth* newspaper interviewed twenty-three bookmakers:** *Truth,* 20 February 1925.

'[An] increase in burglaries in city premises': *Round Table,* March 1924, vol.xiv.

'In the police strike riots seventy-eight shops were smashed': *Round Table,* March 1924, vol.xiv.

The hapless Nicholson was left isolated: Robert Haldane, *The People's Force,* p.180.

As is so often the case, until this time: Victorian Parliamentary Debates, 15 July 1925, p.151; *Argus,* 21 March, 4 April and May– July 1925.

Do you know that the Commissioner of Police was found: Robert Haldane, *The People's Force,* p.197.

Nor was Blamey necessarily a good judge of character: John Hetherington, *Blamey.* p.63.

Another version, admittedly third-hand at best: Kevin Morgan, *Gun Alley.*

Blamey was finished: Royal Commission on the Alleged Shooting at and Wounding of John O'Connell Brophy, VPRS 3992 and VPRS 2570. Brian Hardiman, in his paper *Police Accountability,* says that crucial files on the affair are missing from the archives.

His interim findings on the CIB: AM Duncan, *Interim Report,* 1937, pp.8, 9, 12–15.

When questioned, both men freely admitted their actions: Police File 46/8682/14.

When interviewed many years later, Victorian chief commissioner: Alan Dower, *Deadline,* p.21.

4. Chief Commissioner William John MacKay

Scots-born MacKay has been variously described: Larry Writer, *Razor,* p.116; Susan Borham, 'Corruption in high places'.

Razorhurst, Gunhurst, Bottlehurst, Dopehurst: *Truth,* 23 September 1928.

Even the rather more sedate *Sydney Morning Herald:* *Sydney Morning Herald,* 10 and 11 July 1928.

It was during the debate on the proposed legislation that Linda Littlejohn and Jessie Street: Letter from L Littlejohn and J Street to members of the Legislative Assembly. Street's son Laurence Whistler Street became chief justice of the Supreme Court of New South Wales and conducted the inquiry into the involvement of Premier Neville Wran in the Murray Farquhar scandal; see 'MacKay's Legacy: Cops and Crooks in Cahoots'.

At the time, the City of Sydney was infested with criminals: Lance Hoban, *A Centenary History of the New South Wales Police Force,* pp.60–1.

The special powers conferred later came to be an instrument: Justice JRT Wood, *Royal Commission into the New South Wales Police Service,* vol.1, 1997, pp.53–6.

The detectives have now such a firm grip on the underworld: *Smith's Weekly,* 31 October 1931.

According to his admiring biographer, Vince Kelly: Vince Kelly, *The Bogeyman.*

The whole system in connection with starting price betting prosecutions reeks with injustice: New South Wales Parliamentary Debates, 3 March 1936.

First, you narrow the terms of reference: Trevor Haken and Sean Padraic, *Confessions of a Crooked Cop.*

Variously described as a man who would believe the best: Vince Kelly, *The Bogeyman; Truth,* 7 March 1937.

It has been my unpleasant duty and **Without in any way seeking to minimise:***Royal Commission into SP Betting Report,* 1932, p.116.

Kelly told the officer in charge: *Truth,* 20 April 1947.

Reilly had long had good police connections before Kelly: David Hickie, *The Prince and the Premier,* p.130.

At first it was known as the 'Basher Squad': Basher squads were nothing new in policing. In the 1920s they had been used in Sheffield, England, by Sir Percy Sillitoe, much to the delight of the press, and he went on to use the same tactics in Glasgow.

At the beginning of February 1946: David Hickie, *The Prince and the Premier,* p.274.

5. Ray 'Gunner' Kelly and Co

One of the best detectives of the New South Wales police: *Sydney Morning Herald,* 4 February 1960.

For a time Kelly, born in New South Wales in 1906: *Sydney Morning Herald,* 25 August, and 11, 12 and 18 September 1930; *Argus,* 29 August 1930.

The next year Kelly worked with the riot squad: Interview with Tim Girling-Butcher for *Sin City.*

Although some of the photographs of him appear to show: Evan Whitton, *Can of Worms II,* Chapter 1: The Police.

Those Kelly took on and groomed included Murray Riley: Smith was the son of James Smith, the ex-boxer whose arm was swallowed by a shark in what became one of the great murder cases of the 1930s, the Shark Arm Murder.

If I was investigating Sir Robert Askin: Evan Whitton, 'Detective accused of corruption'.

No one can open one (an illegal casino) without the permission of the Premier: Kevin Perkins, *The Gambling Man.*

Krahe had joined the police as a cadet in 1940: David Hickie, *The Prince and the Premier,* p.280.

After he'd arrest you, the paying began: George Freeman, *George Freeman.*

I never had run-ins with them at all: Interview with Tim Girling-Butcher for *Sin City.*

An incident that backed up Freeman's assessment took place in February 1972: Tony Maguire, 'The case of the missing victim'; Andrew Keenan, 'Purge of corruption seems doomed to fail'; Jennie Curtin, 'Death of former policeman remains a mystery'; Keith Gosman, 'Heroin in the ice cream'.

He [Krahe] was a crook all right: Richard Hall, *Disorganized Crime,* p.56.

Following a flat-warming party at Brifman's new brothel: Matthew Condon, *Three Crooked Kings* and 'Desperate measures'.

However, Krahe's champion Bill Jenkings wrote: For an account of the careers of Kelly, Krahe and Fergusson, see Evan Whitton, *Can of Worms II* and David Hickie, *The Prince and the Premier.*

6. MacKay's Legacy

Such actions and attitudes were not uncommon: *Sydney Morning Herald,* 10 August 2013.

On 10 May 1972 Roger James: *Age,* 20 and 22 May and 1 July 1972.

Scotland Yard sent over Detective Superintendent Bob McGowan: In a curious twist, the Scotland Yard officers were later gaoled in England on fraud and conspiracy charges. After he retired McGowan was sentenced for a Value Added Tax fraud and O'Hanlon received seven years for accepting bribes from London pornographer James Humphreys.

One result of Duncan's death: James Morton and Susanna Lobez, *Gangland North, South & West.*

There was no evidence against him in my inquiry: Conversation with James Morton, 11 November 1996.

I was a cadet when Fred Hanson was commissioner: Conversation with James Morton, 22 November 2012.

In 1967 Allan, or possibly his then assistant Don Fergusson: PN Grabosky, *Wayward Governance;* David Hickie, *The Prince and the Premier;* Evan Whitton, *Can of Worms* and *Can of Worms II.*

More seriously, in 1968 he made some extraordinary decisions: *Canberra Times,* 1–8 July 1968; *NSW Police Journal,* 5 July 1968.

As for the baccarat clubs: Quoted in David Hickie, *The Prince and the Premier.*

By 1974 Hanson was slacking off: Richard Hall, *Disorganized Crime,* p.209.

After Hanson retired it is alleged that he flew drugs down from Cairns: David Hickie, *The Prince and the Premier.*

Johnny James organised the meat for the Barbecue Set: Conversation with James Morton, 29 November 2013.

Beck found Darlinghurst police station in 1977 to be in complete disarray: Quentin Dempster, *Honest Cops; Sun-Herald,* 30 May 1982.

Lennie McPherson and George Freeman may have been the Mr Bigs of Sydney crime: Conversation with James Morton, 6 November 2006.

It's a sad state of affairs pervading Sydney at the moment: Quoted in Malcolm Brown, 'Indecent proposals'.

Jim Lees, a devout Christian, was the next to be appointed commissioner: Malcolm Brown, 'Nemesis of crims and corruption'.

People survived because of being an embarrassment: Email to Susanna Lobez.

the death of 24-year-old drug dealer and socialite Maria Hission: Fashion designer and lover of solicitors, models and criminals, Hission lived in Rose Bay, Sydney. A darling of the drug dealers known as the Windsor Castle Set, she disappeared on Christmas Eve 1975 after she had dinner with her mother. Her body surfaced off North Head two weeks later and was identified through her jewellery. She had been tied to an anchor after being shot in the head with a .32 bullet. Almost certainly her body had been dumped from a boat. Ten days later an associate of the Double Bay Mob refused to answer any police questions about the suggestion that he had borrowed a boat on the night of her disappearance, and was later said to have left Australia. It seems that Hission had only reluctantly become involved in the heroin trade and wanted out. Parrington was unable to make an arrest.

7. Whistleblowing v The Brotherhood

In December 1971 computer expert Philip Neville Arantz: A Lauer, Royal Commission transcript, 18 November 1996, pp.34428–9.

Arantz was not the first officer to draw attention to the practice: R Blissett, 'Vale CIB', *NSW Police News,* vol.67, no.10.

Arantz's punishment was swift and harsh: In 1993 MP John Hatton raised the issue in parliament during a debate on the final report of the joint select committee on police administration, commenting that 'psychiatry is a weapon in the police force', adding that psychiatric advice had been the 'weapon' used to dismiss pioneer whistleblower Philip Arantz from the force in 1971 after he had leaked crime statistics.

I was the odd one but there were so many others: PN Arantz, *Collusion of Powers;* Keith Gosman, 'Baling out of the force'.

There was no way you could work if you didn't 'weigh-in': Jenny Gregory, 'The deconstruction of memory', p.78.

Greg Wheadon, son of a chief inspector: Ellen Connolly, 'Police whistleblower awarded $660,000', *Sydney Morning Herald,* 3 February 2001.

On 26 October 1993 questions were raised in parliament: Parliament of New South Wales, Legislative Assembly, 26 October 1993, p.4410.

There was also sexual harassment and drunkenness: This is common among police worldwide. The celebrated English detective Reg Spooner, called to investigate the body of a man found in a car, simply released the handbrake and watched the vehicle move slowly downhill so another division had the responsibility.

Geoff Schuberg found the situation to be similar: Interview for *Sin City.*

If you didn't agree with something you were expected to look the other way: Deborah Locke, *Watching the Detectives,* p.88.

'No police officer can claim that he or she has always followed the strict Victoria Police code of ethics': Simon Illingworth, *Filthy Rat,* pp.50–1.

In fact over the years and in various states officers have spied on each other: Malcolm Brown and Jennifer Cooke, 'The circle of power'.

In Western Australia in 1985, *The Daily News* revealed that Police Commissioner Bill Bull had spied on Assistant Commissioner Spears: *Daily News,* 14 November 1985.

Illingworth, called a 'maggot' and a 'filthy rat': Email to Susanna Lobez, 13 March 2014.

A decade after the shutters hit the fan: George Brouwer, *Past Patterns—Future Directions,* p.82; Selma Milovanovic, 'Corruption watchdog probes 35 police'.

I went out in the morning and my car was completely vandalised: *Four Corners,* 9 February 1998.

partly because of the spectacle of a person being publicly disloyal: *Four Corners,* 9 February 1998.

Whistleblowers are always accused of being mentally ill: Email to Susanna Lobez, 26 February 2014.

It was well known in those days: Interview for *Sin City.*

Untangling corruption almost always leads to the disclosure of secrets and the erosion of

underground loyalty: Simon Illingworth, *Filthy Rat,* p.130.

'It was the equivalent of a gold miner': Simon Illingworth, *Filthy Rat,* pp.144, 158, 171.

Her position was based on an early study of Australian whistleblowers: *Sydney Morning Herald,* 7 February 1998.

8. Victoria from the 1960s

It is rather amazing: Cited by PD Beattie, Motion of Condolence, Death of Colin James Bennett, Queensland Parliamentary Debates, Legislative Assembly, 18 June 2002.

In 1963 at a United Nations seminar in Canberra: 'Confessions and admissions—judges suspicious', *Age,* 1 May 1963; Julius Stone, radio broadcast, 12 May 1963.

The next year, during the investigation and questioning of three Italian men: *Age,* 12 September 1964.

From then on discussion of these corruption allegations was front-page news in *The Age:* 'Corruption claim, det. charged; others to be accused', *Age,* 19 October 1965.

In March 1966 Thompson dismissed charges: 'SM finds detective did neglect duty', *Age,* 9 March 1966.

During the year of Mr X, police morale was said to be at an all-time low: *Age,* 25 October, and 1, 2 and 9 November.

And this was the case in Victoria of one-time head of the homicide squad Jack Matthews: Gideon Haigh, *The Racket.*

Wyatt had two useful friends: Gideon Haigh, *The Racket,* pp.101, 151.

In 1959 Wyatt went to live in Ascot Vale with Elva Isabella Moran: *Age,* 8 and 9 December 1971.

Wyatt, however, was a principal witness: *Canberra Times,* 11 March 1970.

It would have been naive to suppose that responsible ministers and officials: Quoted in Russell Skelton and Fergus Shiel, 'The myth of a clean police force'; *Canberra Times,* 1–10 December 1971; Peggy Berman and Kevin Childs, *Why Isn't She Dead?;* Gideon Haigh, *The Racket;* Geoff Wilkinson, 'The power of Peg'.

Later Wyatt would be portrayed by some as a loveable rogue: Gideon Haigh, *The Racket,* p.155.

If the Victorian police thought that after the successful prosecution of Matthews: Celebrity criminal the late Mark 'Chopper' Read has claimed that Wainer, who died in 1987, was not all he might have been and would patch up shot criminals with no questions asked. Mark Read, *Chopper from the Inside,* pp.166–7.

Beach began by advertising in the newspapers: Barry Beach QC, *Report of the Board of Inquiry into Allegations against Members of the Victoria Police Force;* George Brouwer, *Past Patterns—Future Directions.*

There were, of course, the usual criminal stalwarts giving evidence of brutality: Robber and escaper Peter Gibb's criminal career ended when he suffered a heart attack after a bashing in January 2011. He had put a child in a deep freeze, he said, for a joke, but those who saw him do it lacked his sense of humour. 'Piggy' Palmer was acquitted of a 1974 murder but was later sentenced to twelve years following a string of armed robberies. Jockey Smith, who had escaped from prison, was shot by police in December 1992. In 2007 docker Joseph Power was found to be too ill to stand trial for an attack on a sex worker and was to be questioned over the disappearance of Julia Garciacelay in July 1975. Laurie Prendergast, a friend of enforcer and killer Chris Flannery, simply disappeared from his driveway one day in August 1985. Quinn died after being set on fire in July 1984 in Pentridge Prison, where he was serving a life sentence for a double murder.

they gathered in what the president of the Police Association, LJ Blogg: Robert Haldane, *The People's Force,* p.290.

9. Two Coppers, Two States

At the beginning of August 1978, painter and docker turned brothel owner Joey Hamilton: Hamilton also complained that in 1981 many members of the Caulfield car-crimes squad were regularly partying at his brothel in Glen Eira Road, Ripponlea, and requiring free sex from the prostitutes. Some officers were transferred and others fined by the Police Discipline Board: George Brouwer, *Past Patterns—Future Directions,* pp.64–5.

it needs to be recognised that apparently he had throughout his service been somewhat encouraged: George Brouwer, *Past Patterns—Future Directions,* p.68.

Including the 135 days of preliminary legal argument, the trial lasted 420 days: *R v Higgins [1994] 71 A Crim R 429; The Queen v Alistair Farquhar MacRae* [1995] VSC 108; George Brouwer, *Past Patterns—Future Directions; Age,* 7 April 1993; *Sunday Herald Sun,* 18 November 2001 and 24 April 2004.

Evan Whitton was one and he remembered one of the more memorable exchanges: Evan Whitton, *Can of Worms II,* Chapter 1: The Police.

They and four Queensland officers witnessed the unsigned confession: B Stannard, 'How we got Finch'.

In 1988 Ralph, along with drug dealer Morres George, was convicted of conspiracy: 'Career check for supergrass', *Sydney Morning Herald,* 7 July 1988.

Ten years after the killing the police could not produce anything like a complete set of papers to ICAC: Robert Klitgaard, *Controlling Corruption.*

Overall Huckstepp, who came from a Jewish family named Krivoshaw: John Dale, *Huckstepp.*

As for Drury, he was treated appallingly by his superiors: HF Purnell, *In the Matter of an Inquiry into the Investigation by the New South Wales Police Force of Circumstances Surrounding the Shooting of Detective Senior Constable M.P. Drury 6.6. 1984;* Quentin Dempster, *Honest Cops.*

[redacted]

[redacted]

10. Noble Cause Corruption

In their study of police ethics, US writers John P Crank and Michael A Caldero thought: John P Crank and Michael A Caldero, *Police Ethics,* pp.2, 6.

'There is no way you can effectively catch criminals: *Four Corners,* 7 August 2000.

The work of any investigator ... is made much easier if a suspect can be induced to confess: Torquil Dick-Erikson, 'Confessions in evidence', p.864.

The widely read American manual *Criminal Interrogation and Confessions:* Fred E Inbau et al, *Criminal Interrogation and Confessions;* WS White, 'Police trickery in inducing confessions', pp.581–629.

In any high-profile murder case the investigating officers: Christopher Bray, '"Hell, someone's cut this girl in half!"'.

Queensland's Crime and Misconduct Commission found that between 2001 and 2005 officers had prisoners removed: Robert Needham, *Dangerous Liaisons.*

I can remember witnessing people in the CIB getting full, free and voluntary confessions: Interview for *Sin City.* Later Stewart would tell Tim

Girling-Butcher that one of the detectives involved was Ray Kelly.

The third category, known as internalised false confessions: Gudjonsson and MacKeith, 'Retracted confessions', p.187; Saul M Kassin, 'False confessions', p.249.

Although he denied direct involvement in any scrumdowns: In England the practice was known as swifting.

In New South Wales, Chief Justice Laurence Street set the tone: *R v Lattouf and Carr,* NSWCCA 287/1978.

It was not until the 1991 case *McKinney v R:* [1991] HCA 6; (1991) 171 CLR 468.

The necessary information shall be obtained by the police: *Advertiser,* 28 January 1914.

In practice the third degree did not go away: Royal Commission on the Alleged Shooting at and Wounding of John O'Connell Brophy, VPRS 3992 and VPRS 2570. VPRS 3992, Unit 2590, File 29916; Robert Haldane, *The People's Force;* 'Police treatment of suspects', *Argus,* 19 June 1936; *Advertiser,* 20 June 1936.

There were allegations in the 1930s that police officers in Queensland had been resorting to force: *Morning Bulletin,* 6 June 1930.

An inquiry by the Police Complaints Commission headed by judge Eric Pratt: Police Complaints Tribunal, *Report by Police Complaints Tribunal; Telegraph,* 25 March 1986; PN Grabosky, *Wayward Governance,* chapter four; *Sunday Mail,* 16 March 2003.

Police perjury—unlike some perjuries—carries no risks: CH Rolph (ed), *The Police and the Public,* pp.146–9.

Frustrated by the failure of conventional criminal investigations: Bob Bottom, *Without Fear or Favour;* Donald Stewart, *Recollections of an Unreasonable Man; Daily Mirror,* 26 November 1981.

In his essay *Miscarriages of Justice in Serious Cases in Australia:* In Carrington et. al. (eds), *Travesty!*

11. Drugs

It's amazing how many coppers are in this business: *Sydney Morning Herald,* 6 August 1977.

Judge Anthony Collins told Gudgeon: *R v Gudgeon* [1995] QCA 506; Evan Whitton, *Can of Worms II; Sydney Morning Herald,* 25 April 1986.

In the 1990s the force's drug squad: Office of Police Integrity, *Ceja Task Force,* Seamer paragraph 2.3; Fraser, *Snouts in the Trough,* p.147.

At that time we were doling out samples of our wares: Damian Marrett, *Wired,* p.125.

Unit 2 of the drug squad: Office of Police Integrity, *Ceja Task Force: Drug Related Corruption, Third and Final Report,* 2007, p.4.

Attwood was ordered to lift its game: After the major crime squad vacated its office at St Kilda Road, renovators tinkering with a ceiling tile were startled when thirteen pistols fell from the ceiling onto their heads. Andrew Fraser, *Snouts in the Trough,* pp.183–4.

Even more unfortunately for the force, he was replaced by Detective Sergeant Wayne Strawhorn: Conversation with Susanna Lobez and James Morton, 10 December 2013.

'If they didn't have a green light to deal drugs in Victoria, they were flat-out revving the car on amber!': Damian Marrett, *Wired,* pp.66–7.

In a classic example of the ability of the police to load members of families: Andrew Fraser, *Snouts in the Trough,* pp.150–2; Damian Marrett, *Wired.*

In the three years from 1998 nearly sixty clandestine laboratories were discovered: John Silvester, 'Cops, robbers, drugs and money'.

Ferguson was additionally convicted of money laundering: *R v Ferguson; R v Sadler, R v Cox* [2009] VSCA 198.

The full disaster of the 1990s Victoria Police drugs policy became brutally clear: *R v Strawhorn* [2008] VSCA 101.

After this spate of cases Sergeant Bill Patten: John Silvester, 'End-of-year gangster wrap'.

[redacted]

Miechel eventually went down for a minimum of fifteen years: *R v Miechel* [2006] VSC 359.

[redacted]

The Attorney-General was sure that the public would be happy: *Advertiser,* 9 October 1981.

The president of the South Australian Police Association: *Advertiser,* 9 October 1981.

Look—this report has not even scraped the surface: *Advertiser,* 2 April 1982.

It seems that during a drug bust in August 1986: Bob Bottom, 'The tape that trapped Moyse'; Chris Masters, 'Suppression City'; Candace Sutton, 'Masters lifts lid on Adelaide', *Advertiser,* 2 October 1988.

Over the months Moyse had made more than $100,000: *Advertiser,* 19 January 1999; *Australian,* 3 September 2010.

After the conviction of Moyse, Octopodelis gave evidence: *Sun-Herald,* 23 October 1988.

Ranks have closed in the police: Chris Masters, 'Suppression city'.

12. Sir Terence and Co

In 1934 Mr Justice Macrossan, sitting in Brisbane: *Courier-Mail,* 17 January, 28 February and 24 March 1934.

'Graft paid to police said to run into millions': David Burnham, *New York Times.*

Queensland police were part of a political machine: Conversation with James Morton, 28 November 2013.

Queensland had always had something of a laissez-faire attitude to prostitution: Des Sturgess, who later became Director of Public Prosecutions in Queensland, wrote of seeing Bischof give evidence in the Southport taxi-driver murder case, 'I didn't believe much of it'.

Young is a man of poor moral character: Quoted in P James, *In Place of Justice,* p.109.

After the inquiry concluded, the unkind joke was that he was 'the only man in Queensland who could not find a tart in the National Hotel': Phil Dickie, *The Road to Fitzgerald and Beyond;* Peter James, *In Place of Justice;* Evan Whitton, *The Hillbilly Dictator,* chapter 2.

Thousands of pounds' worth of pay-offs were changing hands: Judith Summers, *Soho,* p.216.

In September 1971 she told Superintendent Norman Gulbransen: David Hickie, *The Prince and the Premier.*

I have been charged because of untrue malicious statements: Quoted in P James, *In Place of Justice,* p.116.

On 4 March 1972 Brifman was found dead in her flat: David Hickie, *The Prince and the Premier,* pp.284–8.

Murphy, born in 1927, was 'very corrupt and very sinister': Conversation with James Morton, 3 November 2011.

Certainly Murphy had come under some fire in the 1983 Stewart report: James Morton and Russell Robinson, *Shotgun and Standover;* Tony Koch, 'Rat-Pack leader takes evidence to the grave'.

Glen hit the pot over the Sundown murder: For a detailed account of the early years of Lewis, Hallahan, Murphy and Herbert, see Matthew Condon, *Three Crooked Kings.*

Less worthy was Hallahan's relationship with robber and standover man: [Unreported] *R v Hallahan,* Brisbane District Court, 14 August 1972; *Sun-Herald,* 10 July 1988.

Bischof's successor was Ray Whitrod: Domenico Cacciola, *The Second Father,* p.106.

The last straw for Whitrod: Ray Whitrod, *Before I Sleep;* Evan Whitton, *Trial by Voodoo.*

Williams, accepting the evidence of these fine officers: Australian Royal Commission of Inquiry into Drugs, pp.119–20.

Milligan, probably realising on which side his bread was buttered: Milligan was released from his 10-year sentence in January 1986 and lasted until October, when he was charged with possession and supply of heroin. Given bail, he absconded.

Gay brothels arrived: Tony Koch and Matthew Fynes-Clinton, 'The house at Kelvin Grove'.

In December 2010 Moore received a wholly suspended fifteen-month sentence: *Brisbane Times,* 3 December 2010.

In 1985 DPP Desmond Sturgess QC: Desmond Sturgess, *The Tangled Web.*

During the first months of 1987 *The Courier-Mail:* Phil Dickie, 'Fateful trail had dramatic end'.

Hall's investigation soon led to the Rat Pack: P Wear, 'Time to remember an unsung police hero'.

13. The Fitzgerald Commission and after

Few did, but the first of the brave was Aboriginal sergeant Col Dillon: In 2000 Dillon retired as the highest-ranked Indigenous officer.

Herbert should never have had indemnity: Conversation with Susanna Lobez, 30 November 2011.

Other officers were prosecuted, including Allen Bulger: Elizabeth Allen, 'Players in a vast drama'.

Brian Austin, who was one of those named by Lane: Frank Robson, 'After the fall'.

Herbert's old friend and adviser Jack Rooklyn escaped prison: Phil Dickie, *The Road to Fitzgerald and Beyond.*

That year Gold Coast detective sergeant John Swift: *R v Swift* [1999] QCA 94.

Unfortunately, cynical, short-sighted political attitudes: 'Fitzgerald breaks his silence on QLD corruption'.

14. In and out of the Wood

In 1993 Police Commissioner Tony Lauer: Quoted in *Sydney Morning Herald,* 22 October 1996.

At the beginning of the Wood Commission in December 1994 Lauer again held himself hostage to fortune: Kate McClymont, 'Lauer called back to police inquiry'.

In the final report a total of 284 police officers were adversely named: Kate McClymont, 'Police corruption defined by Chook's crotch cam'.

A state of systemic and entrenched corruption: Royal commission final report, 1997.

The contract of Assistant Commissioner Ray Donaldson: *Sydney Morning Herald,* 24 June 2010.

By 2007 twelve people involved in the commission had committed suicide: Fowler died in May 2013. He had been suffering from bladder cancer. Malcolm Brown, 'Holding judgement'.

But it was decided to begin a global search for what Nixon described as 'a new commissioner-cum-saviour': Christine Nixon, *Fair Cop,* p.97.

The position was hawked around senior officers in Great Britain: For an account of Ryan's time in Australia, see Sue Williams, *Peter Ryan,* chapters 12 and 13.

My view is that he had good ideas but he was appalling at implementation: Conversation with James Morton, 30 November 2013.

The Wood Royal Commission actually made recommendations: Conversation with James Morton, 18 November 2013.

Another problem came when police cadet Kim Hollingsworth: John Silvester and Andrew Rule,

Underbelly: The Golden Mile; Ben Hills, 'How the police used Kim, then threw her out'.

Patison, one of six officers convicted of offences: *R v Patison* [2002] NSWSC 1248; *R v Jasper* [2003] NSWSC 287; *R v Caccamo* [2005] NSWCCA 257; *Operation Florida,* vols I and II; *Sydney Morning Herald,* 29 June 2004.

It was a long, uphill struggle: Clive Small and Tom Gilling, *Betrayed.*

15. The Twenty-First Century

He came from an era of policing when rules were bent to get results: Tony Barrass and Trevor Robb, 'Dark horse'.

On 28 March 2002, 38-year-old Sidney John Reid: *Daily Telegraph,* 1 October 2001; *Weekend Australian,* 28 August 2004.

While he admitted fabricating evidence, Lewandowski said he still believed the brothers: Antonio Buti, *Brothers;* Avon Lovell, *The Mickelberg Stitch;* John Flint, 'My shame'.

During this period, under Commissioner Bob Falconer: Tony Barrass and Trevor Robb, 'Dark horse'.

The next year Geoffrey Kennedy QC was appointed: Nick Taylor, 'Corruption list dents confidence'.

Four years later, in 2006, the final report of the commission concluded: Kennedy, GA, *Report of the Royal Commission into Whether There Has Been any Corrupt or Criminal Conduct by any Western Australian Police Officer,* final report, vol.1, part 2, pp.1–4.

In particular, Don Hancock was not on the take: Jim Kelly, 'Murdered Hancock "not on the take"'.

The report did not please everybody: John Silvester and Selma Milovanovic, 'Rogues' gallery emerges from ex-cop's testimony', *Age,* 5 June 2004.

When it was suggested that Tony Lewandowski should be given police protection: John Flint, 'My shame'.

In 2009 Minniti was found guilty of corruption: Corruption and Crime Commission of Western Australia, *Report on an Investigation into Inappropriate Associations between Western Australian Police Officers and Pasquale Minniti.*

The tapes apparently disclosed a conspiracy: Alan Sharpe and Vivien Encel, *Murder! 25 True Australian Crimes.*

Two officers faced criminal charges: *Crime and Misconduct Commission v Deputy Commissioner Stewart and Anor (No 2)* [2012] QCAT 382; Robert Needham, *Dangerous Liaisons;* Daniel Hurst, 'Bad cops avoid charges'; 'Original judgment stands—officer loses pay over procedural breach', *Morning Bulletin,* 8 September 2012.

However, in 2010–11 thirty Gold Coast officers were subject to internal discipline: Mark Solomons, 'Public trust sinks as more rogue officers revealed', *Courier-Mail,* 29 November 2011.

They're not nabbing the crooks as swiftly as they used to: Jessica Elder, 'Big boys slip net as cops get tough', *Gold Coast Bulletin,* 5 August 2011.

One of the most egregious examples of collective noblecause corruption: Office of Police Integrity, *The Victorian Armed Offenders Squad—A Case Study,* 30 October 2008; Kate Hagan, 'Ex-detectives admit to bashing suspect', *Age,* 26 February 2008. Paul Anderson's highly entertaining novel *The Robbers* is a thinly disguised portrait of the squad.

In February 2010 charges of perjury against Ashby were dropped: Kate Hagan, 'Perjury charges against Deputy Police Commissioner Noel Ashby dropped', *Age,* 9 February 2010.

In November 2010 the OPI admitted that it was incapable of dealing with an allegedly corrupt officer: Liam Houlihan, 'Lewis Moran police officer friend probed', *Herald Sun,* 7 November 2010.

Sir Ken had briefed him on a sensitive report about murders committed by parolees: Richard Baker and Nick Mackenzie, 'Bugged: Sir Ken Jones targeted by the OPI', *Age,* 3 June 2011.

Kellam's report, tabled in the Victorian Parliament: Joel Cresswell, 'Sir Ken Jones resigns'; Anthony Dowsley, 'Chorus of approval greets Overland's resignation'; Chip Le Grand, 'Simon Overland cleared'; Chip Le Grand, 'Call for reforms of IBAC's powers'.

Like the Roman god, a mythological gatekeeper: Michael McKenna and Natalie O'Brien, ' Mark Standen's fall a long time coming'.

In 1982 the Stewart Royal Commission into drug trafficking: For an account of the incident and Standen's early career generally, see Charles Miranda, *Deception,* pp.73–8.

In 1990 AFP drug-registry officer Michael Anthony Wallace: *R v Wallace* [2007] NSWCCA 63.

Harrison's final report, which is understood to have found widespread corruption in the AFP: I

Harrison SC, *Report of the Harrison Inquiry into Allegations of Corruption Within the Australian Federal Police.*

In 2005 Michael Nicholas Hurley: Clive Small and Tom Gilling, *Smack Express,* p.184 and throughout.

In May 2010 Jalalaty pleaded guilty: *R v Bakhos Jalalaty* [2010] NSWSC 1561; *R v Standen* [2011] NSWSC 1422.

In April 2013 Victorian Police Commissioner Kenneth Lay: John Silvester, 'Blitz on rats in the ranks'.

16. Controlling Corruption

There are three kinds of men in the department: Barker and Roebuck, cited in M Punch, *Conduct Unbecoming: The Social Construction of Deviance and Control,* pp.7–8.

More recently, about forty years ago sociologist William Ker Muir Jr: William Ker Muir Jr, *Police: Street Corner Politicians.*

If Bill Bloggs joins the Met: Email to James Morton, 17 May 2013.

One former Victorian officer: Conversation with Susanna Lobez and James Morton, November 2013.

Sociologist Maurice Punch has argued: Maurice Punch, *Conduct Unbecoming,* p.2.

Sections of the public felt that Victoria's armed robbery squad: Fitzroy Legal Service Community Centre, *Police Shootings in Victoria 1987–1989;* James Morton and Susanna Lobez, *Gangland Melbourne;* Tom Noble, *Untold Violence.*

In one of New South Wales' first integrity tests: 'Anatomy of an integrity test', *Daily Telegraph,* 23 December 1997.

I don't think it can. It's universal and endemic: James Morton, *Bent Coppers,* p.376.

Police corruption also has to be seen not as deviance but as the way things used to be done: Conversation with James Morton, 28 November 2013.

The general, if perhaps optimistic, view: Richard Hall, *Disorganized Crime,* p.65.

Ethical decision-making must be taught and reinforced: Email to Susanna Lobez, 23 February 2014.

If there is to be further corruption it will not be the kind of corruption of the past: Conversation with James Morton, 28 November 2013.

At the moment, all is quiet on the Western front: Email to James Morton, 22 February 2014.

There have also been allegations that Operation Mascot: Neil Mercer, 'Bent officer's pre-emptive strike'.

Philosopher George Santayana: George Santayana, *Life of Reason,* pp.1905–6.

SELECT BIBLIOGRAPHY

Books

Alatas, SH, *The Sociology of Corruption: The Nature, Function, Causes and Prevention of Corruption,* Donald Moore Press, Singapore, 1968.

Anderson, P, *The Robbers,* Hardie Grant Books, Richmond, Victoria, 2012.

Anon, *Police Corruption,* Communist Party of Australia (Marxist-Leninist), Melbourne, 1970.

Arantz, PN, *A Collusion of Powers,* privately published, Sydney, 1993.

Barker, T, *Police Ethics: Crisis in Law Enforcement,* Charles C Thomas, Springfield, Illinois, 1996.

Barker, T, and JB Roebuck, *An Empirical Typology of Police Corruption,* Charles C Thomas, Springfield, Illinois, 1973.

Berman, P, with Childs, K, *Why Isn't She Dead!,* Gold Star Publications, Melbourne, 1972.

Bezzina, C, with Collins, B, *The Job: Fighting Crime on the Front Line,* Slattery Media Group, Docklands, Victoria, 2010.

Blackburn, E, *Broken Lives,* Hardie Grant Books, Melbourne, 2001.

Bottom, B, *Without Fear or Favour,* Sun Books, South Melbourne, 1984.

—*Bugged,* Sun Books, Sydney, 1990.

—*Inside Victoria,* Pan Macmillan, Sydney, 1991.

Bottomley, K, *Criminology in Focus: Past Trends and Future Prospects,* Martin Robertson, Oxford, 1979.

Brown, G, and R Haldane, *Days of Violence—The 1923 Police Strike in Melbourne,* Hybrid Publishers, Melbourne, 1998.

Brown, M, and P Wilson, *Justice and Nightmares: Successes and Failures of Forensic Science in Australia and New Zealand,* University of New South Wales Press, Sydney, 1992.

Bryett, K, and A Harrison, *Policing in the Community,* Butterworths, Sydney, 1993.

Buti, A, *Brothers: Justice, Corruption and the Mickelbergs,* Fremantle Arts Centre Press, Fremantle, Western Australia, 2011.

Cacciola, D, C Cacciola, and B Robertson, *The Second Father: An Insider's Story of Cops, Crime and*

Corruption, University of Queensland Press, St Lucia, Queensland, 2011.

Cahill, WA, *The Policeman's Manual,* Queensland Police Department, Brisbane, 1913.

Carrington, K, M Dever, R Hogg, J Bargen, and A Lohrey, (eds), *Travesty!: Miscarriages of Justice,* Pluto Press, Sydney, 1991.

Condon, M, *Three Crooked Kings,* University of Queensland Press, St Lucia, Queensland, 2012.

—*Jacks and Jokers,* University of Queensland Press, St Lucia, Queensland, 2014.

Crank, J, and M Caldero, *Police Ethics: The Corruption of Noble Cause,* Anderson Publishing, Cincinnati, Ohio, 2004.

Dale, J, *Huckstepp: A Dangerous Life,* Allen & Unwin, Sydney, 2000.

Dale, P, *Disgraced? The Cop at the Centre of Melbourne's Gangland Wars,* Five Mile Press, Scoresby, Victoria, 2013.

Dempster, Q, *Honest Cops,* ABC Books, Sydney, 1992.

—*Whistleblowers,* ABC Books, Sydney, 1997.

Dickie, P, *The Road to Fitzgerald and Beyond,* University of Queensland Press, St Lucia, Queensland, 1989.

Dixon, D (ed.), *A Culture of Corruption: Changing Australia's Police Service,* Hawkins Press, Sydney, 1999.

Dower, A, *Deadline,* Hutchinson, Richmond, Victoria, 1979.

Dowling, S, *Love Letters from the Bar Table,* S Dowling, Bondi Beach, New South Wales, 2009.

Egan, C, *Murderer No More: Andrew Mallard and the Epic Fight that Proved His Innocence,* Allen & Unwin, Sydney, 2010.

Farquhar, M, *Nine Words from the Grave: The Real Story as Revealed by Murray Farquhar,* MF Farquhar, Sydney, 1986.

Finane, M (ed.), *Policing in Australia: Historical Perspectives,* New South Wales University Press, Kensington, New South Wales, 1987.

—*Police and Government: Histories of Policing in Australia,* Oxford University Press, Melbourne, 1994.

Fraser, A, *Snouts in the Trough,* Hardie Grant Publishing, Prahran, Victoria, 2010.

—*Killing Time: Court in the Middle,* Hardie Grant Publishing, Prahran, Victoria, 2010.

Freeman, GD, *George Freeman, an Autobiography,* George Freeman, Sydney, 1988.

Grabosky, PN, *Sydney in Ferment: Crime, Dissent and Official Reaction, 1788–1973,* Australian National University Press, Canberra, 1977.

—*Wayward Governance: Illegality and its Control in the Public Sector,* Australian Institute of Criminology, Canberra, 1989.

Haigh, G, *The Racket: How Abortion Became Legal in Australia,* Melbourne University Press, Carlton, Victoria, 2008.

Haken, T, and S Padraic, *Confessions of a Crooked Cop,* ABC Books, Sydney, 2010.

Haldane, R, *The People's Force: A History of the Victoria Police,* Melbourne University Press, Carlton, Victoria, 1986.

Hall, R, *Disorganized Crime,* University of Queensland Press, St Lucia, Queensland, 1986.

Henry, VE, *Patterns of Police Corruption and Reform: Comparing New York City and Queensland,* Griffith University, Brisbane, 1990.

Herbert, J, and T Gilling, *The Bagman: Final Confessions of Jack Herbert,* ABC Books, Sydney, 2004.

Hetherington, J, *Blamey,* Angus & Robertson, London, 1954.

Hickie, D, *The Prince and the Premier,* Angus & Robertson, North Ryde, New South Wales, 1985.

Hoban, LE (ed.), *A Centenary History of the New South Wales Police Force, 1862–1962,* Government Printer, Sydney, 1962.

Hunt, N, *The First Police Union: The Police Association of South Australia—100 years,* Wakefield Press, Kent Town, South Australia, 2011.

Illingworth, S, *Filthy Rat: One Man's Stand Against Police Corruption and Melbourne's Gangland War,* Fontaine Press, Fremantle, Western Australia, 2008.

Inbau, FE, JE Reid, JP Buckley and BC Jayne, *Criminal Interrogation and Confessions,* Jones Bartlett, Boston, 2004.

Irving, T, and RJ Cahill, *Radical Sydney: Places, Portraits and Unruly Episodes,* University of New South Wales Press, Sydney, 2010.

James, P, *In Place of Justice: An Analysis of a Royal Commission, 1963–1964,* Shield Press, Deception Bay, Queensland, 1974.

Johnston, WR, *The Long Blue Line: A History of the Queensland Police,* Boolarong Press, Brisbane, 1992.

Kappeler, VE, RD Sluder, and GP Alpert, *Forces of Deviance: Understanding the Dark Side of Policing,* Waveland Press, Prospect Heights, Illinois, California, 1998.

Kelly, V, *The Bogeyman: The Exploits of Sergeant CJ Chuck, Australia's Most Unpopular Cop,* Angus & Robertson, Sydney, 1956.

Klitgaard, R, *Controlling Corruption,* University of California Press, Berkeley, California, 1998.

Lane, D, *Trial and Error,* Boolarong Press, Brisbane, 1993.

Latch, B, with B Hitchings, *Mr X: Police Informer,* Dingo Books, Melbourne, 1975.

Lewis, C, J Ransley, and R Homel, (eds), *The Fitzgerald Legacy: Reforming Public Life in Australia and Beyond,* Australian Academic Press, Samford Valley, Queensland, 2010.

Linnell, S, *Don't Tell the Chief: The Untold Story of Police, Power and Politics,* Wilkinson Publishing, Melbourne, 2010.

Locke, D, *Watching the Detectives,* ABC Books, Adelaide, 2003.

Lovell, A, *The Mickelberg Stitch,* Creative Research, Perth, 1985.

—*Litany of Lies,* Bookscope, Perth, 2010.

McCoy, AW, *Drug Traffic,* Harper & Row, Sydney, 1980.

McKenzie, N, *The Sting,* Victory Books, Carlton, Victoria, 2012.

McNab, D, *The Dodger: Inside the World of Roger Rogerson,* Pan Macmillan, Sydney, 2006.

McNamara, G, *Dirty Work,* New Holland, Sydney, 2010.

McWilliams, R, *Our Police Force,* Sydney District Committee, Communist Party of Australia, Sydney, c. 1936.

Marrett, D, *Undercover,* HarperCollins, Sydney, 2005.

—*White Lies,* HarperCollins, Sydney, 2006.

—*Wired,* UCIC Press, Malvern East, Victoria, 2007.

Marshall, A, *This Is the Grass,* Australiana Book Society, Sydney, 1962.

Masters, C, *Inside Story,* Angus & Robertson, Sydney, 1992.

Milne, K, and T Weber, (eds), *Police in Australia: Development, Functions and Procedures,* Butterworths, Sydney, 1977.

Miranda, C, *Deception,* Allen & Unwin, Crows Nest, New South Wales, 2012.

Moffitt, A, *A Quarter to Midnight,* Angus & Robertson, Sydney, 1985.

Morgan, K, *Gun Alley,* Simon & Schuster, Sydney, 2005.

Morton, J, *Bent Coppers,* Time Warner, London, 1993.

Morton, J, and S Lobez, *Gangland Melbourne,* Victory Books, Carlton, 2011.

—*Kings of Stings,* Victory Books, Carlton, 2011.

—*Gangland Queensland,* Victory Books, Carlton, 2012.

—*Gangland North South & West,* Victory Books, Carlton, 2013.

Morton, J, and R Robinson, *Shotgun and Standover,* Macmillan, Sydney, 2010.

Muir, WK, *Police: Street Corner Politicians,* University of Chicago Press, Chicago, Illinois, 1977.

Newburn, T, *Criminology,* Willan Publishing, Devon, 2007.

Nixon, C, with J Chandler, *Fair Cop,* Victory Books, Carlton, 2011.

Noble, T, *Untold Violence: Crime in Melbourne Today,* Victory Books, Carlton, 2011

—*Walsh Street: The Cold-Blooded Killings that Shocked Australia,* Noble House Enterprises, Melbourne, 2000.

Northcote, J (ed.), *Corruption and Reform,* University of Queensland Press, St Lucia, Queensland, 1990.

O'Sullivan, J, *Mounted Police of Victoria & Tasmania,* Rigby Publishers, Adelaide, 1980.

Perkins, K, *The Gambling Man,* Polynesian Press, Tonga, 1990.

Philips, D, *William Augustus Miles (1796–1851): Crime, Policing and Moral Entrepreneurship in England and Australia,* University of Melbourne, Parkville, Victoria, 2001.

Porter, C, *The Conviction of the Innocent: How the Law Can Let Us Down,* Random House, North Sydney, 2007.

Prasler, S, R Wear, and J Nethersole, *The Fitzgerald Vision,* University of Queensland Press, Brisbane, 1990.

Prenzler, T, *Police Corruption: Preventing Misconduct and Maintaining Integrity,* CRC Press, Boca Raton, Florida, 2009.

Priest, T, *Enemies of the State,* New Holland, Sydney, 2009.

Punch, M, *Conduct Unbecoming: The Social Construction of Deviance and Control,* Tavistock, London, 1985.

Read, M, *Chopper from the Inside,* Sly Ink, Melbourne, 1991.

Rolph, CH (ed.), *The Police and the Public,* Heinemann, London, 1962.

Sadleir, J, *Recollections of a Victorian Police Officer,* Ringwood, Victoria, 1973.

Shand, A, *The Skull: Informers, Hitmen and Australia's Toughest Cop,* Black Inc, Melbourne, 2009.

Sharpe, A, and V Encel, *Murder! 25 True Australian Crimes,* Kingsclear Books, Alexandria, New South Wales, 1997.

Silvester, J, and A Rule, *Tough: 101 Australian Gangsters: A Crime Companion,* Floradale and Sly Ink, Melbourne, 2002.

—*Underbelly: The Golden Mile,* Sly Ink, Melbourne, 2010.

Small, C, and Gilling, T, *Smack Express: How Organised Crime Got Hooked on Drugs,* Allen & Unwin, Sydney, 2009.

—*Betrayed: The Shocking Story of Two Undercover Cops,* Allen & Unwin, Sydney, 2010.

Stewart, D, *Recollections of an Unreasonable Man,* ABC Books, Sydney, 2007.

Sturgess, D, *The Tangled Web,* Bedside Books, Brisbane, 2001.

Summers, J, *Soho: A History of London's Most Colourful Neighbourhood,* Bloomsbury Publishing, London, 1989.

Swanton, B, *Police of Sydney 1788–1862,* Australian Institute of Criminology, Canberra, 1984.

Thompson, J, *Snitch: Crooked Cops and Kings Cross Criminals by the Man Who Saw It All,* Allen & Unwin, Sydney, 2010.

Ward, R, *The Australian Legend,* Oxford University Press, Melbourne, 1958.

Ward, RH, D Bracey, and R McCormack, *Managing Police Corruption: International Perspectives,* University of Illinois Press, Chicago, Illinois, 1987.

White, J, *Journal of a Voyage to New South Wales,* Angus & Robertson, Sydney, 1962.

Whitrod, R, *Before I Sleep: Memoirs of a Modern Police Commissioner,* University of Queensland Press, St Lucia, Queensland, 2001.

Whitton, E, *Can of Worms,* The Fairfax Library, Sydney, 1986.

—*Can of Worms II,* The Fairfax Library, Sydney, 1987.

—*The Hillbilly Dictator: Australia's Police State,* ABC Books, Crows Nest, New South Wales, 1989.

—*Trial by Voodoo,* Random House Australia, Milsons Point, New South Wales, 1994.

Williams, S, *Peter Ryan: The Inside Story,* Viking, Sydney, 2002.

Wilson, D, *The Beat, Policing a Victorian City,* Circa Press, Melbourne, 2006.

Writer, L, *Razor: A True Story of Slashers, Gangsters, Prostitutes and Sly Grog,* Pan Macmillan, Sydney, 2001.

Wrout, B, with B Quine, *Kill the Morans: The Real Story of the Moran Crime Crew,* Five Mile Press, Scoresby, Victoria, 2012.

Articles, Chapters, Reports and Manuscripts

Adshead, G, 'Cops on take', *West Australian,* 4 November 2001.

Alexander, C, 'Is Macca's supersizing our cops? Fast food perks for law officers', *Crikey,* 9 January 2013.

Alexandra, A, 'Dirty Harry and dirty hands', in Coady et al (eds), *Violence and Police Culture,* Melbourne University Press, Carlton, Victoria, 2000.

Allen, E, 'Players in a vast drama', *Courier-Mail,* 14 May 2007.

Aubin, T, 'Fitzgerald inquiry: a who's who after 2,000 pages', *Sydney Morning Herald,* 12 November 1988.

Australian Royal Commission of Inquiry into Drugs, *Report to the Queensland Government on the Alleged Involvement in the Illegal Drug Trade by Queensland Parliamentarians and Senior Police,* Government Printer, Queensland, April 1980.

Ball, R, and D English, 'Police drugs links alleged', *Advertiser,* 8 October 1981.

—'A family affair', *Advertiser,* 10 October 1981.

Barrass, T, and T Robb, 'Dark horse', *West Australian,* 15 September 2001.

Beach, B, *Report of the Board of Inquiry into Allegations against Members of the Victoria Police Force,* FD Atkinson, Government Printer, Melbourne, 1978.

Board of Inquiry into Allegations of Corruption in the Police Force in Connection with Illegal Abortion Practices in the State of Victoria, *Report of the Board of Inquiry into Allegations of Corruption in the Police Force in Connection with Illegal Abortion Practices in the State of Victoria,* Government Printer, Melbourne, 1971.

Borham, S, 'Corruption in high places', *Sun-Herald,* 30 December 1990.

Bottom, B, 'Fall of a drug dealing policeman', *Sydney Morning Herald,* 4 January 1989.

—'The tape that trapped Moyse', *Sunday Mail,* 8 January 1989.

Bottom, B, and T Reeves, 'The night the Mafia came to Australia', *Sunday Telegraph,* 16 July 1972.

Bottom, B, and D Wilson, 'Marijuana trade thriving in city of churches', *Age,* 8 June 1987.

Bray, C, '"Hell, someone's cut this girl in half!"', *Daily Telegraph,* 6 March 2006.

Brouwer, G, *Past Patterns—Future Directions: Victoria Police and the Problem of Corruption and Serious Misconduct,* Office of Police Integrity, Victorian Government Printer, Melbourne, 2007.

Brown, M, 'Indecent proposals', *Sydney Morning Herald,* 26 February 1994.

—'Nemesis of crims and corruption', *Sydney Morning Herald,* 9 August 2002.

—'Holding judgement', *Sydney Morning Herald,* 9 June 2007.

Brown, M, and J Cook, 'The circle of power', *Sydney Morning Herald,* 13 May 1994.

Burnham, D, 'Graft paid to police said to run to millions', *New York Time* s, 25 April 1970.

Christie, J, Private Papers, State Library of Victoria, undated entry (probably 1897).

Chulov, M, 'The force is with her: The rise and rise of Australia's first female police chief', *Weekend Australian Magazine,* 28–29 September 2002.

Coaldrake, P, 'Changing the system', *Legal Services Bulletin,* 14 (4) 159, 1989.

Coaldrake, P, and J Wanna, 'Not like the good old days', *Australian Quarterly,* 60 (4), 1988.

Condon, M, ' Desperate measures', *Sydney Morning Herald,* 2 March 2013.

'Confessions of a crooked cop', *Bulletin,* 18 April 1978.

Cook, J, 'Force clean-up overdue', *Sydney Morning Herald,* 12 May 1994.

Corruption and Crime Commission of Western Australia, *Report on an Investigation into Inappropriate Associations between Western Australian Police Officers and Pasquale Minniti,* tabled paper no.3504, Legislative Assembly, Parliament of Western Australia, 21 December 2007.

—*Report on the Inquiry into Alleged Misconduct of Public Officers in the Investigations of the Murder of Mrs Pamela Lawrence, the Prosecution and Appeals of Andrew Mark Mallard and Other Related Matters,* Corruption and Crime Commission, Perth, 2008.

'Creed cleared on SA murder charge', *Advertiser,* 3 October 1984.

Cresswell, J, 'Sir Ken Jones resigns', *Sydney Morning Herald,* 2 May 2011.

Crime and Misconduct Commission, *Report on Operation Tesco, an Investigation into Allegations of Police Misconduct on the Gold Coast,* Brisbane, 2011.

—*Report on Regulating Adult Entertainment: A Review of the Live Adult Entertainment Industry in Queensland,* Brisbane, 2004.

Curtin, J, 'Death of former policeman remains a mystery', *Sydney Morning Herald,* 31 August 1990.

David, G, and J Wanna, 'The Fitzgerald Commission: The politics of inquiries', *Canberra Bulletin of Public Administration,* 55, June 1988.

Dick-Erikson, T, 'Confessions in evidence: A look at the inquisitorial system', *New Law Journal,* 22 June 1990.

Dickie, P, 'Fateful trail had dramatic end', *Courier-Mail,* 15 May 2007.

Dowsley, A, 'Chorus of approval greets Overland's resignation', *Herald Sun,* 17 June 2011.

Duncan, AM, *Report on All Aspects of Crime Investigation by the Criminal Investigation Branch of the Tasmanian Police Department,* parliamentary paper, Parliament of Tasmania, no.62, 1955.

Egan, C, 'Let off', *Sunday Times,* 10 August 2003.

Evans, R, 'William John Mackay and the South Wales Police Force 1910– 1948: A Study of Police Power', submitted in fulfilment of the requirements for the degree of Doctor of Philosophy, School of Political and Social Inquiry, Monash University, May 2005.

'Fitzgerald breaks his silence on QLD corruption', *Lawyers' Weekly,* 29 January 2009.

Fitzroy Legal Service Community Centre, *Police Shootings in Victoria 1987–1989,* Melbourne, 1992.

Flint, J, 'My shame', *Sunday Times,* 16 June 2002.

Freckelton, I, and H Selby, 'Piercing the blue veil: An assessment of external review of police', in Chappell, D, and Wilson, P, (eds), *Australian Policing: Contemporary Issues,* Butterworths, Sydney, 1989.

Gawenda, M, and T Thwaites, 'How many rotten apples?', *Age,* 2 June 1983.

Glazer, M, 'Ten whistleblowers and how they fared', *The Hastings Center Report,* vol.13, December 1983.

Gosman, K, 'Heroin in the ice cream', *Sydney Morning Herald,* 10 November 1991.

—'Baling out of the force', *Sydney Morning Herald,* 22 January 1994.

Gregory, J, 'The deconstruction of memory: Exploring childhood memories of class', *Oral History Association of Australia Journal,* no.11, 1989.

Gudjonsson, GH, and J MacKeith, 'Retracted confessions', *Medicine, Science and the Law,* vol.28, 1988.

Haldane, R, '"Wildcat" strike: The story of William Thomas Brooks', *Police Association Journal,* May 2009.

Harrison, AE, GR Hohenhaus, and GA Pitman, *Queensland Police Department Submission for the Commission of Inquiry before Mr GE Fitzgerald (Commissioner and Chairman),* unpublished report prepared by three serving members of the department for Acting Commissioner of Police RJ Redmond, 1988.

Harrison, I, *Report of the Harrison Inquiry into Allegations of Corruption Within the Australian Federal Police,* 18 April 1997, not publicly released.

Hills, B, 'Scams and scoundrels: Royal Commission into Police', *Sydney Morning Herald,* 3 February 1996.

—'How the police used Kim, then threw her out', *Sydney Morning Herald,* 21 November 1996.

Hurst, D, 'Bad cops avoid charges', *Brisbane Times,* 22 July 2009.

Independent Commission Against Corruption, *Report on an Investigation Relating to the Raid on Frank Hakim's Office,* Sydney, 1989.

Ironside, R, 'Policeman's "joint account with killer"', *Courier-Mail,* 25 July 2009.

Jacobsen, G, 'A long history of police corruption', *Sydney Morning Herald,* 12 August 2011.

Kassin, SM, 'False confessions: Causes, consequences, and implications for reform', *Current Directions in Psychological Science,* 17, no.4 (2008): 249.

Keenan, A, 'It began with the first constable', *Sydney Morning Herald,* 17 September 1985.

—'After the war, the parasites move in', *Sydney Morning Herald,* 23 September 1985.

—'Entrepreneurs frame a market', *Sydney Morning Herald,* 24 September 1985.

—'The new assault on corruption', *Sydney Morning Herald,* 25 September 1985.

—'Purge of corruption seems doomed to fail', *Sydney Morning Herald,* 28 February 1988.

Kellam, M, *Report for the Independent Broad-Based Anti-Corruption Commission,* tabled in the Parliament of Victoria, 19 February 2014.

Kelly, J, 'Murdered Hancock "not on the take"', *Sunday Times,* 7 March 2004.

Kennedy, GA, *Report of the Royal Commission into Whether There Has Been Any Corrupt or Criminal Conduct by Any Western Australian Police Officer,* Perth, 2004.

Kidman, J, and S Barrett, 'How elite agents went off the rails', *Sydney Morning Herald,* 22 June 2008.

Koch, T, 'Rat-Pack leader takes evidence to the grave', *Australian,* 23 December 2010.

Koch, T, and M Fynes-Clinton, 'The house at Kelvin Grove', *Courier-Mail,* 11 December 1984.

Le Grand, C, 'Simon Overland cleared', *Australian,* 26 November 2013.

—'Call for reforms of IBAC's powers', 27 November 2013.

Lewis, C, 'Police Accountability Queensland Style', unpublished honours thesis, Griffith University, Queensland.

Littlejohn, L, and J Street, Letter to Members of the Legislative Assembly, NSWSR, Col. Sect. Special Bundles, 5/8918.

Lucas, GAG, *Report of the Committee of Inquiry into the Enforcement of Criminal Law in Queensland,* Government Printer, Brisbane, 1977.

McClymont, K, 'Lauer called back to Police Inquiry', *Sydney Morning Herald,* 21 October 1996.

—'Police corruption defined by Chook's crotch cam', *Sydney Morning Herald,* 19 May 2013.

MacCormack, S, 'The formative years', *New South Wales Police News,* January 1988.

McDonald, P, 'Life and crimes of Colin Creed', *Advertiser,* 11 April 1996.

McKenna, M, and O'Brien, N, 'Mark Standen's fall a long time coming', *Australian,* 7 June 2008.

Maguire, T, 'The case of the missing victim', *Bulletin,* 19 January 1982.

Masters, C, 'Moonlight State', *Four Corners,* 11 May 1987.

—'Suppression City', *Four Corners,* 6 October 1988.

—'Moonlight reflections: Hidden Queensland', *Griffith Review,* no.21, spring 2008.

Mercer, N, 'Bent officer's pre-emptive strike', *Sydney Morning Herald,* 6 May 2013.

Milovanovic, S, 'Corruption watchdog probes 35 police', *Age,* 21 July 2005.

Molomby, T, 'Miscarriages of justice in Britain: The Guildford Four and the Birmingham Six', in Carrington et al (eds), *Travesty! Miscarriages of Justice,* Pluto Press, Sydney, 1991.

Moore, A, 'A Secret Policeman's Lot', in John Shields (ed.), *All Our Labours: Oral Histories of Working Life in Twentieth Century Sydney,* University of New South Wales Press, Sydney, 1992.

Needham, Robert, *Dangerous Liaisons: A Report Arising from a CMC Investigation into Allegations of Police Misconduct (Operation Capri),* Crime and Misconduct Commission, Queensland, 2009.

Office of Police Integrity, *Ceja Task Force: Drug Related Corruption, Third and Final Report,* Victoria, 2007.

Police Complaints Tribunal, *Report by Police Complaints Tribunal: Barry James Mannix,* Brisbane, 1986.

Police Integrity Commission, *Research Report, Project Odin: Identifying and Managing High Risk Officers in the New South Wales Police,* Sydney, September 2009.

Punch, M, 'Rotten orchards: Pestilence, police misconduct and system failure', *Policing and Society,* vol.13, no.2, June 2003.

Purnell, HF, *In the Matter of an Inquiry into the Investigation by the New South Wales Police Force of Circumstances Surrounding the Shooting of Detective Senior Constable M.P. Drury 6.6. 1984: Advice,* Crown Solicitor, Sydney, 1990.

Reports Commissioned by the Hon. KT Griffin, Attorney-General, South Australia, into Alleged Corruption in the South Australian Police Force, Government Printer, Adelaide, March 1982.

Robson, F, 'After the fall', *Sydney Morning Herald,* 11 August 1995.

Royal Commission on Alleged Chinese Gambling and Immorality and Charges of Bribery Against Members of the Police Force, *Report of the Royal Commission on Alleged Chinese Gambling and Immorality and Charges of Bribery Against Members of the Police Force,* Government Printer, Sydney, 1892.

Royal Commission on the Alleged Shooting at and Wounding of John O'Connell Brophy, *Report of the Royal Commission on the Alleged Shooting at and Wounding of John O'Connell Brophy, a Superintendent of Police,* Government Printer, Melbourne 1936.

Seggie, R, 'Aspects of the Role of the Police Force in New South Wales and its Relation to the Government 1900–1939', doctoral thesis, Macquarie University, 1988.

Shanahan, CP, *Report on the Anti-Corruption Commission Investigation into any Involvement by Western Australia Police Officers in the Death of Andrew Petrelis,* Corruption and Crime Commission of Western Australia, 17 May 2007.

Sherman, L, 'Becoming bent: The moral careers of corrupt policemen', in Sherman, L (ed.), *Police Corruption: A Sociological Perspective,* Anchor, New York, 1974.

Silvester, J, 'Cops, robbers, drugs and money', *Age,* 18 March 2003.

—'End-of-year gangster wrap', *Age,* 30 December 2006.

—'Blitz on rats in the ranks', *Age,* 27 March 2013.

Skelton, R, and Shiel, F, 'The myth of a clean police force', *Age,* 12 June 2004.

Skolnick, JH, 'Corruption and the blue code of silence', *Police Practice and Research,* vol.3, no.1, 2002.

Stannard, B, 'How we got Finch', *Bulletin,* 22 November 1988.

Stewart, DG, *Report of the Royal Commission into Drug Trafficking,* Australian Government Printing Service, Canberra, 1982.

—*Report of the Royal Commission of Inquiry into Alleged Telephone Interceptions,* parliamentary paper, Parliament of the Commonwealth of Australia, no.155, 1986.

Sutton, C, 'Masters lifts lid on Adelaide', *Sun-Herald,* 2 October 1988.

Swanton, B, 'The promotion of police integrity', *Police Journal,* vol.LVIX, no.3, September 1986.

Swanton, B, and RW Page, 'New South Wales Police', in Swanton, B, and Hannigan, G, (eds), *Police Source Book 2,* Australian Institute of Criminology, Canberra 1985.

'Sydney's casinos: A fact of life becomes a scandal', *National Times,* 25–30 June 1973.

Taylor, N, 'Corruption list dents confidence', *Sunday Times,* 13 April 2003.

'Too much secrecy in graft hunt', *Australian,* 28 April 2003.

Walker, R, 'The New South Wales Police Force 1862–1900', *Journal of Australian Studies,* vol.15.

Wear, P, 'Time to remember an unsung police hero', *Courier-Mail,* 13 May 1998.

White, WS, 'Police trickery in inducing confessions', *University of Pennsylvania Law Review,* vol.127, issue 3, January 1979, pp.581–629.

Whitton, E, 'Detective accused of corruption', *Sun-Herald,* 2 November 1993.

Wilkinson, G, 'The power of Peg', *Herald Sun,* 21 December 2002.

Wilson, P, 'Miscarriages of justice in serious cases in Australia', in Carrington et al (eds), *Travesty! Miscarriages of Justice,* Pluto Press, Sydney, 1991.

Withers, K, 'Australian city probes police gang', *Sun,* 7 September 1991.

Wood, JRT, *Royal Commission into the New South Wales Police Service: Final Report,* Sydney, 1997.

'You can't buck the system', *National Times,* 25–30 June 1973.

BACK COVER MATERIAL

Legal proceedings against a former police officer have forced parts of this book to be redacted. Bent law officers exist in every era, sabotaging the work of their colleagues and putting the community at risk.

James Morton and Susanna Lobez have illustrated, in several *Gangland* books, that Australia almost certainly has out-ganged other countries. Now their spotlight is turned on corruption within the police services and identifying which state wins the bent cop handicap.

Morton and Lobez examine the problems that started with the First Fleet and spread through to the present day, looking at the trouble caused by greed, power, drink, sex, money and, most recently, drugs. They compare the experience in Australia with corruption in America, England and Hong Kong, concentrating in particular on organised corruption at the highest levels, including judges, lawyers and politicians, through to the petty criminals who work our streets.

Which state has the shadiest cops? The answer will surprise you.

James Morton, a former defence lawyer, is one of Britain's leading experts on crime, and the author of more than twenty books including the bestselling *Gangland* series.

Susanna Lobez is an actor-turned-barrister-turned-broadcaster. She has been an ABC specialist legal presenter on *The Law Report* (radio) and *Law Matters* (TV). She has written feature articles for *The Age* and columns for the *Sunday Herald Sun.*

They are also the co-authors of the bestselling *Dangerous to Know and Kings of Stings.* James Morton is also the co-author of *Shotgun and Standover,* an account of the Painters and Dockers' union. They have written eight books together.

A

B

C

D

H

M

N

Q

R

T

U

V

W

Y

Z

Printed in Dunstable, United Kingdom

91335469R00252